LOITERING IN THE LAKES

The beautiful Lake District is the setting for the true narrative account of many years of camaraderie and companionship on the mountains.

Four friends, with a love for mountaineering, got together and formed a club — Sally's Ladies — and were soon joined by others.

Related in this book are the well-composed walks, the pitfalls, fun and excitement which was encountered.

As the author states in her book:
'The purpose of Sally's Ladies, and the goal towards which they aspired, was to achieve a complete understanding of mountains by climbing them, lingering among them, looking, listening, and feeling.

The account of how far they succeeded is by no means complete, but a time always comes for a chapter to be closed . . . .'

LOITERING IN THE LAKES

D.W. Ball

ARTHUR H. STOCKWELL LTD.
Elms Court   Ilfracombe
Devon

© D.W. Ball, 1987
First published in Great Britain, 1987

All rights reserved.
No part of this publication may be reproduced
or transmitted in any form or by any means,
electronic or mechanical, including photocopy,
recording, or any information storage and
retrieval system, without permission
in writing from the copyright holder.

ISBN 0 7223 2174-0
Printed in Great Britain by
Arthur H. Stockwell Ltd.
Elms Court   Ilfracombe
Devon

To
The Mountains

We came, we saw, they conquered.

Seascale, 1987.

Illustrations set between pages 128 & 129

CONTENTS

Climbing Song	9
Foreword	11

Part 1

SCARTHWAITE DAYS

The Beginning	15
New Boots	23
Scarthwaite	27
The First Recruit	32
Sally's Ladies	38
Blizzard on the Pike	46
Winter in Spring	58
South Traverse	65
Dress Circle	75
Glaramara	84
The Best Ridge	96
The Timed Walk	105
October Cameo	114
Farewell to Scarthwaite	118
Interim	127

Part 2

WESTERN WANDERINGS

Strands	133
Minor Misfortunes	147
Mary's House	159
Red Pike (Wasdale)	164
Eskdale in May	178
The Last Recruit	186
Full House	198
Summer Parting	207
Arctic Easter	209
Heat Wave	215
Over The Green	224
Terrace Route	245
Treasure Of Heights	253

THE S.L. CLUB

FOUNDER MEMBERS

Primrose Woodward (Prim) — *President*
D. Wilson-Ball (Cis) — *Secretary*
Catherine Grudgings (Cath)
Marjorie Coppen (Cop)

Elected Members

Doris Marshall (Doris)
May Shaw (May)
Hilda Norman (Hilda)
Daisy Price (Daisy)

CLIMBING SONG

It's a springing step on a climbing track,
For the heart is high and the will is strong
When the blue hills call where the dawn wind breaks,
And the breath of the morning is the wanderer's song —
    The song in the heart for the tramp of feet
    To the eagle's haunt where the great rocks meet.

O, the dew's on the heather and the harebells chime,
The gorse is all aflame where the sweet becks fall,
The heart's like a lark with the music in the air
Where the long grass ripples and the curlews call —
    And the song in the heart soars clear and free
    For the hills of the west that are turning to the sea.

The mountains beckon, and the great sky sweeps
To the surging rocks where the white clouds roll,
The tramp is steady and the heart is strong,
For the hills are calling to the wanderer's soul —
    To reach, O pilgrim, that far mountain crest
    Climb, climb on, and there alone find rest!

FOREWORD

In the beginning, there were four of us — Prim, Cath, Cop and myself — and our first visit to the Lakes was in the summer of 1945. We came, we saw, and the mountains conquered, a victory so overwhelming that they lured us back every subsequent Easter. We were hooked for life.

Gradually, we collected other congenial companions, strong walkers like ourselves, until by 1950 there were seven of us. An eighth was added some years later, but we never exceeded that number.

None of us was particularly young, for all had seen the thirty years' milestone come and disappear. Apart from one who enjoyed private means, we earned our bread the hard way, each having achieved a position of high responsibility in her respective work. In short, we had reached maturity, a state gleefully jettisoned each Easter. When we came to the Lakes we let our hair down and became alive.

We were a tough lot, hard-going, quarrelsome without being vindictive, rude to each other but paradoxically courteous, and wholly uninhibited. Differing widely in character, we still blended harmoniously. Our aim was to become complete mountaineers. In this, some of us succeeded to a very high degree and others not so high, but anyone lacking that objective could not have become one of us, for each newcomer was thoroughly vetted beforehand.

We were neither interested in covering great distances across the fells nor in standardised walking. We chose our pace, loitered, and cared nothing about getting from A to B in a specified time. We walked with open eyes and minds, observing, learning and absorbing until the very essence of the mountains was distilled into our hearts.

In the hills lay happiness.

Part 1

SCARTHWAITE DAYS

THE BEGINNING

How did you get from Nottingham to Grange-in-Borrowdale in 1945 without a car? You went by train. This was simple for Cop, who could travel direct from London to Keswick, but a marathon for the rest of us, involving many changes. The first was at Leeds, where our slow, crowded train arrived too late for us to catch the connection to Appleby. After Leeds, we were obliged to change at Skipton, Carnforth and Oxenholme. All the trains were packed, and part of the journey was done in the luggage van, jammed in with twenty-two other passengers, two large dogs and six bicycles. We had left Nottingham at seven o'clock that morning, and it was seven in the evening when we reached Keswick.

A taxi was waiting to take us up Borrowdale to the village of Grange. Grange View, the house where we were to stay, later became the headquarters of Lakeland Rural Industries, but in those days it was the private residence of Mrs Sally Coates.

The evening was so warm and calm that we abandoned unpacking and went strolling, first to the twin arches of the bridge, then to the Bowder Stone, the massive perched boulder reputed to weigh two thousand tons, which has a ladder up which people can climb to the top.

"Trippers' stuff," I said.

"True," agreed Prim. "I suppose it's something everyone ought to see once, but I've no patience with it!"

The trunks of the birches on Grange Fell gleamed white in the twilight, and the air was full of the scent of meadowsweet. Across the river rose the green-brown ridge of Catbells and Maiden Moor, but Skiddaw, at the foot of the valley, was veiled in cloud.

My bed was very hard. I assumed that they went in for that type of bed in the Lakes, and hoped I should get used to it, but hard bed or not, I knew I had come to a very special part of England, and I was filled with excitement and anticipation.

The following day being Sunday, we lazed, absorbed, and made plans. We intended to climb all the well-known fells, such as Scafell Pike, Great Gable, Helvellyn, and Skiddaw, and as many more as we could. Also, there was the immediate neighbourhood to be explored. The barometer was high, the weather was warm and settled, and we were ready. Skiddaw, rising in perfect symmetry at the foot of our own valley, was an obvious first choice.

* * *

The bus to Keswick was so full when it reached Grange that we doubted whether it would pick us up. It did, and eleven more people got in after us, and we were a solid mass until we reached the outskirts of Keswick, when the bus pulled up, and the driver said, "Will some of you get out now, for decency's sake. I'm only allowed eight standing." In those days, several bus companies plied up and down Borrowdale.

We began Skiddaw, through the pine woods and up the steepish slope to the Halfway House, which no longer exists, but was then in its heyday, serving refreshments. Tea was seven pence a cup.

As we gained height Derwentwater lay at our feet, and beyond that rose the great fells at the head of the dale. We walked slowly because there was so much to see, and the day was almost unbearably hot, but on reaching the summit we entered a world of swirling damp cloud, eerie and fascinating. It was the most interesting part of the walk.

On the way down, dalliance at the Halfway House, lying on the warm turf and drinking more cups of sevenpenny tea, caused us to miss the Borrowdale bus, and we had to take a taxi up the valley.

There was no thrill in Skiddaw. Like the Bowder Stone, it was something to be done once and then forgotten. To look at it is beautiful, to climb it is boring.

* * *

We did the Honister round in a heat-wave.

Honister Pass is neither particularly long nor excessively steep, but walking on a motor road is never attractive. Under a brilliant blue sky, we meandered up to the quarry and down the far side of the pass, with Prim, armed with map, telling us the names of the fells on either side. I paid little attention, because my concern was with my feet. Someone had advised us to take our oldest, strongest shoes to the Lakes, but had omitted to point out that the linings of the shoes should be perfectly smooth. My shoes were old and strong enough, and I had had them nailed, but the linings were badly worn, and my feet were gradually being rubbed sore and about to blister — and this in the middle of a long walk.

Turning into the Buttermere Hotel (now a Youth Hostel) for drinks, we had a prolonged laze on the verandah before tackling the Newlands Pass. In the afternoon heat, it was a slog up and down into the Newlands valley, where we stopped at a farm which gave us tea in the backyard among the ducks and hens. The sun grilled us, and Cop's legs, in brief shorts, looked about to burst into flame.

My tortured feet were giving me hell, and with still two miles to go to Grange a large blister burst, and I sat on the road and changed into plimsolls. Then I limped along cursing, with Cath prodding me on like a driver with an unwilling mule.

In retrospect, it was a very good walk, especially for Prim and Cath who were untroubled by the heat. This was the first time we were late for dinner, and marked the beginning of a habit which was to become second nature to us over the years. For the next two days there were no long excursions. My feet were so sore that I was obliged to stick to plimsolls, and Cop's legs were badly burnt.

Prim said, "This is a good opportunity to do all the bits and pieces one is supposed to do in this area."

So first we went to the chemist's in Keswick to buy things for sunburn and blisters, had coffee and biscuits at Storm's Café — that dark, dingy place where everyone gravitated — then began on the bits and pieces, starting with Watendlath.

There was no motor road to the hamlet in those days, but the track from Ashness Gate was wide and easy. Walpole, with his Herries books, made Watendlath famous, but to see a notice on one building: 'This is where Judith Paris lived', struck me as utterly ridiculous. Watendlath's only attractions are the tarn, the old bridge, and the track climbing from the village over the fell to Rosthwaite.

We walked through Manesty Woods to the landing stage at Brandelhow, and took the launch to Keswick. Friar's Crag was suffering from such an influx of tourists that we spent a mere five minutes over Ruskin's 'Fifth finest view in Europe' before going up Castle Head, where we found no people but an abundance of litter. We walked back to Grange via Portinscale, Brandelhow and Manesty.

*   *   *

We climbed Helvellyn on the hottest day of the year.
  Getting down-dale was easy, but in Keswick we queued for an hour for the Grasmere bus. Alighting at Wythburn, we draped scarves and handkerchiefs from our heads to protect our necks from the sun. Helvellyn from Wythburn is very simple, but we took almost four hours over it. In that heat it would have been impossible to walk in comfort on the flat, much less to toil up a mountain.
  There was not a breath of air on the top, and almost no view because of heat haze. We were too thirsty to eat our sandwiches, and tried not to think of long, cool drinks. It was suggested that we went down to Thirlspot, where we might get tea, as there certainly would not be any if we descended to Wythburn.
  I shall never forget that roasting descent. Even the sun-lovers, Cath and Prim were scorched. Cop lost the heel of her shoe and walked with a drunken roll, and laughing at her made us hotter still. When we reached a stream we lay on our stomachs and put our faces in the water. The stony track gave way to boggy ground, which soaked and refreshed our feet. At the stream, Cath had changed into white tennis shoes, but soon they were the same colour as my black plimsolls.
  The King's Head, at Thirlspot, welcomed us into their cool dining-room, though with dirty, sweat-streaked faces and muddy legs we looked like tramps. We did not care what we looked like, and the tea was heavenly. Then, waiting outside for a bus, we were picked up by a passing Rolls-Royce in spite of our appearance, and enjoyed a luxurious ride back to Keswick — but we had to queue for the Borrowdale bus.

* * *

After Helvellyn came a gentle day when we walked to Stonethwaite and up the Langstrath, following a track beside the beck until we came to a succession of waterfalls and deep, clear pools.
  "Let's paddle," we said, and dumped our rucksacks and took off our shoes and socks. After some dabbling, Cath lost patience.
  "Paddling is no good. I'm going to swim."
  She stripped, and Cop followed suit, and they jumped in the pool. They splashed and swam up and down for some time, until I called, "There are two hikers coming down the valley," when they climbed out and hastily got back into their clothes.
  We wandered on, finding an ideal picnic place, and having drinks from tiny waterfalls. We had borrowed a cup from Mrs

Coates, and somehow the handle got broken. We were having a lazy, enjoyable afternoon, climbing about on the rocks and sitting with our feet in the beck, when Prim, bending over a waterfall, slipped on a mossy stone and fell in. She got up, and promptly fell in again, and we laughed so much that we almost joined her in the water. She sat draped in a mac while we spread her clothes on the rocks to dry. When they were more or less dry she got dressed, and we went back for tea.

On Sunday afternoon, we walked along the Catbells road to have tea at Swinside, and returned over the hump of Catbells itself, entranced by the view of Skiddaw and Blencathra, Derwentwater and Bassenthwaite, the Helvellyn range, the Solway Firth. There were hills and more hills on every side — and Prim with a map identifying them.

* * *

There is magic in the very name of Great Gable, and climbing it gave us the best day of all.

We walked up Honister and through the quarry yard, to climb to the old drum house and onto the Grey Knotts — Brandreth plateau — to a fresh wind and glorious views of Buttermere, Crummockwater, the long trough of Ennerdale, and the sunlit Irish Sea. Over Green Gable, a slither down to Windy Gap, which lived up to its name, and we started to climb Great Gable. It was indeed rock climbing, for instead of slanting left to the usual track, which was not so obvious in those days, we attacked the rocks straight ahead, mounting by a series of small ledges close to the north face. Half-way up, Cath was vertically above my head, and it occurred to me that it would be hard lines on me if she fell. But we all loved the spice of danger involved and the thrill of handling hard rock.

The view from the summit cairn was spellbinding. Great End, Scafell Pike, the crags of Scafell — there close at hand! When I first saw them from Gable top those greatest fells of Lakeland put a spell on me from which I have never since been free, nor wished to be.

We descended by the Breast Track, taking the loose stones and shale fast, to Styhead Tarn and down the pass, heading for tea at Seathwaite Farm. We could not finish all the home-made biscuits, so pocketed them to eat in our bedrooms at night. Then we raced to Seatoller, and caught the bus just as it was leaving.

* * *

The days were flashing past, and there was still Scafell Pike to be ticked off. It was Prim's idea that we should approach it by the Langstrath, because on the map there was a definite track from the head of Langstrath up to Esk Hause.

The Langstrath valley is about four miles long, and we walked steadily, passing the foot of Stake, with the valley head slowly coming nearer, until the track suddenly petered out and vanished. We went doggedly on through swampy tussocks to the end, vainly searching for the missing track, or indeed for the least sign that anyone had ever passed that way before. Prim said she felt like writing to Bartholomew to tell him to correct his map. There was a laborious climb up steep, bumpy grass, than which no going is viler, for it is a treadmill. With much puffing and sweating and not a little cursing we emerged on Esk Hause, near Angle Tarn.

Soon we were standing by the 'shelter' at the top of the Hause, Great Gable ahead, Great End to the left, and the Scafell range tantalising, near. It was the Promised Land, unattainable because time was running out. We had spent so long over getting up the wretched grass out of the Langstrath that it had taken the heart out of us. There would be no Scafell Pike that day. After eating the rest of our food by Sprinkling Tarn, we carried on to Styhead and down the pass to Seathwaite Farm for cups of tea, then ran to Seatoller to catch the bus — and were late home for dinner.

* * *

More tiring than any long walk was the day of queues, endured because we felt we ought to see a little more of that part of Lakeland about which most people talk so enthusiastically. In Keswick, we stood in a queue for the Grasmere bus, after which there was standing room only on the bus itself.

Grasmere's attraction lies in its lake and the surrounding heights, the village itself being pleasant but unremarkable. We inspected the Wordsworth graves, and went to Dove Cottage, where we sat on a wall and argued.

"Do we have to go inside?"
"Are any of us Wordsworth fans?"
"I had enough of Wordsworth when I was at school."
"Well, it is supposed to be one of the show places in the Lakes."
"All the Americans make a bee-line for it."
"We aren't Americans."
"Still, perhaps we should go in — just once."
Having finally made up our minds to go inside, we saw the notice

'Closed until 2 p.m.' It was then 1.30, and we unanimously agreed that it was not worth waiting, and caught a bus to Windermere. We walked down to the lake shore at Bowness. The crowds, the noisy activity round the boats, the general fun-fair atmosphere made it difficult to realise that we were still in the Lakes, and we left Bowness forthwith.

Then came a succession of four queues — for a bus from Windermere to Ambleside, then from Ambleside to Keswick, then for tea at Storm's, and finally for the Borrowdale bus.

It was a very boring day. Nevertheless, I was glad to have seen the Grasmere-Windermere area, if only because it made me realise the great beauty of Borrowdale.

* * *

Our final day was unbearably hot, but it was our last opportunity for Scafell Pike.

There was the crowded bus to Seatoller, the walk to Seathwaite, with a pause for tea and biscuits at the farm, then Styhead and up Esk Hause. Goodness, it was a roaster! We stopped by the enchanting Sprinkling Tarn, where the shimmering blue with its illusion of coolness had an almost hypnotic effect. I could have stayed there happily for the rest of the day, and Cath and I were still sitting dabbling our feet in the water long after Prim and Cop had gone on. We never noticed them go, and they were nowhere in sight when we ultimately reached the top of the Hause and climbed up the Great End col to the desolation of boulders beyond.

The ribbon of track, white against the grey stones, went up and down and on and on, and we grew hotter and hotter. Near Ill Crag we rested on some boulders which were almost too hot to touch. It was as though we were being slowly fried, and we sat dripping in a silent trance, without the energy to move. It was only when I accidentally glanced at my watch that we realised it was too late to carry on to the Pike, and we should only get home about dinner time if we raced. Accordingly, and unwillingly, we raced, and made Grange View just as the dinner was going into the dining-room.

Prim and Cop arrived an hour and a half later. They achieved the Pike, and rushed all the way back. Cop, whose face radiated heat, complained, "Prim shot down Grain Gill like a race-horse — just to have time for a cup of tea at Seathwaite! Then we had to run all the way to Seatoller!"

Later that evening we had the tiresome business of packing, of stowing away the heavy raincoats with which we had burdened ourselves all through a heat wave, because someone had told us, "It always rains in the Lake District."

It was almost dark when we went for a final stroll over Grange bridge. Cop, still recovering from the mad gallop down Grain Gill, did not come. The dale was very quiet and peaceful. The fells were dark shadows, the river a silken ribbon, and one bright star hung over Skiddaw.

It was over, and we realised that in a fortnight we had barely scraped the surface of the treasure of the Lakes, but it would be there, waiting, and we should be back. We knew we should be back!

NEW BOOTS

On this, the first of the Easter meetings which were to continue unbroken for many years, Cath and I set off from Nottingham alone. Prim and Cop were to join us in two days' time. As in the previous summer, it was a long, tedious train journey involving many changes, taking thirteen hours to get from Nottingham to Keswick, and making us wonder why we had embarked on it, which feeling was immediately dispelled the moment we caught sight of the fells.

The old, nailed shoes had been discarded, and we had each bought a pair of walking boots, of which we were inordinately proud. We could scarcely wait to try them, so on the first afternoon we decided to go to Watendlath, the easiest walk we knew. We went over the fell from Rosthwaite, and the boots felt fine, and everything was delightful until we reached the group of larches from which one looks down on the tarn and the old farm buildings. On descending the track, we found the place seething with visitors. This was doubly annoying, because by then we were becoming very conscious of our feet, and inclined to be hyper-critical. We needed a rest, but not cheek by jowl with half the universe, so we walked on through the village, not stopping until we reached Ashness Gate, by when we had had more than enough of the new boots.

The worst was yet to come, for there was no bus up the dale for another hour, and we were faced with two miles of road walking. At first, we pretended that our feet felt fine, but soon abandoned that because it was so manifestly untrue. Cath grumbled about her ankles being bruised to the bone, and my feet felt flayed. We cursed whole-heartedly as we tramped along.

"Damn all boots!"
"Damn all walking!"
"Damn the fells and the whole blasted Lake District!"

The last half mile was a pilgrimage through a purgatory of fire, and when we reached Grange, I was sorely tempted to consign my new boots to the nearest dustbin.

But next day, after a rainy morning the sun came out in the afternoon, and we walked along the Catbells road — in boots. I fully expected we should abandon them after the torture of Watendlath, but Cath, lacing hers up with grim determination, had said, "I've bought these damn things, and I'm jolly well going to wear them if it kills me!" After that I felt obliged to follow suit, and pulled on my own boots with loathing. They felt awful. We pounded along the road, not saying much but feeling very uncomfortable, until we got to Swinside Inn, where we had tea, and tried not to remember that we had several miles of walking to get back to Grange. Strangely enough, this walk back through Brandelhow and Manesty woods, was less of an ordeal, no doubt because our feet had been tortured until they had no more feeling left in them.

To our amazement, Prim had arrived when we got back. She had reached Grange in the middle of the afternoon. She explained, "I was told at the station that there would be all the changes of trains that we had last year, so I asked if I could borrow their timetable, and I found it was possible to get a direct train to Appleby. It's much quicker!"

* * *

On a cloudy day with a keen wind, the four of us went up the rough road by Castle Crag and climbed the slate gully to Lobstone Band, to emerge into a desolation of swampy grass and a howling gale.

After dashing about, trying unsuccessfully to find a sheltered spot in which to eat our sandwiches, we sat on the wet grass, shivering and gobbling, and saying rude things about the dreary morass surrounding the insignificant pool of Dale Head Tarn.

So far, the walk had been devoid of interest, but what followed was amply rewarding. We climbed up Scawdel Fell, more popularly known as High Spy — which sounds more like the name of a children's game than a fell. To me, it is Scawdel Fell, just as Saddleback is Blencathra. From Scawdel Fell, we had a fine ridge walk over Narrow Moor and Maiden Moor to Catbells, with views so splendid that we forgot about the wind, and strode along with joy — apart from my feet, of which I was becoming increasingly conscious. I had brought a pair of shoes in my rucksack, and halfway along Maiden Moor I changed into them, then pelted after the other three who had got well ahead. To change from heavy boots to light shoes on a downward slope needs caution, because your feet feel so unencumbered that with the first few strides you are liable to go head over heels, which I did. As I was bringing up the rear no one noticed, and I escaped facetious comments. Cath, with no spare shoes, valiantly endured her boots to the end without complaining.

Dropping down the nose of Catbells, we headed for Swinside Inn and tea, followed by that most enchanting of walks through the woods back to Grange.

* * *

Planning to go to Wasdale to see the deepest lake, we made short work of Honister and the track to the old Drum House, which we had renamed the Gallows because the thick wooden beams leaning drunkenly on the slate platform looked exactly like a structure formerly used for executing felons.

The simplest way to Wasdale would have been over Styhead, but we had rejected that, as we should have been on high ground for only a few minutes at the top of the pass, and that was not enough. It was far better to go by the Grey Knotts — Brandreth plateau, a truly delectable place in which to linger. At the cairn on Brandreth, where the north face of Gable leaps into view, I let out a yell of delight.

"Shall we climb it?"

"No, we are going to Wastwater," I was told, and we swung off for Beck Head, and the track down Gavel Neese which is too bumpy and steep for comfort. Across the gulf of Styhead there was the cairn on the Pike and the black, precipitous cliffs of Scafell, half veiled by streamers of cloud. Prolonged halts to look at and discuss the scenery combined with the unease of the track underfoot delayed us to such an extent that when we finally got down to Wasdale any hope of reaching the shore of the lake was abandoned.

At Burnthwaite Farm, where they provided us with coffee, we sat in the barn to eat our sandwiches, lingering over them because it was warm and snug among the hay, and this was not one of the wind's friendly days. When we eventually emerged, dark clouds were massing low on the hills, ominous signs of rain, though they assured us at the farm that the clouds meant nothing, and there would only be a short shower at most. Unconvinced, we decided to go straight back over Styhead, hoping for tea at Seathwaite.

Before we had gone far up the pass we had several halts, first to inspect the Napes Needle at close range, then to trace the line of the Corridor Route to the Pike, and finally to listen to faint shouts coming from Gable. We thought someone must be calling for help, but the howling gale prevented us from hearing distinctly.

The wind was increasing in intensity, but fortunately it was at our backs. Then came the rain and sleet, driving at us with horizontal spears, deluging and soaking us in a matter of minutes. At the ambulance box at the top of the pass men were taking out a stretcher to rescue a climber with a broken leg on Gable. This was what the shouting had been about. I did not envy them their job in those appalling conditions.

We had not a dry stitch on us as we went down to Stockley Bridge. Prim was the least wet, having put on a cape over her mac, and though this imprisoned her arms, she darted from rock to rock like a ballet dancer, and was the only one to avoid slipping and falling into oozing pockets of mud — not that we minded slipping, for when you are thoroughly wet, with water running down your back next to your skin, you cease to care about anything. In fact, you enjoy it!

We dashed on past Seathwaite Farm because we were too wet to sit down for tea, and did the mile and a half to Seatoller at the double. The bus ride from there to Grange was uncomfortable, like sitting in a bath of cold water. On reaching home we stripped and gave all our clothes to Mrs Coates. Spin-driers had not been invented then. She put all our things through the mangle before hanging them round the kitchen fire to dry. I took off my sodden boots and emptied the water out of them.

Because we travelled light in those days, spare clothing was minimal, and we improvised. I came to dinner in my pyjama trousers and an old sweater which should have been discarded years ago. We all looked a little bizarre, as though we were part of a fancy dress parade. We larked about, poking fun at each other, until the resultant noise was like a drunken party. If it is possible to get intoxicated on the after-effects of a soaking, then we were. It was our initiation into genuine Lakeland rain — the real stuff.

As for our boots, we had learnt a valuable lesson, because from that day they were as comfortable as slippers, and my advice to anyone with troublesome new boots is not to try to break them in gradually, but to put them on and sit with feet immersed over the boot tops in a bucket of water for about an hour. That will do the trick!

SCARTHWAITE

The Nottingham-Appleby-Penrith route was a great improvement on the twelve hour journeys of previous years. We did not leave Nottingham until mid-morning, and at Penrith we abandoned the railway altogether, having discovered that an express bus was just about to start for Keswick. We were in Borrowdale much earlier than we had anticipated, which pleased us mightily. After a year's absence we could not get there fast enough.

Cath and I had acquired bright yellow oilskin capes, thick enough to keep out even Lakeland rain. Their one disadvantage was that when we wore them our arms were imprisoned — an awkward factor when dealing with rock.

Mrs Coates had left Grange View and gone to live at Scarthwaite, a beautiful slate house at the far end of Grange, where the Catbells road turns right. Maiden Moor swept down almost to her garden wall. Every Easter, Scarthwaite was to become our second home. Mrs Coates took no other visitors during our annual stay, which delighted us, because it meant that we could do and say exactly what we liked without having to be polite to strangers — or to each other.

* * *

On the first morning, I was roused from sleep by Cath.

"Get up! Come and look at the view! Look at the blue sky and the sun! It's perfect!"

I rushed to the window, and, yes, it WAS perfect! There were the golden-brown hills, with streaks of snow on Rosthwaite Fell and Glaramara, and broader bands of glistening white at the head of the dale. It was the Promised Land.

The call of those sunlit, snowy hills was so strong that we almost ran to Seathwaite, even passing the farm without going in for coffee. Styhead Tarn was partly frozen over, but we did not linger there, for there was deep snow on Esk Hause, in perfect condition, so firm that our feet scarcely marked the compact granulation of the surface. Sprinkling Tarn was a sheet of grey ice in a glittering white bowl, and Great End towered in a rampart of black buttresses and snow-filled gullies. In the keen, almost sparkling air we felt as though we had been let out to play, and thoroughly enjoyed ourselves, until pangs of hunger took us up to the 'shelter' at the top of the pass. As the wind was rising, we thought this would be a good place in which to eat, but soon discovered that 'shelter' was a misnomer, because there was none. There were plenty of rocks, and we burrowed among them. Mrs Coates had packed enough food for lunch and tea, but we ate everything.

Presently, it began to snow, hard pellets which bounced off you, and our hands became numb. We emerged from our holes, to stand arguing about whether to go on to Angle Tarn or to go down to Seathwaite for tea. Tea won, and we decided to go down Grain Gill. Running and sliding down the hause, we swung right for Grain Gill, and found ourselves on a steep, polished slope of smooth snow. Having started down before realising that it was not the top of Grain Gill, it was easier to carry on than to struggle back, but the angle was too acute for comfort. We descended in ways varying from crouching glissades to plain hell-for-leather slithering, but none of us lost complete control.

At the bottom of the slope we cut over to the correct route, down which we slid until the snow ended and the mud began and lasted all the way to Stockley Bridge, by which time our feet were well plastered.

After eating everything on the table at Seathwaite Farm, there was time to stroll the mile and a half to Seatoller and the bus — a pleasant change from the usual mad rush along that road.

* * *

We looked forward to more frolics in the snow on the high fells, but in vain, for with the morning came hammering, relentless rain. The tops of the near fells whitened with fresh snow, and a dozen new gills leapt down the hillsides.

Although the sitting-room was very comfortable, by afternoon we were tired of being indoors, and set off in the rain for our favourite walk along the flank of Catbells to Swinside Inn for tea. The walk was the attraction, not the tea which was invariably bread and butter, jam, and ginger cake. Best of all was coming back through the woods, close to the water, when we would quote poetry and argue about it. We surprised ourselves by the number of poems to do with lakes which we could dredge from the depths of memory.

The woods gave some shelter from the rain, and we began collecting branches and fir cones to burn on the sitting-room fire. Everyone put the cones in my open rucksack, almost filling it, which was all right until I forgot and bent down to pick up a branch, and all the wet cones showered out over my head.

"Use your own rucksacks in future!" I said.

It rained for twenty-four hours, then stopped, and next came a great wind which shrieked and thundered against the house with the sound of the sea crashing on rocks. It whistled under the doors and through every crevice, and Cath's towel, hanging near the bedroom fireplace, blew up the chimney, and I grabbed it just before it disappeared.

Mrs Coates, very concerned about us, laid down the law for once. "You must not go on the tops. It's not safe with this wind. You are not to go!"

We told her not to worry. Some of us had been out to post letters, and the wind was bad enough in the valley, without going any higher. But we felt like prisoners. It was a wasted day, apart from an evening venture through the woods under Castle Crag, when we almost got blown away.

During the night the gale dropped, but the rain returned, and having spent the morning seething with frustration, by afternoon we had had enough. We would go out whatever the weather. It would not be the first time we had got a soaking. We would go by the Castle Crag track, and have tea at Seatoller Farm. The decision having been made, our spirits rose.

The rain was fierce when we set out, and up by Castle Crag it turned to sleet. We went on, not caring what it did. Cath and I were quite happy in our oilskin capes, though with arms imprisoned she was unable to get through a narrow grike in a wall, and stuck halfway, like a cork in a bottle, and we had fun pulling her loose.

A downward track, inches deep in mud, took us to the foot of Honister, but there was no tea at Seatoller Farm. All their visitors had stayed indoors because of the inclement weather, and there was no room to cater for outsiders. After some grumbling and snarling, we walked to Seathwaite. We knew we should get tea there, and, dripping as we were, another mile or two would make no difference.

A miracle happened while we were having tea in that dark, familiar room, for we came out into sunlight and a beautiful evening. Amazed and delighted, we simply could not believe it, but there it was, and we immediately began planning, our wet clothes drying on us as we walked back to Seatoller. Styhead the next day!

* * *

A perfect spring morning, and we were impatient to go, but we rushed about, collecting our gear and getting in each other's way to such an extent that we missed the Seatoller bus and had to wait for the next one, sitting meanwhile on Grange bridge and looking at a Skiddaw white from head to foot.

It was warm walking to Seathwaite, and we took our time, meandering up to a sun-bright Styhead Tarn, so different from when we last saw it, and so attractive that though it was scarcely midday we decided to remain there and picnic. Lolling by the water's edge, we ate every scrap of our food, and still we lingered, until Cop demanded, "Are we going to sit here all day?" and we finally collected ourselves.

We went on, down to Wasdale Head, where we visited the tiny church and the climbers' graves in the churchyard. We then realised that the afternoon was half over, and stood and argued about what to do next, and how to get back to Borrowdale without returning over Styhead, and Prim said, "The alternative would be to go over Black Sail, Scarth Gap, and Honister. We might even have time for food at Gatesgarth Farm!"

The thought of three high passes was a little daunting at that time of day, but we set off, and it seemed a long grind to the top of Black Sail, because we were beginning to feel hungry. A rough track took us down to Ennerdale, a deserted valley, the only building in sight being the small, barn-like Black Sail Youth Hostel. We made for that, hoping we might get a cup of tea, perhaps even something to eat, but were disappointed. The caretaker would not even give us a drink of water. All we got out of him was that there was "A bit of a sketchy track, though he didn't think we should find it" which went up onto the Brandreth plateau.

It was then 5 p.m., and we were hungry — and hunger means fatigue. We turned out rucksacks and pockets, searching for forgotten scraps of food, no matter how stale. We found nothing, until Cath, scrabbling in the corners of her rucksack, unearthed a small bar of chocolate. This was manna from heaven. The bar was meticulously divided into four, and we each ate our ration, making it last as long as possible.

Then, locating the very sketchy track, we began to climb out of Ennerdale. We went steadily, not speaking much, because we had had enough and wanted to get it over. When we reached the Brandreth plateau the Gallows looked far away, and we headed directly for it over the swampy, undulating terrain. We were very tired indeed on the rough track down to the quarry and the road walk to Seatoller, where we were lucky to find a bus about to leave.

We were late for dinner, and, as usual, left Prim to make our excuses, and Mrs Coates, eyeing us up and down and shaking her head, asked, "Now, is it worth it?"

Weary, dirty, hungry, we answered with one voice, "Yes!"

We learnt a valuable piece of fell-craft that day. Never eat all your food at once!

* * *

The holiday ended with a gem of a spring day, when we walked up Honister and climbed Dale Head, not a strenuous fell, but one where you think you should be getting to the top long before you actually are. We ate our sandwiches by a snow cornice which projected over the green map of the Newlands valley.

Then, each choosing the line of descent she favoured, we dropped to Dale Head Tarn and cut across to Scawdel Fell. I had a slight mishap at Newlands Beck when my foot slipped off a stone and I sat in the water, thus drawing rude comments from the others about clumsy footwork, and a request that I walked in the rear so that they would not have to look at me while I dripped.

Scawdel Fell to Catbells, always a fine ridge walk, was at its best that day, with all the high fells clear, deep blue Derwentwater surrounded by a pinkish haze of larches, and snow-capped Skiddaw and Blencathra ahead. Coming off the nose of Catbells, we got tea at a small nearby café, thus avoiding the extra half mile of road-walking to Swinside and ginger cake.

We came back through the woods, listening to a symphony of blackbirds and thrushes. It was the final bitter-sweet walk.

THE FIRST RECRUIT

Mrs Coates had given names to her three 'guest' bedrooms. They were 'Langstrath' which had three beds, 'The Pines' which had two, and 'Riggside' with one. She could accommodate six people, and Prim was concerned because there were only four of us, and therefore Mrs Coates, with two vacant beds, was losing money. We needed to expand, to find several others who were good walkers, and, equally important, who would fit into the pattern of our ways. We decided that if we started with one at a time we could break them in gradually, as it were.

Doris was our first recruit (or victim). She was a keen walker, and anxious to have a go in the Lakes, but being organist at a large church in Nottingham, she was unable to come until after the Easter weekend, so after the usual train journey via Appleby, only the original four assembled at Scarthwaite to be welcomed by a beaming Mrs Coates. The winter had passed, and we were home again.

It was so good to be back in Borrowdale that on the first morning, which was sunny and warm, we opted to leave the tops for the time being and have a leisurely walk, with plenty of time to stand and stare. Idling up Honister, we saw an owl asleep in a tree, and sat down to have a long discussion about it. That, plus several rests by the stream, made it lunch-time before we got over the pass to Buttermere, where we called at Miss Nelson's cottage, at Gatesgarth, for a pot of tea to have with our sandwiches. We also ordered afternoon tea for 3.30, in spite of Mrs Coates having given us sufficient food for two meals.

Having eaten, we turned to the lake. Prim and Cop went off along the lakeside track, while Cath and I started to climb Scarth

Gap. Half-way up, we sat on the grass to argue about it.

"What do we do when we get to the top?"

"Come down again."

"Then what is the point of going?"

"We might see over the other side."

"What should we see?"

"I don't know. Pillar, I suppose."

"It's too hot to go up just to come straight down again."

"Let's not bother!" and we remained lying on the fell-side until tea-time.

It was a waste of a good day, but we were not to realise that until later. Walking back over Honister after tea, we were diverted by Prim's demonstration of how to run, with knees slightly bent, down a steep slope. We tried, but found it very difficult to keep in balance. Some can do that sort of thing with ease, but others can't.

Talking to Mrs Coates that night, Prim learnt that John Cockbain, a dalesman who lived at Seatoller, had a taxi for hire, and promptly made use of this information, for the following morning the up-dale bus was so packed that it did not stop at Grange, whereupon she rang up John and instructed him to fetch us. She said we would wait on Grange bridge, and he would know who we were as she would be wearing a red beret.

He took us to Seathwaite, thus saving a mile and a half of road walking, and we went up Grain Gill and on to Great End. Although the day was calm and warm in the valley, a mighty wind was sweeping the top, a factor of little consequence, for in the sharp, clear air the view was magnificent — the plunging screes of Gable, Kirk Fell, Pillar, the patchwork quilt of stone walls at Wasdale Head, Lingmell, the grey, bouldery wilderness of the Pike, Bowfell — and more and more! The eye could scarce believe the wealth of hills!

Great End is strong, powerful rock with no soft touch, the true territory of the mountaineer. I fell in love with it that day — a love which I have never lost.

Descending by Styhead, we had tea at Seathwaite Farm and strolled to Seatoller, where we missed not only the bus but also John's taxi which had just gone to Keswick. Waiting for its return made us late for dinner, but Grange Fell was bright pink in the sunset, while the Maiden Moor ridge was dusky blue. Things like being back in time for dinner just did not matter.

* * *

On Easter Monday the weather changed. Clouds massed and there were heavy showers and much wind. We went over the fell to Watendlath, not for love of the place, but merely because it was handy for providing a little leg-stretch in poor weather.

That year, we had all bought oilskin coats. They were ex-army stores, green and brown camouflage, and ideal for the Lakes. We did not try them on when we purchased them, but as they were made for men we judged there would be plenty of room in them, which would be a good thing, because we were tall and hefty, with the exception of Prim, who was of average height. On the way to Watendlath it began to rain, so we got out the oilskins and put them on, and fell about with laughter.

"We look just like escaped convicts!" exploded Cop.

It did look as though we were wearing some bizarre kind of uniform, but the oilskins fitted, except for Prim's. Hers came down to the ground, completely hiding her legs and feet, and she looked like a perambulating tent. We howled, and so did she.

"I can always shorten it when I get back!"

That evening Doris arrived, ready to do some real walking, but possibly with some private misgivings after hearing our chatter about walks and expeditions. She listened, looked thoughtful, and said little.

By morning the weather had turned diabolical. The wind howled, the rain lashed down for the next three days. A flat greyness obliterated the view from the windows of Scarthwaite. Expeditions optimistically planned in the evening were cancelled the next morning. Apart from going into Keswick, semi-paddling to Seathwaite, and walking half-way up Honister to see the maddened, thundering Hause Gill, we were house-bound. On every short foray we attempted, the relentless rain attacked viciously. We spent hours round the fire, talking endlessly about the fells, telling Doris all that she should be seeing, and cursing the weather. Poor Doris!

Then, after the third day, conditions improved slightly, just sufficient to be bearable, and that was enough for us. Donning oilskins and sou'westers, we went to do Dale Head, Hindscarth, and Robinson — the three fells whose names sound like a group of solicitors.

At the top of Honister we sheltered under a wall during a violent hailstorm. Then we battled against a savage wind up Dale Head, and crouched among the summit rocks to eat our sandwiches — a hurried meal before beginning the switchback down from Dale Head, up onto Hindscarth, down from Hindscarth, up onto

Robinson. At times the wind halted us in our tracks, but it was grand. Descending Robinson, we reached Buttermere Moss, an extensive swamp which cannot be avoided. We walked steadily across, but Doris rushed at full speed and sent clouds of water over herself — thereby learning how not to cross a large swamp.
We followed a steep, grassy track down to Buttermere, where we had tea and waited for the bus which would take us over Whinlatter to Keswick. It arrived as the heavens opened, and of the scenery on the way to Keswick we saw nothing, for beyond the bus windows was a solid wall of water.

* * *

Rossett Gill, in Langdale, was described in guide-books as "The steepest and roughest track in Lakeland," which at once put it on our list of "musts", and on a cold, overcast day we set out to do it.
To reach Langdale meant going to Ambleside and taking another bus from there, but the 10.30 bus from Keswick to Ambleside was already packed when we reached the bus station, and the next one did not leave until 11.30.
"That puts paid to Rossett Gill!" I said, and cursed, and we went into Storm's to have coffee, and to decide what to do next. We felt very let down.
Then Prim, who had been saying nothing, exclaimed, "We can still do it! If we caught the 11.30 to Ambleside, then ate our lunch on the Langdale bus, we should still have time to do the walk and get home at a fairly respectable hour."
"Late, you mean!"
"Well, not too late — perhaps."
So we did that, and duly arrived at the Old Dungeon Ghyll Hotel, Langdale, and went in for a pot of tea. That we knew we should have been getting on with the walk increased our enjoyment of the tea.
The head of Langdale divides into two forks, and we took the left, more obvious one. After half a mile we discovered it was the wrong one, and had to come back and start again on the other fork. For a mile or more we traversed flat, swampy grass, gradually approaching a wall of snow-streaked fells, until we came to a sheep-fold where the track divided into two, the right fork going over Stake Pass and the left to Rossett Gill, which, viewed head on, certainly looked steep.
We attacked with gusto, becoming so warm that we shed some clothes. The track was like a staircase with all the steps misplaced.

Soon we were high enough to feel the wind, which plucked and tore at us. The rocks became patched with ice. At the top of the Gill we emerged into winter, for Esk Hause was under deep snow. Storm clouds were beginning to pour over the mountains and the wind howled, and we put on all the clothes we had taken off, plus our oilskins.

Half-way up the Hause, the clouds arrived. Enormous hailstones bombarded us, bringing us to a halt. With the force of the wind behind them, they hurt, and we crouched almost flat while they hammered our backs. Only when the storm had passed could we carry on through the snow to the top of the Hause, and I shall never forget the grandeur of that ring of black, snow-capped mountains under a lurid red sky. For that alone, it had been worth struggling up Rossett Gill.

The steep, upper slopes of Grain Gill were under snow. Where the track went was anybody's guess, so we simply plunged down, and there was much falling and rolling. I did not fall, and my smug feeling lasted until the snow gave place to bog. I fell in that, and the mud went inside my sleeves up to my elbows. I noticed Doris striding through the bog with careless abandon and obvious enjoyment. The choice of a new recruit had been good.

Racing from Stockley Bridge to Seatoller, we caught the bus by the skin of our teeth, but only because it was running ten minutes late. We reached home only slightly late for dinner.

* * *

We spent one isolated day of spring wandering over Loughrigg Fell, described by Prim as, "A pleasant easy walk for a warm day." We ambled up from Grasmere, via Red Bank, dallying shamelessly, but eventually reaching the summit, where we did some map work, identifying all the fells in sight. Loughrigg has one of those long, meandering tops with rocky outcrops, pools, heather banks, and many patches of bog, through most of which we paddled on the way to Ambleside.

That evening we made ambitious plans for the next day — our last. And with the morning came teeming rain, but we could not stay indoors. We were desperate. Mrs Coates, packing up lunch, thought we were crazy. With no specific goal in mind, we went up Honister, and by the time we reached the top of the pass, water was pouring off oilskins and running down our necks.

Prim, grinning, suggested, "What about going up Dale Head?" This evoked a roar of protest. Then we stood and argued, getting even wetter, and finally decided to go down to Buttermere and eat our lunch in Miss Nelson's cottage.

We dashed down the pass, and arrived at the cottage looking as though we had fallen in the river, and Miss Nelson took us in, explaining that we could not use her sitting-room because her two guests, being sensible, had stayed indoors that day. She made us a large pot of tea and we camped in a huddle in her narrow passage, thankful to be out of the rain and wind.

Then we fought the elements over Honister once more, and there was great stripping and drying when we got back to Scarthwaite — plus satisfaction because the day had not been wasted.

After that, the weather no longer mattered to us — until the next Easter.

SALLY'S LADIES

Doris, swamped by organ engagements, could not come to the Lakes this Easter, so Prim invited May. We all knew May, a keen naturalist who lived in a village not far from Nottingham. Forthright in manner and with a pronounced sense of humour, we thought she might fit in well with us.
"But can she walk?" I asked Prim.
"Of course she can walk. Living in the country, she must be used to hiking over fields and up and down hills."
"What about mountain walking?"
Prim said, "I hope so. That is what we shall find out."
Again we journeyed north by train, and by late afternoon were in Borrowdale, wildly excited and bubbling with anticipation as we told May all that we proposed to do, to which outpouring she listened poker-faced. We unpacked our gear that night, so that no time would be wasted in the morning, and Cath gave me a bar of chocolate, with the warning, "This is your emergency ration, and you are not to eat it unless it is absolutely necessary." I stowed it in my rucksack, and forgot it was there.

* * *

The first day was like summer.
Prim always scorned boots and May hadn't any, so immediately after breakfast they set out for the bus, leaving the rest of us struggling with our laces. We caught the up-dale bus by doing the last hundred yards over the bridge at the double.
It was warm walking up Honister, and there were more cars going over the pass than in previous years, petrol having become more plentiful. At the Gallows we stopped to discuss where to go next, but did not finally decide until we reached the cairn on

Brandreth. Then we separated, Cath, Cop and I to climb Gable, while Prim and May did the Gable South Traverse. Prim thought that climbing Gable might be too much for May's first expedition, and the Traverse should be a fairly easy walk. We arranged to meet near Styhead Tarn at four o'clock.

We continued over Green Gable and down to Wind Gap, through which a gale roared like an express train, sweeping Cath off her feet three times in quick succession. After the Gap there was no wind, the air was dead calm, and we were soon up the rocky shoulder and sitting by the main cairn on Gable.

I took a few bearings with my new compass, but learned little from them, as Prim had gone off with the map. We lounged, sunning ourselves by the cairn, until we estimated that there was just time to get to the tarn by four o'clock. Then we went down by the Breast Track. The large, rough boulders of the scree patches took longer than we had anticipated, but we made it exactly on time.

After waiting for a while, we concluded that the other two had got there early and gone on down the pass. We agreed to have a further ten minutes' rest, but within that time they appeared round the rocks. May's face was expressionless, and Prim looked slightly guilty. They flopped on the grass beside us, and I fetched water from the beck while Cath produced something for them to eat. Then they described their walk in detail, or rather, Prim talked while May seemed lost in thought. They had done a fair amount of rock scrambling while searching for any sign of a track, and at times they had encountered pockets of wind so strong that they were obliged to progress on all fours. Also, they had witnessed the aftermath of an accident where a man who had fallen eighty feet was being lowered on a stretcher.

"What was the Traverse really like?" I asked in a low aside to Prim, who was sitting next to me.

"It was marvellous!" she whispered back. "We must do it again, because you would love it, but I'm sorry it was so tough for May's first go. I feel awful about that."

As we started down the pass, May asked, "Do we get the bus at Stockley Bridge?" adding that her feet were beginning to get sore, and we dare not tell her about the long trek from Stockley Bridge to Seathwaite and the even longer one from the farm to Seatoller.

I said, "Walks which start as a pleasure often end as a penance. You'll get used to it."

"Like hell I will!" she answered, pulling a face.

At Seatoller the bus was packed, so we hired John's taxi, Cath sitting in the front and the rest of us jammed in the back. Cop sat on me, and with every bump in the road she bounced, deliberately. Sun-scorched and late we arrived home, and Mrs Coates, eyeing us up and down, exclaimed, "You're proper daft!"

Then she filled us with gorgeous food, after which we were comatose round the fire. We always brought a small library of Lakes books with us, and I was asked to read aloud. Meanwhile, the others yawned, until Prim said she was going to have a bath, and departed, and Cop woke up.

"I might as well go to bed!" And she went off with her candle. A few minutes later, there was a lot of banging upstairs. We went to investigate, and found she could not get out of the lavatory in the dark.

"Let me out, you silly fools!" she was shouting.

We found her trying to open the door outwards, having forgotten that it opened inwards. We made some caustic comments on her intelligence before we, too, went to bed.

* * *

The next day, the warm, sunny weather would have been ideal for the tops, but there was a general feeling of inertia, and every suggestion was turned down, until Prim in disgust said, "I suppose we could always go up Catbells!" This, for some reason, met with approval. May wished to go into Keswick first to buy dressings for her feet, and Prim told her that we only went into Keswick when the weather was bad, but as it was not going to rain at all this holiday we might as well go and get it over. We split into two parties, Cath and I to go up Catbells and the others to Keswick to do their shopping. Then they were to come across on the launch and meet us on the top of Catbells for lunch.

Taking the Manesty track, we lazed up our fell in slow motion, stopping every few yards to look at various things, or for no specific reason, but we eventually reached the ridge and walked along until we came to a place where we could see the track coming over the nose. It was lunch-time, and we expected the others to come in sight at any moment.

We waited, ate our sandwiches, and went on waiting. The lake was blue, the larches shone green, larks sang, and the afternoon stole away. It became chilly, and we realised that the sun had gone and there were a few spots of rain, and still the others were missing. We gave them up for lost, sure that they had gone elsewhere, and went on down the nose, Cath laughingly observing, "Well, we've done Gable and Catbells so far this holiday."

"The lion and the lamb!" I said.

We were half-way through tea at Swinside Lodge when the trio walked in. Because the room was full they were unable to sit near us, so explanations were postponed. When we had finished our tea we left, to return home through the woods, the way we always took from Swinside to Grange. We walked slowly to give them time to catch up, but first, with time to spare we went along the lane to pick violets, then entered the woods by another gate.

We dawdled, and sat for half an hour on a log, but the others did not come. Then we realised that it was dinner time, and rushed home, and, to our indignation found them already there. When asked what the hell they had been playing at, they said the idea of coming up the nose of Catbells had never occurred to them, nor had they got off the launch where we expected. They had climbed Catbells by the path we had taken, and must have been about half a mile behind us all the while. After tea, they had gone through the usual gate into the woods (when we were up the lane picking violets) and had then hared along to catch us.

A silly day spent chasing each other!

* * *

On a grey, windy morning, Prim proposed that we should climb Helvellyn via Dollywaggon Pike, but at breakfast time the clouds were so thick and heavy that we began to have doubts. Prim waved these aside.

"We can always go somewhere else if it is not fit when we get there."

"What does she mean?" May asked me, suspiciously.

I shrugged. "Heaven knows!"

We always rooted through the sandwiches before we set out, to make sure that someone else carried the biggest packet, and on this particular morning we found among them some round, coloured objects which mystified us. We had no idea what they were, though Cath suggested that they might be some kind of very hard plum. Then Mrs Coates enlightened us, introducing us to Pasche eggs. She did them for us every subsequent Easter, wrapping each egg in onion skin and hard-boiling them until the shells had a most attractive, marbled appearance. It seemed a shame to eat them.

It rained most of the way over Dunmail Raise, but had stopped when we got off the bus at Tongue Gill. The track up to Grisedale Tarn was fairly steep, and as we gained height the temperature dropped sharply. When we had lunch, huddled beneath the rocks near the Tarn, our fingers went numb, and we put on all the extra clothes we carried.

The Dollywaggon Pike track was very good, rising in fascinating zigzags, unspoilt by clumsy feet as it is now. We were soon on the top, meeting a fierce wind, but the view more than compensated for that. The entire Lake District lay around us, and we could have identified every ridge and peak had it been possible to open the map without it being torn away.

It was a splendid high-level walk from the cairn on Dollywaggon to Nethermost Pike then to Helvellyn top, where we sat by the shelter wall among a horrible mess of discarded papers and tins, and finished our sandwiches. The shelter failed to keep out any wind.

Plunging down to Thirlspot, we had tea at the King's Head, then waited for the Keswick bus. This was full and would not stop for us, so Prim promptly went to find the landlord of the King's Head, and talked him into fetching his son from the barn to drive us to Keswick. The car was small. Prim sat in front and talked to the driver, and the rest of us travelled in a heap in the back.

We were late home, so no washing and changing was done. The sweet at dinner was a luscious concoction invented by Mrs Coates. She called it "Scarthwaite Pudding." It was a rip-roaring success.

* * *

On Wednesdays a bus ran from Keswick, via Whinlatter, to Buttermere. We used it to get to the start of the Red Pike-High Style-High Crag ridge, and planned to catch the last bus back to Keswick after the walk.

We always seemed to have plenty of time early in the day, so at Buttermere we went into the Victoria Hotel (since modernised and renamed the Bridge Hotel) for coffee and biscuits. All the interior doors of the hotel bore plaques bearing the names of famous people who had stayed there. We went round reading the names, and wandered upstairs, where May opened the door of the room where Mary Queen of Scots had reputedly slept, but there was someone in bed, so we retreated hurriedly and began the walk.

"We'll have lunch by Bleaberry Tarn," Prim said.

We found the going fairly steep, and having dallied so long in Buttermere, gave up the idea of lunch by the tarn, and had it by Sour Milk Gill. Red Pike went up in a series of terraces. The final section steepened considerably, and it was disconcerting to find chunks of the shaly rock coming off in our hands when we tried to pull up on them.

We were soon on the summit, where we remained for some time, absorbed and entranced by the superlative view — by the lake below and the serried ranks of fells. On the ridge to High Stile we paused every other minute to look at Pillar, for this was the first time we had seen it at close quarters, and the soaring magnificence of the Rock held us spellbound.

From High Stile we continued to High Crag, from whence we had to get down to Scarth Gap and Gatesgarth. Then we lost Cop, and went scouting about for her among the rocks. We finally spotted her crabbing along sideways down the face of High Crag. We left her to it, and took a less hazardous line to the top of Scarth Gap. We found her waiting at the bottom of the pass, and she admitted that she had had a rough ride and it was a wonder she had any boots left.

"It is also a wonder you did not break your silly neck!" she was told.

Then we discovered that we had exactly twenty minutes left in which to do nearly two miles along the road to Buttermere village to catch the bus. Alternatively, we could have tea at Miss Nelson's at Gatesgarth, and walk back over Honister. The vote was unanimous. We had tea. Then we were over the pass and down at Seatoller in an hour, good going, but still we were late for dinner. It had been a very rewarding day. Red Pike, High Stile and High Crag are true mountains, towering over Buttermere. To see them from the valley is an inspiration, but to traverse that rugged skyline is heaven.

That night, it was proposed that we became a mountaineering club. The idea met with loud approval and noisy enthusiasm, and was promptly put into action. Prim was elected President, as, apart from being the best mountaineer, she also planned and led the walks, organised the Easter meetings, and was always ready to make charming excuses for us when we transgressed. I was made Secretary, my job being to write detailed accounts of the Easter meetings, provide each member with a monthly club bulletin, and be general dogsbody. Cath and Cop were to be Founder Members, as they had been in from the beginning.

Someone said, "We ought to have some rules," and, being in that frame of mind, we produced three:—
1. Never to eat porridge.
2. Never to get back in time to wash.
3. Never to walk anywhere if it was possible to ride.

We could, with advantage, have added never to scream when

Mrs Coates brought in the pudding, for at times she must have thought she was entering a den of wild animals.

The club must have a name. We hesitated over Scarthwaite Fell Club, and finally decided that that would have to do until we could think of something better.

* * *

On Sundays we never did much walking, apart from the Catbells flank to Swinside, or up the Castle Crag track, or on the lower slopes of Grange Fell, and we were always in for Sunday lunch, which was invariably excellent. This particular Sunday was an exception, for after a very large lunch we suddenly took a notion to walk, not on any track, but straight up the fell-side onto Maiden Moor and along the ridge to Scawdel Fell. As this would mean going without any tea, Mrs Coates promptly brought in the teapot and a large cake, and I am ashamed to say that within half an hour of finishing lunch we had also had tea. Only crumbs remained of the cake, apart from a piece which Cop saved to eat on the ridge.

We certainly did Maiden Moor the hard way. Climbing straight up, contending with all the old tough heather and bracken roots, soon had us puffing and panting, while the upper section was steep enough to have us on all fours, hauling ourselves up the rocks. Just then it began to rain heavily, and we had to hold onto the rocks with one hand and struggle into our oilskins with the other.

On the top the wind was strong and all views were wiped out, and we sat on the wet grass, eating chocolate and grumbling gently. The sensible thing would have been to go straight back down the fell, but that did not occur to us. Having set out to do a ridge walk we intended to do it, even if the weather did its worst — which it did.

Fighting along, the wind hurling sheets of water over us, we reached Scawdel Fell and slithered down to the all-prevailing bog of Lobstone Band, then down the slate gully which had become a rushing stream, and to the Castle Crag track, where we were below the wind and only had to contend with the heavy rain, which was nothing. Although we were so wet and muddy, there was that contented feeling of achievement which is always the reward of a walk done in adverse conditions.

* * *

When the final day of the holiday came we gave up all hope for one last top, for the rain sluiced down. We spent the morning in Keswick, mooning round the shops and doing nothing in particular. Then, suddenly the rain stopped and a watery sun appeared, and we decided to salvage what was left of the day by going up Styhead and back down Grain Gill. The sun was lighting up fresh snow on Esk Hause!

In the ensuing rush, we reached home at 12.55, bolted lunch, and caught the 1.30 up-dale bus. There was no time for lacing boots. We did that on the bridge at the beginning of the Seathwaite lane, gave them a smear of dubbin and parked the grease tin under a tree to collect on our return — and as far as I know it is there to this day. Then on to Seathwaite and Stockley Bridge at the double.

We were half-way up Styhead when it began to rain.

"It's only a cloud. It will soon pass over," we said, fooling ourselves.

At the top of the pass it was blowing, raining, and snowing hard. Black clouds seethed over Great End, yet through tiny gaps in the gloom the sun was shining on the Irish Sea. Conditions were uncomfortable but thrilling. In Grain Gill the stream had turned into a roaring torrent, which we had to cross and recross several times, not an easy manoeuvre. Then we got below the snow-line, and there was just rain and bog. The track, such as it was, was under water. We were too wet for tea at the farm, and the bus ride from Seatoller to Grange was like taking a cold bath. Mrs Coates dried our clothes as well as she could, because we had to pack.

Later that night, when Prim and I were in the kitchen settling up the holiday account, Mrs Coates told us that we were known in the village as Sally's Ladies. Each Easter, as soon as we put in an appearance, word went round, "Sally's Ladies are here again!"

And we returned to the sitting-room to tell the others that we had got the perfect name for the club — SALLY'S LADIES. Thus the S.L. Club was born.

May had acquitted herself well in her first year. From the beginning, she loved the mountains whole-heartedly, in spite of her initial ordeal, which was worse than any of us realised at the time. Many weeks later we learnt that she had broken two toe-nails on the Gable South Traverse.

She said, "My only fear was that you would do walks as strenuous every day, and if you did I might conk out!"

BLIZZARD ON THE PIKE

We needed another walker. If our number was made up to seven, we could guarantee that half a dozen would be at the Easter meeting, thus allowing for the times when the odd one would be absent. For example, there was Doris, still a church organist, though she intended to resign as soon as possible, as she hated missing the Lakeland Easters. If all seven of us turned up, Mrs Coates could easily put up an extra bed in 'Riggside', Prim's room. So we invited Hilda to join us. She had done extensive walking in Switzerland and would be used to the hills, so there would only be a matter of getting her used to Sally's Ladies!

Cath and I had bought a car, a second-hand Hillman Minx. Hilda and May already possessed cars, but would not be using them this Easter. Prim was to bring Hilda up by train, which, she said would give her a good opportunity to prime Hilda about the Easter gathering. May was to come in the car with Cath and myself, and would share the driving. Cop would be coming by train from London.

We enjoyed the journey by the Ilkley-Skipton route, and planned to have tea at the King's Head at Thirlspot, but we hit trouble near the top of Dunmail Raise when the car refused to go in any gear above second. The selector was bent, and neither we nor an AA patrolman could move the gear lever. We crawled at ten miles an hour back to a garage in Grasmere, but they could do nothing because the mechanic was not available. We went on to the next garage, which was at Ambleside. They could do the job, but were uncertain how long it would take. We crossed all our fingers and spent the next hour over tea in a café. On returning to the garage we were overjoyed to find the car ready and waiting. Racing to

Keswick and up Borrowdale, we arrived at Scarthwaite a few minutes before Prim, Hilda, and Cop walked in. Hilda looked affable, though slightly anxious. She had a large framed rucksack with a pair of boots swinging from it.

That evening, we argued about where to go the next day, and went to bed without making any plans, knowing that Prim would produce some in due course. The night was quiet and peaceful, and we were sure the weather would remain settled. All mountaineers are optimists.

* * *

Brilliant sunlight made an ideal day for Dale Head, Hindscarth, and Robinson. Honister took some time because the Mellbreak pack of foxhounds was hunting off Grey Knotts, and we stood watching until they were out of sight.

From Honister top up Dale Head is a lengthy walk, as far as you can see and twice as far beyond that. I kept telling May that the summit cairn would be just over the next rise, and after a while she stopped believing me. As we climbed we got into the wind, the sun disappeared, and dark clouds began to form over Gable.

We battled against a rising wind on the ridge to Hindscarth. Then came the rain, and we donned oilskins and sou'westers, and Hilda produced a thin plastic cape without any fasteners, the sort of garment adequate for a light summer shower at ground level. We goggled in disbelief, and Prim whispered in an aside, "I warned her. I told her to bring an oilskin!"

"I wonder if she realises she's in for a soaking."

"She soon will!" chuckled Cath.

In vicious wind and rain we made Hindscarth, then Robinson, where there should have been a magnificent view of the Red Pike-High Crag range, but there wasn't. We told Hilda what she should have seen, but she was too wet to care. Ploughing through Buttermere Moss, Cop, a compulsive talker, slipped and fell full length, and lay reclining on one elbow until she had finished what she was saying. Then Hilda sat down with a tremendous splash, which annoyed her intensely.

The rain was sheeting down at Buttermere, where we rushed into the Victoria Hotel tea-room for a pot of tea. As we sat and dripped we became surrounded by individual pools of water, and Cop's hands were stained bright blue from the dye in her gloves. We looked at each other and exploded with laughter. Only Hilda remained dead serious and harassed, exclaiming, "We shall catch cold! We must get home!"

When she had said it three times, Cop asked, "How do we get home?"

"We walk over Honister." Prim blandly replied.

"Oh, Prim, we can't!" wailed Hilda.

Her cry fell on deaf ears, and we sallied forth into the wind and driving rain and headed for the black clouds massed low in the pass, but as we passed the Buttermere Hotel, Prim swerved and dashed inside, while we stood in a huddle and waited. Some of us realised that she was about to do something, and the others were too wet and disconsolate to think at all. She came out to tell us that she had rung up Seatoller but John was not there. She had then rung up Swinside and arranged for Middleton's taxi to collect us, and we were to go into the hotel to wait. We made a mad rush for the door. The hotel lounge was chilly without a fire, but at least we were out of the rain and jubilant at the idea of an easy ride, though Hilda worriedly persisted in her plaint, "We must get home!"

"We are going to get home," we assured her.

Cop adding, "You can always start walking if you are in such a hurry!"

The six of us squashed into the taxi in layers, and on reaching Scarthwaite prised ourselves loose with difficulty. Mrs Coates made tea for us, and carried off our wet clothes. Then we rushed upstairs and five of us put our cold feet into the bath simultaneously, and when we had finished Hilda lay in the bath. She was convinced that being soaked to the skin would have dire effects, though we assured her it never did.

After an outsize dinner, we sprawled, warm and comatose, round the fire, and Prim, reading aloud about Dale Head, kept stopping to rub her eyes.

"I can't see properly. It's the wind."

"What wind?" Cop wanted to know.

"Dale Head wind, of course!"

"Oh!" said Cop. "Mine is another sort — from over-eating," which caused Hilda to regard her with disapproval.

Prim finished the piece she was reading, and I suggested, "Now read Baddeley."

To which Cop retorted, "She's been reading badly!"

"Heaven preserve us!" I said in disgust.

"This intelligent conversation is too much for me," said May, with a prolonged yawn. "I'm off to bed."

* * *

Several days of wild, wet weather curbed our activities considerably. The first of these days was a complete loss as far as any outdoor pursuit was concerned. There was an uncomfortable sortie to Keswick, and we tried to be philosophical round the fire, but it did not work. There was some reading aloud. I read and the others listened in the intervals between their own private conversations. You need to be very good tempered to do this type of reading aloud!

By Sunday afternoon the rain had diminished to a thick, murky drizzle, and Cath, Cop and I, tired of being cooped up, decided to go for a walk. We could not go far, as we intended to be back for tea, so Cop made one of her bright suggestions, "Let's go halfway, and then come back!"

"Half-way to where?"

"I don't know or care," she said. "I'm like a sheep. You lead and I'll follow."

We went along the Catbells road, and after a mile it began to rain very heavily. Cath and I cursed because we had come out in ordinary coats, but Cop in her oilskin was quite happy. We rushed back home, and I discovered that it was my oilskin Cop had taken, and we had a slanging match.

We went to evensong in the village church, and it was still raining when we came out. May, staring wistfully at the misty fells, pleaded, "Send us some decent weather, Lord. I've prayed for it!"

"What!" Hilda exclaimed. "How much did you put in the collection bag?"

"What has that to do with it?" demanded May.

"You said you had paid for decent weather."

"I said prayed, not paid!" adding in a loud aside, "the rain must have got in her ears!"

It was still raining the next morning, which meant another frustrated session round the fire. On a plate on the sideboard were our Pasche eggs, ready to take on a walk, and we wondered what to do with them if we did not go. Cop, with a wicked glint in her eye, suggested, "Let's throw them at each other!" at which Prim hastily intervened.

"I think we should take Hilda to Watendlath after lunch, whatever the weather."

This caused a storm of protest. We thought nothing of Watendlath. We were sick of going there.

"Have you an alternative suggestion?"

We had not, so Watendlath it was. Going over the fell from Rosthwaite we were bombarded by a vicious hailstorm. We had tea at one of the Watendlath farmhouses where they insisted on keeping the door open, in case they missed any customers, and we sat, snarling, in the draught.

Strolling down to Ashness Gate, we took a notion to visit the Lodore falls, which should be spectacular after all the rain. On reaching the Lodore Hotel, we scattered in all directions. Prim and I, on the back path, had almost reached the falls when Cath raced after us, shouting that the bus was coming. Cop was roaming somewhere on the far side of the beck, and by the time we had found her the bus had gone. May and Hilda, who had started to walk back to Grange, also missed it, as they did not know it was coming until it passed them.

Then, after each of us had told the others what half-wits they were, we walked home, and as we tramped along the rain stopped, the sky began to clear, and our spirits soared. The wet spell was ending, and with it our time of inaction.

* * *

The Warnscale Bottom track at Buttermere looked interesting, and the weekly bus from Keswick, via Whinlatter, made the walk over Honister unnecessary.

On reaching Buttermere village, our first priority was morning coffee. This they refused to provide at the Victoria Hotel, though they did offer to unlock the attached café for us. We told them we did not like trippers' cafés. At the Buttermere Hotel they did not serve coffee. This made us determined to get it at all costs, and Hilda's suggestion that we did not need it, and should get on with the walk, was ignored.

"We are sure to get it at Miss Nelson's," we said, as we walked by the lake, but before reaching her cottage we came to Gatesgarth Farm. There the coffee was excellent, and we lingered over it for most of the morning before starting up Warnscale Bottom.

A fair track climbed a rocky gorge which echoed with the music of waterfalls. At the top, we emerged among some ruined quarry huts. There we cast about for a sheltered picnic spot, discarding one place after another as being too draughty, too cold, or too uncomfortable, and finally settling between two high walls of slate which made a perfect wind tunnel. In half a gale we ate our Pasche eggs; Cop's rather squashed because she had sat on it; and each trying to swap her lettuce sandwiches for someone else's meat.

May, looking about her, asked "Where are we?"

And Prim replied, "At the top of Warnscale Bottom."

"You can't be at the top of a bottom!"

"You can — and we are."

May subsided, muttering, "Daft!"

A boggy track led to the Gallows, where we paused for Cath to rescue her socks which had slipped into her boots and to put some Elastoplast on May's toe, before making for Brandreth summit. Soon we were ploughing happily through deep snow, and admiring the wonderful cloud effects over the Buttermere and Ennerdale valleys.

Although the wind was keen, we stayed for some time by the summit cairn on Brandreth before plodding back to the Gallows, walking in Indian file through the snow, the front ones constantly stopping to admire the view and the back ones urging them to get a move on because it was cold. In the swamp surrounding the Gallows, May almost lost her outsize boots, and Hilda plunged knee-deep.

Strolling down Honister, we were unlucky over tea at Seatoller, and went on to Rosthwaite, to a table groaning with home-made cakes at the Scafell Hotel. We were not particularly hungry, though Prim, who loved cakes, attacked them with gusto. She said it was in case we had stew, which she hated, for dinner — a weak excuse, as Mrs Coates never gave us stew.

Home in good time for once, there was skirmishing to bag the bathroom, but I did not join in. I had decided to harden my feet by not washing them at all.

At dinner, a large main course was followed by an enormous blackcurrant pudding, and Cop, with clasped hands and enraptured eyes, exclaimed, "I don't care if I am too full! I'm going to eat a lot of that!"

"Pig!" said May.

When we had demolished the pudding and were almost at bursting point, Prim said, "Let's pass the plates up, then we can start on the cheese. I like cheese!"

How we ate in those days, and then sprawled ungracefully round the fire, with the exception of Hilda, who lay on her back on the floor. She said she was more comfortable that way. Cop tried it, but quickly scrambled up again.

"It is not at all comfortable. Nothing is, when you are too full!"

"You can always stand and lean on the wall!" I said.

We discussed writing our own book about the Lake District. It was to be unlike any of the hundreds published, for, as Cop pointed out, "Our approach would be entirely different and original. Anyone can slobber over Wordsworth and the scenery, and we don't want that. It's been done to death."

"And which of us would have to write this unique book?" I asked.

They all looked at me and answered, "You!"

* * *

To all hill-wanderers, there are certain days which remain highlighted in memory, and the day we did the Corridor Route to Scafell Pike was one.

There was the lane to Seathwaite, Stockley Bridge, and the pass, with Styhead Tarn sparkling in the sun. The first part of the Corridor Route was obvious and easy, but after that we found ourselves in a maze of steep rocks instead of the plain sailing we had expected. Obviously we had somehow missed the correct route. We were very close to the great gash of Piers Gill, and had to do some strenuous, but thoroughly enjoyable, rock climbing to get above the ravine to the saddle between Lingmell and the Pike. This was under deep snow. There were a few footprints, which we followed, but the going was laborious through snow so soft and mushy that we sank in above the knees.

Prim, in the lead, suddenly swung left, ignoring the footprints, which went straight on, and we found ourselves on a wickedly steep slope where the snow had hardened almost to ice and we had to kick holds for our feet. It was strenuous going, and we were a little worried about a mass of black cloud which was approaching rapidly from the north. Then Prim stopped and pointed up the slope.

"I think we must be on some sort of a track, because there is a girl in a plastic mac standing up there."

A few minutes later, she exclaimed, "She's still there! She hasn't moved!"

As we drew nearer, the girl turned into a rock covered with wind-blown ice. Then the cloud burst in a blinding hail-cum-snow blizzard, and visibility was nil. We struggled on, panting and fighting every inch of the way, and suddenly, to our immense relief, we almost bumped into the immense cairn on the summit of the Pike. About us, the storm raged in fury, and we knew we must get down quickly. The way we had climbed up near Piers Gill was unthinkable. The Esk Hause route was the only possibility, but we could see neither that nor any other route. We could see nothing in any direction. There was only Prim's infallible mountaineering instinct to point us in the direction of Esk Hause, and it did not fail.

The first downward slope from the Pike was solid ice, difficult to negotiate, especially as the blizzard made it impossible to see anything, but as we topped the next ridge a miracle happened. The storm swept away, the sky cleared, the sun came out, and we found ourselves on an expanse of shining, virgin snow surrounded by dark peaks. It halted us in our tracks, for we knew we might never see anything so glorious again. The grandeur filled our hearts, our whole selves, with such elation that we could scarcely bear to leave it. We loitered joyously, and time raced by before we reached the final ridge connecting the Pike to Great End, and slid down beside a big snow cornice onto Esk Hause. Down Styhead the snow gave way to slush, and the slush to mud. My boots were full of water, swishing round my toes.

The going was fast from Stockley Bridge to Seatoller, where we were fortunate enough to catch a bus. We reached home half an hour late. Mrs Coates took one look at us, laughed heartedly, and offered to make a pot of tea. We declined, kicked off our sodden foot-gear, and straight away sat down to dinner. We were ravenous, tired, and dirty, and full of a sense of achievement. We had seen the glory of the hills that day.

* * *

"Can we have a gentle walk for a change?" asked Hilda.

"An easy walk so that we can get back without having to run the last two miles," added May.

Prim looked at Cath, Cop, and myself.

"I'm easy," shrugged Cath.

"I don't mind where I go as long as I go somewhere," Cop said.

I remained silent. I wanted to do a top, but knew that if I suggested anything I should be reminded that we had done the Corridor Route for my benefit because I had always wanted to do it, and therefore I should be satisfied for the time being.

"All right," Prim said. "We will go to Keswick, eat our sandwiches on Friar's Crag, catch the launch across the lake, and walk home over Catbells. You couldn't have an easier day than that!" Everyone agreed.

We enjoyed an almost deserted Friar's Crag. The day was ideal for splendid views, but we were unable to linger if we were to catch the launch. It was bitterly cold on the water, but we soon got warm climbing up through the trees to the road. We emerged near a house which provided refreshments.

"Shall we have a pot of tea?" suggested Prim.

"No!" said Hilda. "We waste such a lot of time over things like that!"

The rest of us chorused, "Yes!"

"I'm going to have a pot, anyway," and Prim made for the house, and we followed, willingly or otherwise.

After the tea we went up the nose of Catbells, taking our time, and discussing all the fells in sight. On reaching the track which drops down to Manesty, May said, "This is where I leave you. I shall stroll down and get a little peace. You others can go where you like!"

We were all supposed to go down the Manesty track, but it seemed such a tame ending. Prim said, "Why not do the whole ridge?" So we carried on over Maiden Moor and Scawdel Fell, and down to the wet squelch of Lobstone Band.

Hilda, wearing light brown suede shoes, was not happy in the patches of bog, and even less so in the slate gully, which we took fast, having realised that we should probably be late for dinner. Her shoes had no grip on the wet slate, and she dislodged a large piece which landed on my instep, and I swore.

We raced along the Castle Crag track, and Cath and I took a short cut across the fields near Hollows Farm. We had to climb several fences to reach the wall round Scarthwaite garden. I wanted to climb that, but Cath said, "No, Mrs Coates might not like it," so we crossed the field to a gate into the lane. That was locked, and we climbed over. Our short cut made us much later than if we had taken the usual track.

We found Hilda muttering with dismay and annoyance over her ruined shoes.

"I thought we were going for an easy walk. I should not have worn them if I had known. These were expensive!"

Then Cop took her by the arm and led her aside.

"Hilda, let me give you some good advice. Never put on a pair of decent shoes when you think you are going for a gentle walk with Prim, because you could easily find yourself landed on somewhere like Scafell Pike!"

"I'm beginning to realise that." Hilda sounded resigned, and later on asked Prim. "Do you consider we had an easy day, going through all that bog and having to rush home?"

Prim shrugged. "It was not what I would call strenuous. But I've thought of a really easy one for tomorrow." She then proposed that we should go to Langdale, climb by Dungeon Ghyll to Stickle

Tarn, and walk down past Easedale Tarn to Grasmere. That would be very simple, and there would be plenty of time to catch a bus home. Hilda expressed doubts about the time factor. She said we did too much loitering on the way, instead of getting on with the walk.

"What I really like is to make an early start, and get home in time for a wash and afternoon tea."

There was dead silence. Then first one then another began to laugh, until we were roaring our heads off.

* * *

A warm, sunny day found us in Langdale, starting on Prim's simple walk. Instead of going up Dungeon Ghyll, we left the bus at the New Dungeon Ghyll Hotel, and went up Mill Gill by mistake, which was immaterial. In those days the track was excellent, with an enjoyable upper section — a narrow gully between rocks, where you could use your hands to take some of the weight off your feet. I enjoyed that, as my right foot was bruised and swollen where the slate had fallen on it the day before.

We ate our sandwiches by Stickle Tarn, sitting near the water, looking at the precipitous face of Pavey Ark, some of us stifling the urge to go up Jack's Rake.

There was to be a pleasant stroll over the fells to Codale Tarn, then down to Easedale Tarn, pausing for cups of tea at the refreshment hut, and finally taking the pony track to Grasmere. We anticipated that the walk would not be very exciting, and we ambled along, talking and not paying much attention to where we were going. The fell was featureless, its undulations cutting off all landmarks on every side.

After a good half-hour we should have been nearing Easedale Tarn, or at least Codale, but there was no sign of either. It was then that we realised that we had been following sheep tracks, and had lost direction, and because it was such a simple walk we had brought neither compass nor map. Without much idea where we were heading, we walked on, skirting numerous patches of black, oozing bog. There were no other people on the fell.

Prim began to laugh.

"If anyone asked me where I was going, I should feel such an idiot saying either to Grasmere, or Ambleside, or Langdale, and not sure which!" At this, Hilda lost her temper.

"This is ridiculous! I'm going back!"

Then we all laughed, for by then we had no idea which way was forward and which was back.

We walked on, Hilda muttering and grumbling, until we reached the edge of an escarpment, and looked down on a valley.

"That's Langdale!" Prim said.

Our aimless wanderings had taken us in a large circle. Hilda then decided that she had had enough.

"Our best plan is to climb down there. Is anyone coming? May?"

"I might as well, I suppose," shrugged May.

We said nothing. We had no intention of climbing down to Langdale, and no doubts about ultimately getting to Grasmere. We stood watching with interest as Hilda and May scrambled over the escarpment and disappeared. Then Prim said, "Right! Now we'll go to Grasmere!" She set off like a homing pigeon, up and down over rock, fell and bog, and we followed. I found the steep downhill bits trying for my bruised foot, but following behind Cath and putting my hands on her shoulders helped. Once she slipped and sat in the bog, but I removed my hands in time to stop falling on her.

Then Prim sang out, "The outskirts of Grasmere!" and we cut straight down, through gorse bushes and dead bracken. We knew it was too late to catch the bus, so Prim said we would stop at the first house we came to, and enquire about a car. The first house was a derelict farm, from which a cart-track led down to the road. As we walked towards the village, Cop, with a wide grin, said "I've got a better idea than hiring a car. You lie down in the middle of the road, Cis, and we'll telephone for the ambulance, and when it comes we'll say that you've hurt your foot and can't walk any further. Then we'll ask the man if we can go back to Grange in the ambulance with you!"

Prim said, resignedly, "Oh, Cop!"

Soon we reached a group of houses. The first looked empty, but Prim banged on the door to make sure. At the second, nobody was at home. We had just drawn a blank at the third when two people turned in at the gate, to be accosted by Prim, "Do you live here?"

They looked surprised, but directed us to a garage 'just down the road and round the corner'.

So we travelled back to Grange in a large, comfortable car, and wondered how Hilda and May would get out of Langdale when there was no afternoon bus service there.

We had almost finished dinner when they arrived. Having, with difficulty, scrambled down to Langdale, they had tried to thumb a lift, and were eventually picked up by a private touring bus and taken to Ambleside. There they had caught a relief bus to Keswick, but the last Borrowdale bus had gone, so they had hired a taxi to Grange.

Hilda said they had been really worried about leaving us on the fells. This evoked considerable amusement, and I said, "Worried is the wrong word, Hilda. It would have been more appropriate had you been warned about us!"

She admitted, "Actually, we should never have gone down into Langdale."

Round the fire later, we browsed through the guide-books, found nothing about the walk we had done that day, abandoned them in disgust, and began arguing about easy walks in general, a subject on which we held widely differing views.

Prim said, "I shall never dare to plan another walk!" and went on, "and I've never looked such a tramp in the evening in my life. I'm going up to do something about it, and then I'm going to bed."

She gave a tremendous yawn, and departed. As soon as the door had closed behind her, it reopened.

"And I've done with the Langdale Pikes for ever!"

"Amen!" said May.

* * *

Before the holiday ended we had several 'easy' days, wandering by the river and up the Castle Crag track, exploring the fells round Seathwaite, and foraging in Manesty and Brandelhow woods — all enjoyable days in Borrowdale, but my most vivid memory is of Scafell Pike, the untrodden snow, the dark crags, and the silence of the heights. That was a mountaineer's day.

We speculated about Hilda's feelings, considering what effect being lost, soaked to the skin, and ruining a pair of expensive shoes, would have on her, but on the last evening she said, "This has been a wonderful holiday. I've never had one like it. Shall I be coming next year? Will you ask me again? I hope you will!"

She was told, "Of course! You are now one of Sally's Ladies!"

WINTER IN SPRING

This was an Easter of rain, snow, and biting wind, which, combined with the after-effects of a severe attack of flu recently suffered by Prim, made it a mainly unenergetic holiday. Also, it was the year when the chore of getting to the Lakes finally ended, and we could snap our fingers at the shortcomings of the railway. We took two cars, Cath's and Hilda's, and Cop came up from London to Nottingham the day before, in order to travel with Cath and me. Hilda's passengers were Prim and May, and poor Doris was unable to come at all.

    We went by the Ilkley-Skipton route on a grey, gloomy morning. Dark clouds were massed to the west of the Pennines, and we reached Windermere in a heavy downpour which persisted for the rest of the journey. But to us, exiled for the past year, even in rain Borrowdale was beautiful, and we sang at the tops of our voices as we drove up the narrow road to Scarthwaite, to the heart-warming welcome of Mrs Coates. She was so tolerant of the way we turned her fine house into a kind of zoo, and ate all before us like a plague of locusts.

    Prim, Hilda, and May went to bed soon after dinner, Prim because she had been advised to rest as much as possible, and the others because they were worn out, so they said. Then Cop found May's bag of sweets on the mantelpiece, and we ate them. We three stayed up late on that and every succeeding night, and occasionally the others complained of the noise coming from the sitting-room when they were trying to sleep.

    Cath, Cop and I were in 'Langstrath' this year, and to share a bedroom with Cop was like living in an earthquake zone. She strewed her possessions everywhere, but if any of our things strayed by mistake into her part she threw them right and left. We never reached the stage of actually fighting, but sometimes we came very near to it.

* * *

On the first day of the holiday it was fine and reasonably warm, and over breakfast we argued about where to go. Prim was having breakfast in bed, so could offer no suggestions. We finally decided to start in the Langstrath, and then go wherever the whim took us.

We pottered so slowly up the long, lonely Langstrath that it was lunch-time when we reached the foot of Stake. The sun was shining on the flat rocks near the ancient ash trees, and we stayed there, picking out the sandwiches we liked and discarding the others. Then, to our amazement, Hilda said, "I think we have done enough for a first walk, so May and I will just stroll quietly back on the other side of the beck. I don't suppose you others are ready to come."

"You're dead right!" I said.

"We haven't been anywhere yet!" Cath pointed out.

"Well. I'll be damned!" I said, as we watched them go. "They've had enough already!"

"Where next?" asked Cop.

"We'll go up the Stake Pass."

This we did, and at the top of the pass found snow a foot deep. We debated the next move, and I suggested the back of the Langdale Pikes. I wanted to see the 'long, thundering drop into Langdale' as described by H. H. Symonds; and we set off in what we thought was approximately the right direction. The going over the soft, untrodden snow was strenuous, and some of the drifts were deep.

Cath, who was leading, suddenly stopped.

"I can hear rushing water."

We stood listening, and we, too, heard it, but foolishly, I said, "Oh, it will be nothing much," and pushed ahead, and went through the snow into a stream. Cath grabbed me by the collar and heaved, and we both rolled backwards in a heap, a spectacle much enjoyed by Cop. I removed my boots and emptied the water from them.

"This is a mug's game when we don't know where we are putting our feet!" exclaimed Cath, and we agreed. We abandoned the back of the Langdales, and returned to the top of the pass, which was not easy because the cairn was buried under the snow, and took some finding. On the way, Cop fell head first into a snow-drift, and it was our turn to laugh. We raced down the pass, and along the Langstrath to Stonethwaite, where we had large mugs of tea before walking home. We were not late for dinner.

That night, after the others had gone to bed, leaving Cath, Cop and me by the fire, we found May's slab of chocolate, and ate it. That was the last time May left anything edible in the sitting-room.

* * *

On a windy day we set out to climb Gable. Leaving the cars at Seatoller, and walking up Honister, the gusts fretted and plucked at us so forcibly that Cop grumbled incessantly, in spite of being told not to act like an old woman. But on reaching the Gallows, when the full force of the gale shrieked round our ears, she had no breath left with which to complain.

Unlike the soft, laborious mush at the top of Stake, the deep, hard snow on the Grey Knotts-Brandreth plateau made for good going, only spoilt by the piercingly bitter wind. By the Brandreth cairn, we crouched, shivering, among the rocks, but our sandwiches were so tasteless that it was difficult to tell the difference between cheese and meat, and our jaws were almost too stiff to move. It was the most unpleasant picnic I have ever had.

On Green Gable the gale howled. Eyes streamed and tears froze on cheeks. As we fought along, I said, "Isn't it good to know that in a couple of hours we shall be down out of this!" To which Cop replied, "I don't know why we came at all!"

Incredibly, when we got down to Wind Gap, with its huge snow cornice, there was no wind, but neither was there any chance of climbing Great Gable, for the whole of that face of the mountain was sheathed in ice. We watched one foolhardy man attempt it, lose his footing, and shoot down on his back spinning like a top. Fortunately, his feet, not his head, hit a rock.

We turned down Aaron Slack to Styhead, twice stopping to haul Hilda out of the snow. The first time, she had one leg buried to the knee, and the second, both legs went in up to the waist.

After tea at Seathwaite, we strolled to Seatoller and drove home, where we received a dressing-down from Mrs Coates.

"It's proper daft, and I mean DAFT, to go on the tops in conditions like these, and you are not to try. I shall be real worried and vexed if you do it again!"

* * *

The weather was not conducive to mountain climbing, so Mrs Coates had no cause to worry. The fact that Prim was out of action did not prevent her from planning alternative excursions. We had two cars at our disposal, therefore it was a good opportunity to see more of the Lake District.

We set out to drive round to Wasdale, and it was snowing when we reached Cockermouth. This, though unpleasant, would not have deterred us, but when the cable of Cath's windscreen wiper burnt out we were obliged to turn back. We spent the day in Cockermouth, drifting aimlessly about the streets while the wiper was being repaired. Prim suggested a visit to Wordsworth's house, where she was accompanied by an unenthusiastic Cop. The rest of us pretended to be deaf. On the way home it snowed heavily, turning Borrowdale into a white, incredibly beautiful fairyland.

Another day there was the drive to Ullswater, when we started out in a glittering world of white peaks, and ran through alternating sunlight and snow flurries. Fortunately, the sky cleared as we reached the southern stretch of the lake, revealing the splendid fells grouped at its head. We did some useful map work.

One day, to give the car drivers a break, we walked over Honister to Buttermere, round the lake, and back. The road over the pass was icy, and sledges would have been ideal. Having none, we slid most of the way down.

Hilda said she had once spent a holiday in Coniston, and perhaps we might like to go and have a look round there, though we should be disappointed with it after Borrowdale.

"We could always climb the Old Man," said Cath, knowing well that we should not do that when the weather was preventing us from climbing our own fells.

We were not greatly impressed by Coniston on that first visit, though we did cast speculative eyes on the Old Man. Prim directed the drivers along the eastern side of the lake. She said, "We ought to go and have a look at Brantwood — Ruskin's place."

Cop alone replied, "I'll come if I ought, but I don't want to!"

The rest of us paid no heed, and while Cop trailed after Prim, we sat looking at the Old Man and his satellites.

Next, we went to Tarn Hows. To reach it involved a short walk, which the others did while Prim and I waited in the car. Finally, we explored Hawkshead, another of those places where every Lakeland visitor should go once and get it over. At one National Trust building, Prim, who carried a guide-book, said, "This must be the house where Wordsworth lodged."

May sniffed, "And they haven't washed the curtains since!"

We had tea, and when paying for it were asked how many pieces of scone we had eaten. We had no idea, never having been to a place where you paid for part of a scone instead of a whole one, but we made something up, and went out to continue exploring. Neither Cop nor I knew what we were looking for, so we followed Prim who obviously did, while the other three went in the opposite direction. We were taken to Wordsworth's cottage and the Grammar School, then we ran into the others, who told us that Hilda had fallen over a tombstone in the churchyard, but was undamaged apart from her dignity.

* * *

Time passed all too quickly. The weather gradually improved until the valleys were clear of snow, but the heights retained their white mantle. They were seldom visible because of dense cloud. When Hilda and May had reached the last day of their holiday, we persuaded them to go over Styhead to Wasdale. They said they were quite willing, provided the day was fine, which it was. There was even some sunlight. The car was left at Seathwaite, and we idled to the top of the pass, where we had a lengthy rest on the stretcher box.

Then, most suddenly, the air became cold and it began to snow, and Wasdale was a cauldron of black, seething cloud. Neither Hilda nor May liked the look of it.

"It would be foolish to go on." Hilda sounded very definite, and May nodded in agreement.

"We shall have to go back."

It was more or less a fifty-fifty split, and there was no point in arguing. You either want to do a thing or you don't, and they didn't.

"All right," I said, "but we've come up here for nothing!"

We started back, the snow bouncing off us in stinging pellets, and were half-way down the pass when the storm passed and the sun came out, which evoked some annoyance.

"We could have gone into Wasdale after all!"

"We should have gone on!"

"How were we to know!"

"We could always go back up the pass!"

"We are not going back now!"

That was that, so for a diversion, we crossed the beck and went down by a scrambly track with some nice rocks to climb, close to Taylor Gill Force. It was good, until the track lost itself in bog at the bottom, where May slipped and sat down heavily, which she

took in good part after an initial expletive.
"You will not mind me going back to Nottingham looking mucky, will you, Hilda? It's all the same if you do!"
On reaching home, Cath and I, with energy to spare, walked along the flank of Catbells to Walpole's slate seat. Every tree and fell was mirrored in Derwentwater, and we sat watching until we were half frozen. Then we collected larch branches for the fire, and carried them home.

* * *

There was sleet mixed with snow the next morning, and we wore oilskins when we helped to carry the luggage out to Hilda's car. She had offered to take our surplus gear. She and May left in a snowstorm.
"I should not be surprised to see them back at any moment," I said. "I think they are in for one hell of a journey."
Cop airily dismissed that.
"Oh, they will be quite all right in a car!"
"You don't drive a car," Cath reminded her.
Mrs Coates, bringing in our elevenses, said that it had been a record year for accidents on the fells. Also, the milkman had just told her that the 10.30 Keswick-Grasmere bus had been unable to get over Dunmail Raise, and they were waiting for a snow-plough to clear the road.
That night, Hilda telephoned to report that they had been stuck in the snow on Dunmail Raise, and had then driven through torrential rain all the way to Nottingham, and two days later we received a postcard from May —
"I expect you will by now have heard of the terrible ride of two females through a blinding blizzard over the Raise. We now know what it means by 'Snow on high ground'. I think it ought to go on record that Hilda did this journey in nylons and climbing boots."
"Let's hope that conditions will have improved by tomorrow," Cath said, for it was our final day. The sun shone from a cloudless sky, but the high tops remained impossible, and we fretted because it seemed that our few remaining hours would be wasted.
"Why don't you do a little top?" suggested Prim.
So we went up Catbells, and reached deep, crisp snow on Maiden Moor. As we sat in the drifts, eating our sandwiches, the sun blazed down, and the brilliant light was almost painful without sunglasses, and views on every side were perfect. The white Scafells and Gable seemed almost near enough to touch, and the great Helvellyn range filled the horizon with shining clarity.

Cop kept repeating, "We may never see anything like this again!" until we told her to think of something else to say.

It was completely, splendidly beautiful.

We trotted along in single file, Cath leading as trail-breaker, over Narrow Moor and Scawdel Fell, and down to Lobstone Band, where all the bog was frozen except one small patch about a yard wide, where Cath had the misfortune to slip and sit down heavily. She said the wet went right through her clothes to her skin — and it was not funny.

Beyond the tarn, the snow lay in deep drifts, through which we forced an uphill way to the remains of the wire fence half-way up Dale Head. Ten minutes took us down to the top of Honister, and a further fifteen to Seatoller, and the end of the walk.

Not a strenuous day, but a richly rewarding one, and at least we had achieved a top, albeit a minor one.

Adverse weather conditions; Prim being unfit; Mrs Coates' genuine concern for our safety on the higher fells — all had combined to curtail our activities that Easter. Yet to be in Borrowdale, whatever the weather, was in itself enchantment.

And the fells would always be there, waiting for our return.

SOUTH TRAVERSE

We had planned to go to the Lakes by the Scotch Corner-Bowes Moor route, and were well on the way when Prim, who had been studying the map, suggested that we might take in Ripon, Fountains Abbey, and Wensleydale as a more interesting variation.

We had two cars — Cath's, with Prim and myself; and Hilda's, with Cop and May. Our car led, and Hilda followed. I think we had informed her of the detour, but I am not sure. She always vowed that she never had any idea where we were going, and just followed blindly and hoped for the best.

At Ripon, we paused for a lightning dash to the cathedral before driving into Studley Royal Park and stopping at the church. Hilda drew up behind us and waited while we went inside. She and her two passengers were too lazy to get out, and consequently missed the wealth of interesting features gracing the beautiful interior of the church. Cath picked up a leaflet which told visitors what to look for, and we followed the instructions from beginning to end, and when we came out the others grumbled about having to wait so long for us. We said it served them right.

Then to Fountains Abbey, where we were allowed to leave the cars at the gates instead of taking them up a steep, muddy lane to the official car-park. Prim, already familiar with the place, led us up a hill to get a bird's-eye view of the abbey before we explored the ruins at close quarters. This exploration was of necessity cursory, for if there is poetry in stone it is there in Fountains Abbey. It was almost three o'clock before we got back to the cars and our belated packed lunch.

Next, we drove up Wensleydale. At Bainbridge, we pulled up automatically for tea at the hotel, ignoring Hilda's protests.

"We don't need tea! It is late, and we should be getting on!"

"It's a matter of principle," said Cop vaguely.

As we had no idea what she meant, we ignored her, too, and had tea.

It began to rain, and just beyond Hawes our windscreen wipers jammed. I tried to move them by hand, but without success.

"We'll call at the first garage we see," Cath said.

This was at Sedbergh, but as there was no mechanic on duty we drew a blank there. In driving rain and gathering darkness we reached Kendal, and pulled up hopefully at a large garage. There were mechanics there, but they would not fix the wipers because it was after six o'clock and they had stopped work for the day. We said what we thought of them. Then Hilda said, "I will go ahead, and tell Mrs Coates you are on the way," and drove off before we had time to tell her that she might be more useful if she stayed with us.

Prim found a wayside telephone kiosk and rang Mrs Coates to explain the position, then we drove on through the dark and the wet. On Dunmail Raise, where we were in a veritable cloudburst with nil visibility, it would have been of considerable help had we been able to follow Hilda's tail-lights. Cath drove to Borrowdale mainly by instinct, and we arrived safely, and there was Mrs Coates, and we were home again. She said the weather had been very good recently, but there was still deep snow on some of the tops.

"Oh, good!" I exclaimed.

"So you'll be wise to watch it and not try anything daft," she added, trying to look severe.

Cath, Cop and I were sharing 'Langstrath' again. Cath christened us 'The Unholy Three' but I am not sure why, unless it was because we were inclined to be noisy. Mrs Coates was gradually replacing all her beds, and to my delight I discovered that the one I chose had a new interior-sprung mattress. I had been expecting the usual hard Scarthwaite bed, and this new one felt wonderful.

* * *

When the gong sounded for us to get up we took no notice, but lay making stupid remarks.

"Let's cut out morning as well as evening washing."

"Let's go down in dressing-gowns."

"Let's ring for breakfast in bed."

"Nothing to ring."

"Nothing would happen if we did."

Finally, we got up.

After breakfast, Prim said she had some people to see in the valley, and suggested that the rest of us went for a short walk, then we could all come home for lunch, and go out in the afternoon. So we climbed the rough fellside above Hollows Farm. Mrs Coates had told us that there was a reservoir somewhere up there, and we had a vague notion of finding it. I don't suppose we were even going in the right direction, but it was a good excuse for scrambling about on the fell and perching on the rock outcrops, and gazing contentedly at the valley below. As usual, we began quoting things, appropriate or otherwise, and Cop said, "We ought to write a Lakes poem of our own," and started —

"We will go back to the Lakes again,
To dear old Sally Coates,
To rhubarb pie" — "and hard beds!" (cut in Cath)
"And sow some more wild oats!" (finished May)

"Not bad!" commented Cop, patting herself on the back.
"Feeble!" I said. "Worse than the worst of Wordsworth!"
"You make up a better one then!"
"It isn't my time for amusing you. I'd sooner listen to the birds."

After lunch, we went up the Castle Crag track. The sun shone, the high fells soared, and Borrowdale lay serenely below. Cutting down the fell to Rosthwaite, we had a large tea at the Scafell Hotel. Over it, we discussed the walks we intended to do. Prim had them all planned.

"Tomorrow we'll do Greenup and Sergeant Man; Sunday we'll be lazy and do some local walks; Monday we'll do Striding Edge; Tuesday we'll do the Gable South Traverse; Wednesday we'll do Skiddaw — the ordinary route for those who have not done it before and a scrambling way for those who have; Thursday we'll go over the pass to Wasdale and. . ."

Cop drily interrupted, "Friday we'll be laid out; Saturday we'll go home and get to hospital!"

"Well, we'll do Sergeant Man tomorrow, anyway!" retorted Prim.

* * *

In the middle of breakfast the next morning, Prim suggested catching an earlier bus than usual up the dale. The result was frenzied activity — bolting down food and cups of tea, stuffing gear into rucksacks, badgering Mrs Coates for sandwiches, trying to get feet into boots which seemed to have shrunk, and finally rushing through the village like a cyclone.

The Greenup track was good. From it, we got a particularly fine view of Eagle Grag. As we rose, we began to strike patches of ice and snow, and near Lining Crag there was a sudden flurry of hail and one loud roll of thunder.

"I thought it was an avalanche starting!" exclaimed Cop, emerging from a rock outcrop where she had darted when the peal began.

Greenup Edge, notorious for bog, was hard snow, delightful to walk on, apart from the wind which buffeted us as we headed for High Raise. On reaching the summit we hunted for a sheltered niche, but there wasn't one. So, taking five minutes to gobble our sandwiches, we carried on over the white plateau to the spectacular summit rocks of Sergeant Man. We had it to ourselves, and cursed the wind which made it a spot too cold for prolonged lingering.

Starting down in the direction of Grasmere, we were suddenly assailed by a vicious snow-cum-hailstorm. May, who had been carrying her sou'wester by its strings, did not realise that it was half-full of hail stones until she put it on and they cascaded down her neck. Visibility was poor, and we had no idea whether or not we were on any kind of track. We just kept going downhill. Then the frozen snow underfoot gave way to slimy bog, into which most of us fell at intervals. Hilda was cursing incessantly because her new boots were torturing her, and Cop was cursing because the seat of her pants was sopping wet.

We had just slithered down a succession of greasy rocks when the clouds rolled away, the sun came out, and before us lay Easedale Tarn, blue and sparkling. According to some guide-books there should have been a refreshment hut by the water, but only its ruined walls remained, and the fact that we were denied the anticipated cups of tea gave us a raging thirst all the way to tourist-thronged Grasmere. We got tea there, then had a very long, annoying wait in a bus queue, which made us late home for dinner.

* * *

Snow fell in the night, and in the early morning the dale was a Christmas card scene for an hour or so, until its covering of white melted into slush.

As it was Sunday, we coped with a very large midday dinner,

after which Cath and Prim went to sleep by the fire, and Hilda and May went for a stroll along the Catbells road, saying they would be back for tea. Cop said she could do with a proper walk, and looked expectantly at me.

"What about climbing Grange Fell?" It was the first thing which came into my head, and she jumped at the idea.

We began by catching a bus to Rosthwaite, intending to start from there, then found it would have been simpler to start from Grange itself, so we changed our minds. Instead of Grange Fell we would go up to Lobstone Band, climb Scawdel Fell, walk along the ridge, and come down by Catbells.

"Shall we have time to do all that?" Cop wondered.

"Of course we shall if we step out!"

To save time, we climbed a wall and took a short cut across a field instead of walking down the stony lane which curved round to the river crossing. Unfortunately, the short cut backfired at the far end of the field where we were confronted by densely massed tangles of barbed wire. After wasting some time trying to find a way through, we had to go back over the field and climb the wall into the lane we should have taken in the first place.

After that the walk lost its specific object, and we ambled along talking instead of getting down to the job. Eventually, we arrived at the slate gully leading to Lobstone Band, and started up, soon reaching the first patches of snow. Then I glanced at my watch.

"Do you realise that if we are to get home in time for supper we shall have to run all along the ridge — not just walk quickly, but sprint!"

"I'm not going to run!"

"Then we had better not do the ridge."

We stood and argued about it, and threw snowballs at each other, and Cop said, "We can't just go tamely home. We ought to climb something!"

"There's Castle Crag!" I said.

"What, that little thing!"

"It's the only thing we have time for, anyway!"

So we dropped down the gully and climbed the first hill we reached, thinking it was a shoulder of the Crag, then finding that it was not connected and having to come down again. The next try took us over a wall and up a mass of loose slates. A sheep on a higher ledge was knocking down pieces of slate which fell unpleasantly close, so I tied my rucksack over my head, and Cop sniggered.

"You look extremely silly!" I let that pass.

The top of the Crag had some flat slabs just right for comfortable sitting and looking down the valley and to the fells at the head.

Presently, Cop said, "I'm hungry. Did you bring anything to eat?"

"No. You said we should not need anything."

"Well, I've changed my mind!"

We emptied our rucksacks on a flat stone but could only find two tattered sandwiches which must have been there for several days. We ate them. Then we made a steep direct descent from the Crag, skidding wildly down the shifting slates, which we enjoyed, and strolled home. Nothing had been achieved, but the walk had been a pleasant piece of dalliance.

* * *

On the day we did the Gable South Traverse the cars were parked at Seatoller and John took us in his taxi to the top of Honister. When we had discussed the walk the night before, we had wondered if May would be willing, remembering her sufferings on the Traverse during her first walk.

"Oh, yes!" she had assured us. "I'm not afraid of the old Traverse! I might even break my neck this time, let alone my toe nails!"

Snow lay on the Grey Knotts-Brandreth plateau, and there was not a whisper of wind. On Brandreth summit thick mist reduced visibility to a few yards, which was awkward, as we had to make for Beck Head, and could not even see where it was.

"We can't find the way in this," protested Hilda.

"Yes we can. I know the direction," Prim said, and struck off at a tangent. We followed blindly, and suddenly the mist rolled away, and we saw Beck Head a few minutes ahead.

We halted there for lunch, gobbling sandwiches at top speed, eager to get on with the Traverse. We had packed up and were on the move again when there came an indignant cry from Cop.

"I'm still in the middle of my lunch!"

We told her to get a move on, to which she retorted, "I shall take as long as I like!"

"Then you will just have to catch up with us!" Which she soon did, eating as she ran.

After negotiating a mass of boulders, we came 'round the corner' onto the south face proper, and the rest was pure delight on a fair track, beautifully scrambly in parts. We sat under the Napes Ridges, where each different route had its rope of climbers. I envied the two men who were sitting on the top block of the Needle. The mountainside swept down to a green triangle of tiny fields criss-crossed by stone walls, and beyond Wasdale lay the sunlit Irish Sea. The air trembled with the thunder of Piers Gill. It was a glorious spot in which to linger! From the rough start to the rocky finish round the buttresses of Kern Knotts, every step of the Traverse was rewarding.

"I told you it was a good one!" Prim said.

At Styhead there was a snowstorm, which turned to rain as we sped down the pass, going straight through all the patches of bog. We were hurrying to get to Seathwaite, but when we reached the farm Hilda and May said they would go straight home and get washed instead of having tea, and they walked on, leaving us open-mouthed with amazement.

"I'll be damned!" I said, and Prim shrugged.

"Well, it takes all sorts . . ."

After three cups of tea each, rhubarb tart, and shortbread biscuits, came a contented stroll to Seatoller. Cath, Cop and I were dryshod in boots, but Prim's shoe soles had softened in the bog.

"I feel as though I am walking on uncooked pastry!"

"You should get some boots!" Cop told her.

"No, I shouldn't. I like shoes. I don't like boots."

We were full of that complete satisfaction which only comes at the end of a superb day among high hills. It had been the kind of walk I love.

* * *

"We really ought to go to Keswick."

After some of the party had said this so many times that the others were tired of hearing it, we went to Keswick. Cath and I took the car to a garage to have the windscreen wipers repaired, then joined the others in Storm's before drifting round the usual shops. After frittering away the morning, we went home for lunch.

Then Prim said, "Let's go up Walla Crag. We can get a bus up the hill from Keswick, and walk there more or less on the flat. In fact, it is not a walk at all, but merely a very simple little outing." She added that it overlooked Derwentwater and would be a marvellous viewpoint, and we could come down and have tea at the Borrowdale Hotel. May said we could go without her, as she wished to do a solo walk, and have a little peace and quiet for a change.

The Lancaster bus deposited us at the top of Keswick hill, near a gate which bore the words 'Walla Crag'. It seemed too simple for words. We followed a faint track, first across some fields, then over open fell. Before long, we were surprised to be going uphill, which we were not supposed to do. As usual, we had been talking too much. Then the track vanished, leaving us on a wide, undulating moor, and not knowing where to go next. There were several rocky eminences ahead, so we chose the highest, saying, "Perhaps that is Walla Crag," and slogged up steep grass and heather to the big boulders at the top. We could see Derwentwater in the distance, but we were certainly not on Walla Crag. We sat on the top, feeling disgusted with ourselves for losing a little thing like that.

I asked, "What have we climbed?" But nobody had the slightest idea, and Prim said, "I never thought we should need a map, so I didn't bring one. Blow Walla Crag!"

"Where do we go from here?"

"Straight down. I don't know where we shall strike the valley road, but that doesn't matter."

Most of us enjoyed these bee-lines, trackless descents, which often turned into obstacle races, and taught us valuable fellcraft. This time, we plunged down steep, tussocky slopes to a beck, access to which was barred by a high wall which ended in a tangle of barbed wire. Prim went over the wall and Cop climbed up after her, while the rest of us wriggled through the wire. Having got up the wall, Cop was unable to get down the other side, and was running backwards and forwards along the top, to our amusement.

"You look like a monkey on a chain!" I called.

"She's crag-fast!" Prim laughed.

No one offered to help, as we knew that she would ultimately find a way down, which she did, with some grumbling about non-co-operation.

We followed the beck down until we came to familiar ground at Ashness Bridge. Then Prim, who carried a timetable in her pocket, said, "We are just missing the last bus up the dale before dinner time. It is passing the end of the road — now!"

We set off at the double for Ashness Gate, Prim racing ahead, hoping that the bus would be running late. By the time we reached the dale road we were winded and gasping — and then Prim discovered that she had been looking at the winter timetable instead of the Easter one, and that a bus was due in twenty minutes. We were too relieved to be annoyed with her. Of course, we could easily have walked to Grange, but we never did any road walking if we could help it!

* * *

With sun in the valley and snow on the high tops, the final day was a walker's dream. Reluctantly, we gave up the idea of doing Striding Edge for the time being, because Mrs Coates was convinced that we should have an accident on it. There was bound to be snow up there, and we should have loved to go, but we were too fond of Mrs Coates to cause her undue anxiety. But we just had to do one last top, and I suggested Great End. Cath and Cop were all for it, but May and Hilda were not. Prim wanted to go, but after some pondering said, in an aside to me, "I think I had better stay with them, and take them up something gentler. It's a pity, because it is such a good day, but you three go."

So Cath, Cop and I set off, and parked the car at Seathwaite. At the top of Grain Gill the snow was two feet deep and the wind icy, but the strenuous exercise of ploughing through the drifts to the Great End col made us glow to such an extent that we welcomed the wind.

Great End, by its very name a mountaineer's inspiration, was a splendid place for lunching. We were alone on its summit, where the snow was frozen to the consistency of ice. From our solitude we watched other walkers plodding towards Scafell Pike. We had put on our balaclava climbing hats, pulling them down to fit snugly round our necks, leaving only our faces showing. The illusion of warmth thus created may have been mainly psychological, but was undoubtedly pleasant, for we lounged about on the snow most happily, and time had wings. It was only when the cold finally began to penetrate that we reluctantly left the summit.

On the way down, we dropped below the snow-line near Styhead Tarn, and continued down the pass by the more interesting track on the left of the stream, climbing over the rocks by the waterfall, and floundering through the bog at the bottom.

We were in the middle of tea and apple cake at Seathwaite Farm when Prim walked in. She commented on the messy state of the table-cloth, a fair criticism, Cop having upset the milk jug. She listened enviously to our account of the day on Great End.

"A lovely finish to the holiday!"

She told us she had taken the other two up Grange Fell.

"A nice little walk — rocky top — excellent views. You would like it."

"Why didn't May and Hilda come up to Seathwaite with you?"

"Oh, after Grange Fell they went home — to do their packing!" and we all laughed.

We did no packing that night. It was a nuisance struggling with it by candle-light, so we left it until the next morning. We hated doing it, anyway, just as we hated leaving Borrowdale, and Scarthwaite, and Mrs Coates.

Next Easter was so far away, so long to wait, though May commented wryly, "It's only twelve months!"

DRESS CIRCLE

Doris, having completed her contract as church organist, was at last able to spend Easter in the Lakes. Hilda, who was in Europe, would be missing, but fortunately with the return of Doris we could maintain our number at six, and so fill Scarthwaite.
   Prim and I were in Cath's car, and May brought Doris in hers. Cop was coming by train from London. At Scotch Corner the two cars parted. May, bothered by a slipping clutch, went straight on to Keswick, while we detoured to Swaledale. We had that long, lovely dale to ourselves, just us and the brown river and the rolling hills all the way to Keld, where we stopped for tea before taking the high moorland road to Kirkby Stephen. Through Appleby and Penrith, and Keswick, then at last Borrowdale — tranquil silver lake, green-brown fells, snow-touched mountains where the valley ended — we were home!
   Cath and I were in 'The Pines' that year. It was our favourite bedroom.

* * *

We woke to brilliant sunlight, in a dale full of the warmth of spring. On such a morning it was good to be alive — alive and ready for anything!
   I had been reading about the Dress Circle Traverse on Gable. This was higher on the mountain than the South Traverse, and involved handling easy rock, and it sounded like my sort of thing. I suggested it at the breakfast table, where the day's activities were usually decided.
   "What about doing the Dress Circle?"
   Cath and Cop agreed at once, but Prim, who had had bronchitis

for most of the winter, looked thoughtful.

"It could be fairly hard going, couldn't it?"

"It might ," I said. "I don't really know much about it."

She sighed. "I would love to do it. There is nothing I would like better than a good, fierce scramble, but I had better keep off anything too strenuous this year. I should only be wheezing and coughing all the time. I shall have to break myself in more gently. You lucky people can go."

We looked at May and Doris, but they were less than enthusiastic. Doris said that she wished to do her own brand of walking, which did not include climbing rocks, and would be happy to form a select party of one. May looked doubtful, and asked, "Do you guarantee to bring me back sound in wind and limb?"

"No guarantees!"

"Then you can go where you jolly well like. I'm staying in the valley and basking in the sun."

"Then it is just the Unholy Three!" I said; and we set off for Seathwaite.

Getting up to the 1,000 foot boulder in Styhead is an effort on the first day of a holiday, when muscles unused all winter are brought into play, but we soon slipped into the rhythm and mounted the pass. The day was so warm that we dallied for a while by Styhead Tarn to cool off. We had all the time in the world, it seemed.

We ate our sandwiches by Kern Knotts, looking down on the tiny fields of Wasdale.

Then Cath said, "Well, what about it? Don't you think we should make a move?"

I felt I was obliged to confess, "I know where the Dress Circle is, but I am not sure how to get there."

They stared at me with disbelief.

"Haven't you got the map?"

"No, I forgot to bring one."

Cop called me an idiot, and Cath exclaimed, "I like that! You are supposed to be leading this walk, aren't you?"

"I seem to be."

"Well, go on and lead it!"

"Right!" I said. "I'm sure I can find the Dress Circle, but you had better be prepared for some rough stuff."

"She's going to break our necks!" Cop muttered, and I told her she need not come if she was scared.

We set off along the South Traverse track, and when I thought we had gone far enough we began scrambling straight up the mountain. Soon we were among reddish scree and large rocks, sometimes on our feet but more often on hands and knees, working hard and getting rather dirty. There was no sign of a track anywhere, and I thoroughly enjoyed it. On reaching two tall buttresses with a narrow gap between, we got up by putting our backs against one and our feet against the other, and heaving up until we could roll out at the top. Then we found that we were high above the Needle, and had to descend a steep gully to get to its base. Ours was not the orthodox approach to the Dress Circle!

Near the point where the Needle abutted from the fell there rose a perpendicular wall of rock possibly twenty feet high. The top of this was the flat slab of the Dress Circle. The wall looked interesting, and a little awkward in the spacing of hand and footholds.

"Last lap!" I said. "Just that wall, and we are on the Dress Circle!"

Cath inspected the wall, and shook her head. "I'm not climbing that. I couldn't get my big feet on those little holds. I shall sit at the bottom and wait for you."

So I climbed the wall, and Cop followed, and we sat on the top.

We saw three parties of climbers at work on the Needle, and were able to study their technique at close range. The Napes Ridges resembled a spider's web, so festooned were they with ropes. But the Dress Circle bestowed a far greater reward than the watching of rock climbers. It gave that glorious feeling of being perched in space, with the kingdoms of the earth at one's feet — a mountaineer's delight. Across the gulf of Styhead the Scafells were etched against the blue sky, every crag and gully in sharp relief. Incredibly, above the roar of Piers Gill rose the joyous song of larks.

I do not know how long we sat there, but the afternoon was almost spent when I climbed back down the wall to Cath. Cop, following me, could not find the footholds and got stuck half-way, and we roared with laughter at the sight of her spread-eagled against the rock like a squashed fly, yelling, "Get me down, can't you!"

Eventually, when we had finished laughing, I went up and put her feet in the holds, and brought her down.

"You silly fool!" She said, by way of thanks.

We slid and rolled down to the South Traverse track, and along to the top of Styhead, where we had long drinks from the stream.

We were very tired, and so hot that the sweat had made runnels down the dirt on our faces, but the thought of tea at Seathwaite Farm spurred us on down the pass reasonably well, though by Stockley Bridge our feet were beginning to drag, and we had a few minutes' rest

Cath said, "I shall be stiff after this! You might have warned us that we were going to do a rock climb the first day!"

"I didn't know myself."

She added with heavy sarcasm, "If you want to hurry you can go ahead and order tea!"

I protested that it was the last thing I wanted to do, and Cop said, "Tomorrow, A Party will become C Party — or take to its beds!"

As we reached Seathwaite, Prim and May, who had just had tea, came out of the farmhouse, and made some scathing comments. They said they would have been ashamed to be seen with us, as we looked like dirty tramps, staggering along and nearly falling over our own feet. Perhaps they were exaggerating slightly, but we were impervious to their remarks, for our thoughts were centred on a pot of tea. That, and the thrill of achievement. It had been a wonderful day.

* * *

The warm, sunny weather continued, with temperatures soaring until it was more like high summer than spring. Just to lean against Mrs Coates' front door and look at the fells was in itself sufficient beauty.

"I never knew such marvellous weather ever happened in the Lakes!" an incredulous Doris exclaimed over and over again, and we smiled smugly, as though we had done it for her benefit.

In a leisurely way we explored Borrowdale, until we knew every secret track and quiet, forgotten lane in the valley. Borrowdale was becoming popular, but we found those places where tourists did not go, and we loved it all. Sometimes Doris went with us, but often she set off on long solitary walks, effortlessly covering the miles, content to be alone.

One afternoon, we drove to Bampton Grange, on the far east of the Lake District, to visit Hilda, Mrs Coates' niece. She lived in a black and white eighteenth century farmhouse, which had a circular, stone staircase which she called the lighthouse; low doorways; steps up or down into each room; and walls as uneven as the waves of the sea. The ingle nook in the dining-room was as large as a small room. The electric light was the only incongruous feature. We still had candles at Scarthwaite, as the controversy over whether the power cables should go overhead or underground in Borrowdale was then at its height.

Hilda gave us a large tea, and a dozen new-laid eggs to take home.

"Tell my Aunt Sally that's two apiece for your breakfast tomorrow."

We went to Mardale to see Haweswater, and were astonished by its size and appearance. Manchester has made a good job of a project which was, in their opinion, essential. Mardale village has gone for ever, but Haweswater, unlike Thirlmere, retains the characteristics of a lake in a wild, remote setting.

We spent so long looking at Harter Fell, which is in some respects similar to Great End, and also studying possible lines of ascent to High Street, that we were late home for dinner.

* * *

"Haystacks!" said Prim, one morning.
"What about them?" May wanted to know.
"It's a fell, you nit-wit," I said.
"Oh! Are we going to climb it?"
"Yes."
"Not I," said Doris. "I'll walk round Buttermere while you play about on the rocks." Though an excellent walker, Doris was seldom happy when it came to rock scrambling.

At the top of Honister she left us to walk down to Buttermere while we headed for the Gallows and the Grey Knotts-Brandreth plateau. At two thousand feet the air was as warm as it was in the valley, which made the day ideal for appreciative loitering. There were a few walkers making for Great Gable, but none on the Haystacks track, which wound round outcrops and buttresses of rock, and was all the way enjoyable, especially where it skirted the precipitous drop to Buttermere.

For a picnic spot par excellence we had one of Lakeland's greatest treasures — the Innominate Tarn, a gem in a sublime setting overlooked by the arched face of Gable. We were alone, just us and a skyline of mountains, in a profound silence intensified by the breeze rippling the withered stalks of the moorland grass and fluting the surface of the sparkling water. We stayed for a long time in quiet contemplation. I shall always remember the beauty of that place.

We enjoyed the fascinating labyrinth of rock towers and spurs on the summit of Haystacks. The descent to Scarth Gap was steep and rough, for we took it direct, and found the scrambling good fun. We were half-way down when Prim surged ahead, and I realised that she was going to take a photograph of us in ungainly attitudes on awkward rocks. I dashed after her, hoping to get out of camera range before I broke my neck. I succeeded, but she got the others, and the result was a picture which later provoked both mirth and annoyance.

After a pot of tea at Gatesgarth, we walked to Buttermere village. There was no sign of Doris, and we concluded that she had gone to Keswick, via Whinlatter, on the 3.30 bus. It was by then almost 5.30, which was the time the last bus left for Keswick, but Prim suggested that it would be more pleasant to have John come over Honister and fetch us. She went into the telephone kiosk to ring him, but the line was engaged. She tried several times, while Cath and Cop dashed to see if the 5.30 bus was still standing in the hotel yard. It was, but would be going in a couple of minutes. Prim tried again, and still the line was engaged. Then Doris hurtled round the corner. After sitting on a rock near Gatesgarth, waiting for us to come down Scarth Gap, she had eventually realised that she must have missed us. With only a few minutes left to catch the bus, she had had to run all the way to Buttermere village.

The bus engine started as Prim was having a final try, and we suffered a minor panic, uncertain whether to get in or wait for her. To our relief, she was smiling when she came out of the kiosk, and said John would be there to pick us up in three-quarters of an hour.

We watched the Keswick bus leave, and with time to kill, visited the tiny church, beautifully decorated for Easter with primroses, daffodils, and larch branches. Then we went into the Bridge Hotel, and were so engrossed in conversation with the proprietor that we never noticed John arrive, look in vain for us, and drive away again. May spotted his tail disappearing round the corner, heading back for Honister. We rushed out, but he had gone by then, and we were left standing in the road and loudly voicing our annoyance at being stranded on the wrong side of the pass.

"He will come back!" Prim was confident, and in a few minutes he did, having driven to Gatesgarth and back, in case we were wandering somewhere along the road. We went home by the Newlands Pass and the lovely road along the Catbells side of Derwentwater. We were late for dinner, and of course there was no time to wash.

* * *

Cath, Cop and I went to do Helvellyn by Striding Edge. We drove to Ullswater, descending Gowbarrow hill slowly to take in the glorious view of the lake and St. Sunday Crag, but not lingering too much. We were determined to tick off Striding Edge once and for all.

Parking under a tree in the lane near Patterdale, we set off uphill as though we were going to a fire, winded ourselves in a couple of minutes, and had to stop to regain our breath before continuing at a more reasonable pace. Where the lane became the track up to Grisedale Pass, we crossed the beck, and a field, and began to climb the fell-side. This was quite steep, but the sun blazing down on us made it more of a drag than it should have been. I was soon puffing and cursing, and Cath gloating, "You should have slimmed, like me!" did not improve matters.

We had read that a gap in a wall marked the start of Striding Edge. High on the skyline there was a wall, and it had a gap, and Cath, in the lead, sang out, "Do you see that gap? That will be it!"

I did not believe her.

"It can't be. It's much too near. When we get there we shall find we are only half-way up this blasted treadmill."

"Bet you five shillings it is."

"Done!"

I would have given more than five shillings if I could suddenly have found myself at the wall, for the sweltering day made the walk a penance. In fact, it was purgatory. Perspiration poured down my face as I plodded up, eyes on the ground, trying not to think about sitting in the shade with a long, cold drink. I was so hot that I began to wish I had never come.

And suddenly it was over. We had reached the gap and Striding Edge. Toil had ended, joy was to come, and the heat of the day no longer mattered. We sat and investigated our sandwiches, discovering that we were quite hungry, and annoyed because we had forgotten to bring oranges. We said we would have a drink from Red Tarn Beck when we came down by Swirrel Edge, as we should not be really thirsty until then. We deluded ourselves.

Striding Edge was much to our liking, especially the little rock towers. We climbed over each one, a pleasant, if dirty, exercise, and we enjoyed the section where one walks along a narrow crest with a steep drop on either side. The final, and biggest, rock tower gave some excellent scrambling, but the ascent from the neck to the top of the mountain was an anticlimax. What should have been good, firm rock turned out to be loose, bouldery shale which crunched into clouds of grey-black dust underfoot.

After cleaning our hands with snow from a cornice, and deciding not to eat any because it looked so dirty, we sat on the stony summit grass and ate cake and chocolate, but without much relish. We were too parched.

We took the descent of Swirrel Edge almost at a gallop, rushing down and making for the beck, where we drank and drank. But by the time we reached the gap in the wall we were as thirsty as ever. The valley looked far below, and there was no respite from the sun as we strode down, thoughts centred on tea.

"We'll order a pot for six!" said Cop.

In the field leading to Grisedale Beck, I found two half-crowns and a blood-stained bandage. I left the bandage, and paid my debt to Cath with the two half-crowns, and she said she would use them to pay for the tea at the Aira Force café.

With the interior of the car like an oven, we drove at top speed to the café and found it closed. This made us desperate, not necessarily for tea, but for anything drinkable. We felt dehydrated, and Cath said, "We will start for home, and stop at the first place where we can get a drink." We drove up Gowbarrow hill, and a few minutes later, at the Royal Hotel at Dockray, were pouring cider down our throats and groaning with delight. We ordered more and lingered over it, feeling at peace with the world, and also making ourselves late for dinner, which was cooling on the table when we arrived. Mrs Coates greeted us with, "Well, now I hope you are satisfied!"

"Yes," I said, "for the time being!"

"I'm relieved that you have done it, very relieved!"

Mrs Coates had a real thing about Striding Edge. To her it was a very dangerous place where people frequently had accidents. It was laughable, really, because the route we had taken up to the Dress Circle on Gable had been far more hazardous than anything Striding Edge had to offer — but Mrs Coates did not know that.

* * *

On the last day of the holiday, we asked May to choose a walk. After eyeing us suspiciously, she said, with some hesitation, "I should like to go up Grange Fell, and take my time over it, but I suppose that would be too gentle for some of you lot."

"Of course we will go up Grange Fell," we assured her, and Prim added, "We might see if we can find Dock Tarn. It's somewhere in that area."

It was a drowsy kind of day, not conducive to brisk walking, which was an excuse for taking all morning to amble to the top of Grange Fell. It was an entrancing top, a small world of bent and heather and outcrops of lichened rock, where the plaintive notes of curlews bubbled through the silence.

After eating, we walked through knee-high dead heather to another rock-crowned summit, where we sat looking towards Rosthwaite Fell, and speculating on Dock Tarn — some of us.

"Let's find it," urged Prim.

She led us uphill and down, through heather and bog and over walls, until we sighted the Watendlath track below, with another fell rising beyond it, and another after that.

"I am sure it will be up there somewhere between those fells."

"Look here," objected May, "I thought we were just going up Grange Fell. We've done that — and a lot more! Haven't you had enough?"

Opinions differed, but the general concensus was that it was too warm to climb yet another fell. Instead, we sat lazing on the hillside, and looked at the blue-grey dome of Gable, the silvery lustre of Great End where the sun caught the snow still streaking the gullies, and the long, serrated ridge of Glaramara.

Finally, we went down to Rosthwaite to have tea at the Scafell Hotel, then walked by the river back to Grange. The hills were so beautiful that evening that we stayed out until long past dinner time.

Mrs Coates said that according to the newspapers there had never been such wonderful Easter weather for the last fifty years.

'And probably will not be again for the next fifty!' I thought.

On the whole, it had been a leisurely holiday. We had ticked off the Dress Circle Traverse and Striding Edge, but there was so much more, still waiting to be done!

GLARAMARA

All seven members of the S.L. Club were at Scarthwaite, and Mrs Coates put up an extra bed in 'Riggside', Prim's bedroom, but half-way through the holiday, Cop, who was involved in a theatrical production, was obliged to return to London, and then there were six.

With our experience of the Cumbrian climate, we were not anticipating a repetition of the heat-wave conditions of the previous year, and when we set out for the Lakes the best that the weather forecasters could offer was 'Cloudy with sunny periods in the east, and more continuous rain in the west.' Hilda, Doris, and May were in one car, and Cath, Prim and I in the other. We had planned to go by the Ilkley-Skipton route and explore Wharfedale on the way.

At Ilkley it was raining, but because we hated to abandon any project we turned into Wharfedale, drove past Bolton Abbey, and found a spot where we could picnic. The rain was not heavy, but the head of the dale was under a pall of black cloud. Further exploration was uninviting, and we made only a small circular tour, crossing the river at Barden Bridge and re-crossing higher up the dale.

Then Prim directed us to a short cut to rejoin the main road to Skipton. It was up a very narrow and remarkably steep lane. We pulled up on the moorland at the top, and May, whose car had been following, did likewise. She got out and strode over to us.

"What do you think you are playing at, you crazy idiots?"

"It's all right," Prim assured her. "I think this is a bus route. I am sure I once went up here in a bus years ago."

May looked sceptical.

"Well, next time you are going to take off suddenly up a mountainside, just warn us. I don't want my passengers getting heart attacks!"

"They will get over it!" laughed Cath. She had a new Hillman Minx car which went like a bomb.

At Settle, the downpour was so heavy that we splashed along like a boat under a night-dark sky. The rain went with us all the way to Borrowdale, where mist lay low on Catbells and the head of the dale was lost in gloom, but there was no gloom about Mrs Coates, waiting at the door to welcome us. We were home.

Cop arrived at dinner time, and as we relaxed round the fire after the meal the inevitable question arose, "Where shall we go tomorrow?" and provoked a gloomy chorus.

"It is sure to rain tomorrow!"

"I'm too tired to bother!"

"I'm worn out!"

Prim said nothing, neither did Cath and Cop, so I tried a little encouragement.

"We are all tired after the winter, which is why we need to get up the fells." We needed recharging. "So where shall we go tomorrow?"

Cop asked cynically, "Who isn't poorly?"

"I'm not!" Prim and Cath said in chorus, and I said, "Nobody is poorly. They are just bone idle after hibernating all winter."

We left it at that.

* * *

For some inexplicable reason, the first morning of the holiday was spent in Keswick. The weather was cold and showery, but it seemed a waste of time to linger in a town choked with traffic and tourists when we could have been on the hills. Storm's café had closed. Peering through the grimy windows, we saw stacked chairs and tables and an empty counter under a thick layer of dust, and we were saddened. Dingy as it had been with its dull brown paint, it was an integral part of Keswick, especially on a wet day, when you could almost taste the fug of steamy windows and wet clothes.

After lunch, which we had at home, Prim did not ask where anyone wished to go, but announced, "We are going to find Dock Tarn."

"What is special about this Dock Tarn?" May asked. "I have never heard of anyone going to it."

"Not many people know anything about it. That is why we are going!"

We started from Stonethwaite, along the Greenup track. In those days, there was no signpost pointing the way to Dock Tarn and no beaten track to it, as there is now. The elusive Dock Tarn lay hidden somewhere up in a maze of fells, and to locate it needed some map study, which Prim had been doing over lunch.

She led along the Greenup track, and we followed one behind the other. Suddenly, she turned left and struck straight up the fell-side, and we came after. It was not easy going. We were in a litter of boulders, gorse, tangled undergrowth, and the mossy, half-concealed stumps of dead trees, all so steep that we were forced to do some of it on all fours. Doris and Hilda, who had said at the beginning of Greenup that they would only come part of the way, were so involved in the struggle to get up that they forgot to go back.

At the top of the slope, we entered a fascinating world of isolated, tor-like summits, a rough moorland swept by all the winds of heaven. Over outcrops of rock and through patches of bog, we went straight to Dock Tarn, a silent, reed-fringed lake in a lonely cup of the hills. We sat on the stones by the water's edge, and knew that all the hard work to get there had been worthwhile. It was so peaceful, as though we were the only people in the world.

We sat quietly for some time, until someone complained, "I'm beginning to get cold!" And the spell was broken.

Doris said, "I'm not looking forward to going down the way we came up!"

Prim replied, "We are not going down that way," and led on past the tarn and among the outcrops, until we looked down on the Rosthwaite track to Watendlath.

We struck directly down to it, coping with walls, rocks, barbed wire, and swamps, and cursing the heavy rain which had suddenly started. Cath cursed the most because her oilskin had stuck together as though it had been glued, and she had a fight to get into it.

Rushing down the track, we reached Rosthwaite five minutes too late to catch the bus. The rain was sheeting down, and no one wanted to walk to Grange, so Prim went to the telephone kiosk to ring John. He was out, but his mother said she would tell him to come and collect us when he got back, though she was not sure how long that would be. We settled down to a cold, dismal wait under the big yew tree outside the Royal Oak.

Hilda said, "Someone had better ring Mrs Coates and tell her we are late."

Cop guffawed. "If she doesn't know we are late by now, she ought to!"

"I have already rung her," said Prim.

We four, who founded the Club, had always regarded time as unimportant in the hills, and were case-hardened to lateness. Any good walker can stride out from one spot to another, but the loiterer is in harmony with the spirit of the mountains.

In due course, John's car appeared and whisked us home, where Mrs Coates pretended to grumble in case our dinner was spoilt, and then made sure that it was not.

* * *

The tops were so heavily misted that each fell had its upper slopes sliced away. Our world of heights had withdrawn behind a curtain. The valleys remained clear, but who would be content with valley walks? These we reserved for the worst weather of all. We wanted to do something, but had no idea what, and various suggestions were made and discarded, until Prim said, "I know what we can do. We will go up Grain Gill and over Esk Hause to Angle Tarn. We might have time to explore the Hanging Knott part of Bowfell, then we will come back down the far side of Styhead Gill. How is that?" We thought it was good.

We left the track near the top of Grain Gill and climbed the rocks, emerging above Sprinkling Tarn, by which time there was a clamour for food, which we ate in the chill of a spiteful wind.

Then the clouds descended until they almost touched our heads. This started a minor panic, with some of the party deciding that it was futile to go any higher and they wished to start down immediately. We were dismayed, and Cop exclaimed, "If we are not careful we shall be back in time for tea — and a wash!"

This did not prevent Doris, May, and Hilda from packing up and setting off for Styhead, while the rest of us grumbled.

"It's the first time I've ever done the beginning and the end of a walk and left out the middle part!" Prim said.

We sat wondering whether to go on, and then decided against it in case the others started worrying, and still grumbling we followed them.

At the top of Styhead we dropped below the clouds, and were tempted to do some of the Corridor route to the Pike. We had no desire to go tamely down the pass. The other three were waiting by the ambulance box, and on sighting us they set off down the pass, expecting us to follow. Instead, we went climbing among the rocks of Kern Knotts on Gable, a splendid place for scrambling.

We looked down on the tiny fields of Wasdale and the curve of the grey lake, until clouds swirled over Gable and the picture was wiped out, leaving us poised on the rim of a bottomless pit of boiling vapour. It was glorious, and there we remained until it was time to rush down to Seathwaite for tea and apple pasty. After the bleak grandeur of the heights we descended to a different world — one which was about to greet the spring.

* * *

On one occasion, we were obliged to take notice of the time — and we did not care for it.

It was another day of fells with sliced off tops, and we went to Ennerdale, planning to walk round the lake. We drove by Wythop Mill, where the verges of the lanes were gold with celandines and primroses. A solitary shaft of sunlight gave vivid blue to Loweswater, but the only fell clear of cloud was Mellbreak.

Coming down to Ennerdale Water, we called at the Anglers' Inn and ordered tea for four o'clock, then had a leisurely picnic on the lake shore before starting the walk. This began with a grassy track to the left, and petered out at a belt of rocks. Here the party divided, Cath and I to follow Prim and Cop over the rocks, and the other three to sit on the stones by the water. We saw no more of them until tea-time.

Soon, we reached a Forestry Commision road, which enabled us to stride out until we came to the far end of the lake. To get to the other side meant going a long half mile further up the valley to cross the River Lisa at Gillerthwaite. As this seemed a waste of effort, we decided to find our way across by using the remains of what had once been a bridge. There was a notice, 'Bridge Unsafe', so we crossed in slow motion, causing the old timbers to shake alarmingly.

Half the time we had estimated for walking round the lake had gone. We had assumed that we should use the other half in walking back on the far side, but we had not allowed for crossing the half mile between one side and the other, and this was our undoing, for this area was criss-crossed by a maze of streams, some of which had stepping stones, but most had not. It made the going slow and laborious, and when finally we were level with the far side of the lake we were confronted by an impenetrable tangle of barbed wire. It was the end.

Given plenty of time, we might have found a way to get past the wire, but having ordered tea for four o'clock exactly at the Anglers', we were obliged to turn back — and to move fast. Re-crossing all the streams and the ruined bridge, we climbed up to the road and began that most tiring activity — a forced road march. Hot and irritated, and with very wet feet, we pounded along, treating the uphill stretches as though they were flat. Towards the end, we took a short cut over some fields, and were chased by a farm dog. It was a test of endurance rather than a walk, but we made it. We reached the Anglers' Inn at four o'clock precisely — and didn't the tea taste good!

When we were planning the next day's venture, those who had not attempted the walk round the lake protested that they had no energy to do anything strenuous, thereby provoking caustic remarks about laziness from the others.

May said, "Can't you find us a nice, little walk for a change?" to which Prim replied, "I don't know anything else that is easy. We have done all the little walks round here, like Dock Tarn," and May said, "Good heavens!"

* * *

Spring came all at once, and the daffodils in the garden opened overnight. The fells had shrugged off their blanket of cloud and rose clear, almost shining, into the blue sky.

Hilda gave us a shock at breakfast time.

"Doris, May and I are going to climb Skiddaw today."

"What!" exclaimed Cath. "I thought you had no energy!"

"Well, it's only an ordinary walk, isn't it?" from Doris.

Cop said airily, "Oh yes, and it is a good idea for you to do it. Everybody should do Skiddaw once."

"What do you propose to do?" Hilda asked.

Prim answered, "I think we will just have an easy day — for a change."

May eyed her suspiciously.

"I bet you will go up Scafell Pike or somewhere!"

"Oh no, we shall not do anything special."

Actually, we spent the day by the Innominate Tarn on Haystacks. We lingered there through the idyllic spring afternoon, listening to the gentle lapping of the water against the stones and the larks singing high above. We talked very little, for in that setting the light-hearted, idiotic chatter in which we so often indulged would have been out of place.

Dropping down through the rocks to Scarth Gap and the valley, we followed the track under High Stile to Buttermere village, and had tea at the Bridge Hotel before Prim telephoned to John to come and take us home.

Hilda and Doris were not enthusiastic about their day, and May had found it so boring that she had given up half-way. The 'Halfway House' where they had hoped to get cups of tea was a ruin. As a mountain, they thought nothing of Skiddaw.

Cop assured them, "We didn't either, but we didn't say anything. You had to find out for yourselves." At which May called her "A blithering idiot."

Later, when May and I were sitting talking, I teased her a little. "What did you think of Skiddaw?"

May, who never beat about the bush, gave a straight-faced reply. "What did I think? I can tell you that in two words. Bugger Skiddaw!"

Poor Skiddaw, so beautiful and so boring!

Every evening around ten o'clock we used to develop a raging thirst, about which we grumbled incessantly. One night, after Hilda and May had gone to bed, leaving the rest of us moaning about what we would give for a drink, May reappeared with an outsize china jug containing a gallon of water, and a single tumbler. These she set down in the middle of the hearth rug.

"There you are. Now help yourselves — and shut up!"

In the rush to remove the jug and glass before Mrs Coates came in and saw them, we forgot to drink any of the water.

* * *

Cop left on a warm, sunny day to return to London, and we spent the morning commiserating with her before seeing her off on the midday train.

In the afternoon, we were ready to fall in with the suggestion, "What about exploring Gillercombe?"

It was a public holiday, which meant that every well-known track would be chock-a-block with human crocodiles, but few would be making for the high, hanging valley of Gillercombe, and we could be almost certain of finding the solitude we loved.

We walked up Honister by the old, unsurfaced road, which was far more pleasant than the modern metalled one, because we could stop to look and talk about things without being pestered by cars on our heels.

High on Brandreth a light breeze rustled the withered marsh grasses, turning them into a tawny sea, where on sun-warmed boulders we dallied and watched a distant line of walkers heading towards Gable. There were no other travellers on our route, nor was there any track. We made our own way over and around outcrops of rock until very soon we looked down into the green basin of Gillercombe. It was bounded on one side by Base Brown and by Raven Crag on the other, and Green Gable rose at the head.

We climbed down by Raven Crag, an easy descent, though Doris complained that there was too much rock for her liking.

"Will you keep behind me, in case I slip?"

I said that I would, though I could not see what use I might have been, unless I was quick enough to grab her.

We followed the stream to the far end of the valley, where it plunged over an escarpment to descend in a series of cascades to Seathwaite. We descended according to fancy, some of us choosing the section where the rocks were steepest, with plenty of holds, and having great fun working down them. The escarpment was the most enjoyable part, for after that came scree followed by slippery grass straight down to Seathwaite, where the road was lined with cars and thronged with hikers. All the world was out that day, and the top of Styhead must have resembled Piccadilly Circus.

Gillercombe had been a wise choice.

* * *

'We never got to the back of the Langdale Pikes!'

I mentioned this so often when we were discussing where to go that one day we set out to do it.

Leaving the cars at Stonethwaite, we walked up the lonely Langstrath, on this particular morning full of sunlight and the low music of the beck. As usual, we took our time, savouring every detail, and finally reaching the old ash trees at the foot of Stake, and strolling up the pass. At the top, we ate our sandwiches and discussed the next part of the walk, which was to go to the back of the Pikes and return via High Raise and Greenup to Stonethwaite — a good round.

The Pikes seemed comparatively near, but the intervening ground was unpleasant. The bumpy, tussocky grass, swampy for the most part, made slow, heavy going, and before long grumbles were heard. These increased, and after a while we stopped to confer.

"It is stupid going any further in this stuff," Hilda said. "I vote we miss out the Pikes and go straight to High Raise."

"How will you go?" Prim looked mildly interested.

Hilda indicated High Raise, on the left skyline.

"We will go direct!"

"I shouldn't, if I were you." Prim pointed out that to go direct would involve a descent into a swampy basin, followed by a steep climb to High Raise. "That may be the shortest distance, but it will also involve a lot more effort, whereas if we keep on this contour and follow it round to the left, we shall have almost level going all the way to High Raise. That is the way I am going!" and she set off, and we followed.

But when the Pikes were only a stone's throw away, Hilda, May and Doris turned along the contour towards High Raise.

"Well, flaming hell!" I said, as, frustrated and annoyed, we watched them go. The Pikes were so temptingly near, and we could not explore them because half the party had decided to go home.

Prim shrugged. "I suppose we had better go after them, as they don't seem very sure of the way after High Raise. But it is a pity!"

So we started towards High Raise, with a slight diversion to take in the insignificant cairn marking the summit of Thunacar Knott. We found the other three waiting by the top rocks of High Raise, and we sat for a while. The hills were grape-blue, and night's first shadows were beginning to gather in the deep valleys.

Then came the rough track down to the col, the crossing of the swampy edge, the scramble past Lining Crag, and the long trek down Greenup. Hilda, bringing up the rear with me, grumbled without ceasing about her boots. Every step was torture. She really could not stand much more. She went on and on, until at last I said, "Go and jump in the river!" I knew all about new boots, and it was the best possible advice I could give, but she did not take it that way. She assumed that I was being insulting, and refused to speak to me again. We finished the walk in dead silence, which I rather enjoyed, because I wanted to watch the twilight on the hills.

We were very late for dinner, and would have been even later had we explored the Langdale Pikes, but it would have been worth it.

Later on, I thought I ought to put things right, and said to Hilda, "Didn't you know that standing in water is the best thing you could do? Let me have a look at those boots."

On examining them, I found that they had hard-blocked toes, and were half a size too small for her. I advised her not to stand in the river, but to throw the boots in and leave them there, but she would have none of it.

"I am going to break them in if it kills me!"

"It probably will!"

She may have discarded them and bought another pair, or gone back to wearing her old ones, but from that day she never again complained about her feet.

* * *

When Prim said, "We'll go to Watenlath this morning," there was a storm of protest.

"Why go there?"

"I'm sick of going to Watendlath!"

"I've been so many times that I could go with my eyes closed!"

"Not this way," Prim said, "because we shall start from Ladder Brow and climb straight up the fell — without a track."

It was an interesting variation, steep in parts, and we scattered, each choosing her own route. Prim and I found some good scrambling and a tricky traverse among the chaos of rocks near Shepherd's Crag. We all met near the top of the Lodore beck where the water takes its first plunge through the trees, cut across to the Watendlath track, and through the village like steam, for we had no wish to linger there. On the way over to Rosthwaite, we walked towards the sunlit glory of the hills.

In the afternoon, we decided to walk up by Castle Crag, climb the Crag, then follow the fell track to Seatoller, have tea at the farm, and return by the river to Grange.

Though small, Castle Crag is an enjoyable little exercise, especially if one climbs straight up the slates. This we did, though it was not to everyone's liking, and had a prolonged laze on the top. The views were perfect, and harmony reigned — until we were ready to come down, when a heated argument started. I was sitting on a rock away from the others, but I gathered that some of them wished to go down a different way because the way they had come up was dangerous. They were all talking at once, so in the midst of the uproar I slipped away unnoticed, and slid helter-skelter down the slates to the base of the Crag, where I sat on the wall and waited to see what would happen next.

After a few minutes, Prim bounded round a rock to the right, and came to join me on the wall. Her face showed a mixture of annoyance and amusement.

"I found a perfectly simple way down. I knew there would be one if we looked hard enough and used a bit of sense."

"Where are the others?"

"They have gone down through the trees on the far side of the Crag. It is twice as far, and then they will have to climb the fell to get back here."

"How stupid!" I said.

"Idiotic!" she agreed.

We sat in silence for a few minutes, and then she began to laugh.

"Do you know what Hilda said to me! I said I was coming back down this side, and she said, 'You are not to. It's dangerous, and we are responsible for you.' "

"What?" and I looked at her open-mouthed.

"She said they were responsible for me!"

I said, "That is one of the best jokes I have heard for years!" and we both laughed so much that we almost fell off the wall.

"Let's go on," she said, when we had recovered, and we strolled up to the cairn marking the crest of the track.

"What next?"

"We will wait and see who turns up."

It was quite comfortable sitting on the cairn, and we had a lengthy wait before Cath and Doris came puffing up the fell-side. They said they were sick of pushing through undergrowth and climbing over mossy walls. May and Hilda had gone down to Rosthwaite to catch a bus to Seatoller. We continued the walk, and found them there at tea-time.

In an aside to May, I asked, "Did you have a nice walk down the Crag?" and she gave me a dirty look.

"I was thoroughly fed up with all those walls and tree stumps. I am not a flaming monkey!"

"Serves you right!" I said.

"I should have come with you!"

After tea, we went to Longthwaite, and home by the river path.

* * *

The very name of Glaramara was a siren song, and every time we were at Seatoller our eyes were drawn to that craggy, bristling skyline. On the last day of the holiday we ticked it off.

Starting from Mountain View, in ten short minutes we were high on Thornythwaite Fell, skirting the cleft of Comb Gill. The walk was good throughout, first the track up through the trees, then a steepish grassy fell-side with no track, and finally an intricate succession of rock outcrops — this last being the best part.

As we sat eating our sandwiches on a mossy bank beyond the rocks, less than half a mile away up a gentle slope a cairn marked the summit of Glaramara — a magnet which made us bolt the food without noticing what we were eating. Then Prim, Cath and I headed for the cairn, and a couple of minutes later there was a pounding of feet as Doris raced to catch us up. She said she had left Hilda and May sitting on the bank, as they were too comfortable to move, and would wait there until we came back.

Glaramara's topmost rocks gave some fine scrambling, and an all-embracing view of Skiddaw, Grasmoor, Honister Crag, Pillar, Gable, Great End, Esk Pike, Bowfell, the Coniston group, the

Langdale Pikes, High Raise, Helvellyn — fells to the right, fells to the left, fells all around us — such a rich reward for so very little effort!

We longed to go on, to traverse the three-mile top over to Allen Crags and Esk Hause, and back down Grain Gill. We would have done so, had we not left May and Hilda sitting on the bank.

Cath said, "Do you think they will sit and wait until we come back?"

"If we did the traverse we should not be coming back that way, so they would be sitting for a long time!" I said.

Most reluctantly, we turned back to rejoin them, and to stroll down the fell by the way we had come up. There was plenty of time for strolling!

We determined to do the Glaramara traverse the following year. We were equally determined that on all future walks anyone who did not wish to go all the way would not wait for the ones who did, but would be expected to make their own way home.

The next morning was gloomy with dark cloud and rain in the offing — which in no way mitigated the ache of leaving Borrowdale. Nothing could ever do that.

THE BEST RIDGE

Easter came late in April this year, and the waiting seemed interminable, but there was Borrowdale at last, with every fell, every wayside daffodil, every fresh green leaf glowing in the sunlit evening. And then there was Grange, and the tang of wood smoke, and Scarthwaite, and Mrs Coates. We had arrived, all seven of us.
    The blazing fire, the vases of larch branches and daffodils made our sitting-room a shining, welcoming place for a gang of excited people, all talking at once and dumping luggage, on which other people barked their shins, in the middle of the floor.
    The electric light, which had recently been brought underground to the valley, made going to bed a pleasure. Gone were the nights when your room-mate, taking the candle into the bathroom, left you trying to undress in the dark. Cath and I were in 'The Pines', where all was well apart from one thing. Over the years the hard beds at Scarthwaite had been replaced by interior sprung mattresses, until only one of the old ones remained — mine! I cursed it heartily the first night; after that I no longer cared.

*   *   *

The holiday began with a gem of a spring day.
    Just before Easter, I had felt some stiffness at the backs of my knees. This had been diagnosed as something which sounded like sinovitis, but I had been assured that I should be quite all right for fell walking if I bandaged my knees tightly. (Later, it was re-diagnosed correctly as the beginning of arthritis, and tight bandaging was the worst thing I could have done.)
    The bandages were duly put on, and felt most uncomfortable, because my knees would not bend properly, and I was rather

alarmed. If they were like this at the start of the holiday, what awful state would they be in by the end? So I said to Prim, "Let's have a good walk today, in case I don't get another!"

"Where would you like to go?"

"Great Gable!"

"Right!" she said. "Gable by Beck Head. How about that?"

"Perfect!"

John took us to the top of Honister, and we climbed to the pathetic remains of the 'Gallows', where we stayed to watch the Mellbreak foxhounds working on Fleetwith Pike, and saw a fox streaking along the fell-side while the hounds were running in the opposite direction.

It was glorious on the plateau that day, with long clear views, a refreshing breeze, larks singing, and curlews calling. After eating our sandwiches on the rocks above Gillercombe, we moved across to the high col of Beck Head, from which a rough slope of boulders led to the rocks fringing the summit of Gable. We attacked the boulders with gusto, paying no heed when May and Doris said they had had enough and were going to walk back over Brandreth. We hardly noticed them go. Prim was climbing very fast, leaving the rest of us well behind, and taking no notice of Hilda's cry, "Prim, slow down! We don't know which way to go!"

I laughed. "You must be joking! There is only one way to go — up!"

Gable via Beck Head is the best of all ways up the mountain, and soon we were sitting by the Westmorland Cairn, which has a situation far superior to that of the main cairn. It is an airy perch on the edge of the mountain, one from which you feel that you could launch yourself into space and float effortlessly down to Wasdale. There are many wonderful places in the Lake District, but the Westmorland Cairn on Great Gable is unique.

After an hour or more, we started down the rough shoulder to Windy Gap, and then I realised the handicap of my bandaged knees. The track was fairly good in those days, not the gravelly scree into which it has since been pounded, but I found the descent laborious, with every other step a stumble — and a swear-word. I was following Cop, and at one point she slipped, fell, rolled, and regained her feet in one movement — an amazing display of gymnastics which I admired, but resented because I could not do it.

From Windy Gap the track down to the Brandreth plateau was steep, slippery shale, which I took in slow motion, Cath reducing speed to keep with me. At the bottom I collapsed exhausted on a large boulder. My legs had had enough.

"How in heaven's name am I going to get from here to Seatoller?"

"It's a case of having to," said Cath calmly. "We will just take our time."

So we rested while the others forged ahead, Prim well in the lead, and when they were out of sight we resumed our crawl. I had to stop every few minutes, and it was a long, long way to the 'Gallows', and getting down from there to the top of Honister was the last straw. With my two useless wooden legs, I dreaded the walk down the pass.

But I did not have to do it, for at Honister top John's taxi was waiting. It seemed too good to be true! Prim, hurrying ahead, had gone to the Youth Hostel, persuaded the warden to unlock the AA telephone box, and summoned John. My sufferings were over and I was free to ponder on the immense satisfaction the day had brought. If I did not get another top, at least I had done Gable.

It was Cop's day for falling. Returning from her bedroom with a box of chocolates, she caught her toe on a chair leg and measured her length on the hearth rug, chocolates flying in all directions. Again, as on Gable, she did no damage to herself.

"Fools for luck!" I said.

"Not at all!" came the austere reply. "Some people know how to fall without hurting themselves!"

* * *

It was an ideal day for Grain Gill, Allen Crags, and the traverse of Glaramara.

Parking the cars at Seatoller, we walked along the lane to Seathwaite and the track to Stockley Bridge, and with every step I was praying that my stiff, bandaged knees would loosen up. I could have saved myself the trouble, because after a few hundred yards up Grain Gill I realised that they were not going to, and at the rate I was going it would take me all day even to reach Esk Hause.

So, for me, it was goodbye, Glaramara. Prim, Cath, Cop and Hilda went on, while Doris and May said they would go back to Seathwaite with me. I wished that they hadn't, for I was in the sort of mood when it is much better to be left alone to snarl and curse to your heart's content.

It took until lunch-time to get back to Seathwaite, where I left them to picnic by the roadside while I climbed half-way up the fell by Sour Milk Gill. I told them I preferred to eat in a high spot, but the real reason was that it gave me a better view of the ridge of

Glaramara. I spent a long time over my lunch, looking at that ridge.

When I came down, they suggested that we went to Keswick, and I retorted, "I'm not going to Keswick. You go. I'd like you to!" But no, they wished to keep with me, and I thought, 'On your heads be it!' and led them quite a dance that afternoon.

We walked to Seatoller, then down to Mountain View, opposite which the Glaramara track ends. I went over the stile, and docilely they followed. Climbing a little and resting a lot, we meandered up Thornythwaite Fell towards Comb Gill until we were a fair height above the valley. We did that all afternoon, sitting until they complained of feeling cold, then moving on. They must have thought I was mad, because it was obvious we were not going to get anywhere, but I did not care.

At tea-time, we came down and had a pot of tea at Yew Tree Cottage, and I was just wondering what wild goose chase I could lead them on next when the four walkers arived, Prim and Cath striding briskly ahead. They were enchanted by Glaramara top, and all talked at once, describing everything in minute detail for my benefit.

"And what did you do?" they wanted to know.

"Damn all," I said, "except wait for you to come down!"

That night, when the habitual moan about being thirsty was in full swing, Cath suddenly jumped up and exclaimed, "I'm sick of this, and I'm going to do something about it!" and she marched into the kitchen. In a couple of minutes she was back, all smiles.

"I have asked Mrs Coates if we can, in future, have a pot of tea each night before we go to bed."

She looked at me and grinned.

"I told her you must have a hot drink at night, because you fell on your head a few months ago and needed soothing."

The part about the head was true, as I had fallen on a highly-polished office floor, but I demurred about having to be soothed, though May commented rudely, "She's needed soothing for years!"

Mrs Coates brought in the tea, and we cheered, though when she had gone back to the kitchen, Cop said, "I don't know whether I like tea late at night. I would sooner have milk or something."

"You will have tea and like it — or go without!" snapped Cath.

That night, I threw away my knee bandages, and walked properly for the remainder of the holiday.

* * *

When I came down to breakfast the next morning and, as I always did, popped my head round the kitchen door to say good morning to Mrs Coates, I was greeted by a glare. She was sitting cutting sandwiches at the table, and waved the bread knife at me.

"Come here, you!"

I sidled in, wondering what I had done wrong and why she looked so annoyed.

"I'm real put out by you," she went on. "To think you have known me all these years and not felt free to ask me for a cup of tea when you needed one. I'm proper vexed!"

Nonplussed, I could only offer the excuse that she already did so much for us that I did not want to give her any extra work, but she would have none of that.

"Stop talking rubbish! You have had me proper bothered. Now go and get your breakfast — and don't ever be so daft again in future!"

I told the others that I had been ticked off for not asking for late tea and they said it served me right, though I cannot think why.

The weather was superb for what I think is the finest ridge walk in the Lakes, the one which starts at Causey Pike and ends at Buttermere.

We could not use the cars, unless half the party started at one end of the ridge and half at the other, and met half-way and exchanged car keys. No one thought that a good idea, so Prim rang up John, and he drove us to the foot of Causey Pike. Fortunately, he had a very large car by then, and it was a comfortable ride.

Starting up Rowling End, we soon reached the point where the fell begins to arch its spine in a series of bulges. There was a short pull up followed by a small flat terrace, repeated three or four times, and culminating in a scramble over the rocky nose to the top. There were splendid views of Newlands, Grisedale Pike, the Buttermere fells, and the narrow, undulating ridge stretching from Causey to Grasmoor — the way we were going, and it looked good.

We sat on Causey top to eat, then set off, traversing Scar Crags to Sail, and all the while gazing down at the valleys on either side. We trod a pathway through the sky, and I was far more conscious of the sensation of airy space than I had been on Striding Edge. I felt that we had discovered something extremely beautiful.

After the grassy mound of Sail came another narrow col, followed by a climb up Eel Crags, where the track dodged among bands of rock. We emerged on a plateau with Wandope to the left and Grasmoor about half a mile to the right. We walked over to the flat cairn on Wandope, from which our route lay over Whiteless Pike and down to Buttermere. Some of us were looking at Grasmoor — so near, so tempting.

Prim said, "It wouldn't take long. What about it?"

"Yes!" from Cath, Cop and me.

"No!" from the other three, May adding, "We could do it if we wanted, but we don't want."

So we parted, four for Grasmoor and three for Buttermere.

"Order the tea!" we called after them.

We were soon on Grasmoor's massive, bulging summit. Passing a big marker cairn, we began looking for the main one. We knew it must be somewhere close at hand, but failed to spot it. Then we found a level track, which we followed for some distance until it started to descend.

"We don't seem to be getting anywhere," said Cop. "Do you think we should give up and go down to the other three?"

Prim dismissed that idea.

"That cairn is somewhere near, and I am going to find it!" and she went leaping over the skyline and disappeared.

We walked back to the marker, and sat eating chocolate, and in a few minutes she reappeared from another direction.

"I found it!"

We had passed it because it was hidden by the rise of the ground. It is huge, as though someone has tipped up three cart-loads of stones.

We went down over the steep, narrow spine of Whiteless Pike, then Blake Rigg where the track was a green ribbon through bracken, to Buttermere village. The other three were standing in the road waiting for us, and we were amazed to find that they had not had tea.

"Have you ordered it?"

"No."

"Well, have you rung John?"

"No. We only got down half an hour before you did."

"Did you lose yourselves?" I asked, grinning, and they looked annoyed, and said that Hilda had twisted her knee on Whiteless Pike and May had bandaged it with her scarf, and it had slowed them down.

"You could have had tea in half an hour," I said.

"Those who want it can still have it," Cath pointed out, but Hilda said, "I do think we should get home as quickly as possible, don't you? I should like to attend to my knee."

Prim's eyebrows twitched.

"Very well, I will go and ring John. And while we are waiting for him there will be plenty of time for some of you to have a cup of tea!"

And some of us did.

Causey Pike to Grasmoor — I shall always remember that day with joy!

* * *

"What shall we do today?"

It was always a mistake to ask, for it triggered off excuses for not doing much at all.

"My knee is still rather stiff, so I shall have a gentle walk in the valley," said Hilda.

"I'll come with you," said May.

"I'll do a solo — in case you others go rock climbing," said Doris.

This left Prim, Cath, Cop and myself — the four originals.

"What about a laze up the Langstrath?" suggested Cath.

We agreed, but I noticed a speculative gleam in Prim's eye.

We left the car at Stonethwaite and began walking, and it was very, very warm with the sun blazing in our faces. Presently, Prim said, "It might be a good idea to go up to Angle Tarn," but no one replied. I remembered the last time we had climbed steep, trackless grass to get out of the Langstrath, and I did not intend doing that again — ever.

All morning we trailed up the long valley to quarter of a mile or so beyond the foot of Stake, where we ate our lunch. Then Prim repacked her rucksack and got to her feet.

"Who is coming up to Angle Tarn?"

"I'm not!" Cath and I answered in unison.

Cop turned indignantly on me.

"I like that! You are the one who always makes a fuss if we don't go to the top of anything! I wanted an easy day!"

"You don't have to come," Prim said mildly. "I can always go alone," and she started walking.

"Oh, I'll come!" and Cop went grumbling after her.

"I don't like hard labour!" I said, as we watched them go.

We sat on for a while before facing the walk back. Then we made slow progress, for it was scorching hot with not even a whisper of a breeze. We walked in a stupor, and I began to dislike the Langstrath whole-heartedly — a silly featureless valley like an oven.

At Stonethwaite we recovered over tea and biscuits before driving round to Seathwaite to wait for Prim and Cop. The timing was good, and they soon hove in sight, coming at a cracking pace. They dived into the farm, and I followed them in.

"Two cups of tea and two pieces of apple cake," ordered Prim.

"No!" gasped Cop. "The tea is all I want. I couldn't eat anything yet!"

"Then I'll eat both pieces."

"How was the going up to Angle Tarn?" I asked.

"As bad as ever — no track and all that steep grass. It is the last time I shall do it," Cop vowed. "And then Prim rushed me from Esk Hause down Grain Gill to Seathwaite in forty-seven minutes, because she was afraid you might have given up waiting and gone home. She went so fast that I could hardly get my breath!"

Prim, having finished the apple cake while Cop was talking, then said, "I think a better way to Angle Tarn would be up Stake Pass and along the ridge to Esk Hause. I never did think much of the Langstrath."

We drove home, and after dinner Prim asked, "Would anyone like to go for a walk?" and looked surprised when May said, "Aren't you tired?" and replied, "No. Why should I be?" and May groaned.

"I'll go," I said.

We went along the Catbells road. The evening was perfect, with Maiden Moor russet velvet, and blue distant hills, and a singing bird in every tree. On returning, we walked down the village and into the post office-cum-general shop, where Prim asked for a packet of biscuits, blandly telling the shopkeeper that she had brought no money but would pay some time when she happened to be passing. The biscuits were handed over, but I wondered why she had bought them.

"Are you still hungry, after all that dinner?"

"No," she said. "I just thought the biscuits would go nicely with the late tea!"

* * *

On the last day of the holiday we had a new experience. We walked inside a fell. Four of us did this, the other three having declined.

We were invited by Dick, Mrs Coates' son-in-law, to inspect the slate quarry at the top of Honister. Having walked up the old road, we were met by Dick, and taken through a hole into Honister Crag, where we walked for some distance along narrow tunnels and galleries. We each carried a pungent-smelling carbide lamp, which flared wildly in the draught. All the details of the workings were explained at great length. This was interesting, but our main attention was on not bumping our heads on the low roof, not tripping over the loose blocks of slate, and not having our lamps blown out. I have never cared for low, underground tunnels, and was glad when we got back to the daylight, with the sky overhead. It is better to be on a fell than inside one!

We visited the shed where the blocks of slate were being cut by diamond saws, and the noise set one's teeth on edge. I preferred the section where men with chisels and hammers were riving the slate into thin sheets, suitable for roofing tiles. This was craftsman's work, fascinating to watch.

It was lunch-time when we left the quarry, and after eating we had an urge to stand on the top of Honister Crag. It would be more in our line than going inside it had been. Climbing up to the 'Gallows', we reached the top surprisingly quickly after floundering through a stretch of bog and rounding a succession of outcrops of nubbly rock. We were suddenly, almost shockingly, there. The Crag plunged in a tremendous, vertical precipice, a vast gulf of space, at the bottom of which beetle-sized cars crawled up and down the pass. There was a thrill of sheerness and space, and this, to us, was the best part of the day.

After dinner that night came the final session in the kitchen when bills were paid, future plans made, and advice given, and Mrs Coates, rocking steadily in her chair the while, regaling us with the news and gossip of the dale. We loved that Cumbrian voice, that salty yet kindly humour, and her mode of speech. For example, a village gossip was referred to as "She was an endless woman." Most of all, I remember her description of the Parochial Church Council meeting where the vicar said that he expected the people of Grange to raise at least £150 for Church funds, and she had told him, "I doubt you will aim at the moon and land in the midden!"

The following morning we tore ourselves away from Borrowdale. Not having made a detour on the way to the Lakes, we made one on the way back. At Malham Tarn, May, a keen ornithologist, was in her element, but the rest of us were more impressed by the high, limestone bluffs of Malham Cove, which could have provided good scrambling, had we had time.

But our free days on the hills were over for another year.

THE TIMED WALK

On a dull, bleak morning with a nip of winter in the air, the two cars, Cath's and Hilda's, headed north, going by the Ilkley route to carry out Prim's suggestion of a detour to Wharfedale.
The lower part of this dale is not remarkable, but it gradually improves as the hills begin to close in. It was snowing when we went into the beautiful old church at Hubberholme, but the storm had passed and there were gleams of sunlight when we came out, and this, we assured each other, was a good omen. The best of Wharfedale began as the twisting road climbed round hairpin bends, with 1 in 5 gradients, to the wild solitude of the snow-flecked Pennine moors. On reaching the top of the pass, we pulled up to look more closely at our surroundings, and the wind howled and rocked the car. We were completely engrossed — until we noticed that the other car was missing.
"I don't know what has happened to Hilda," Cath said, and she got out of the car and began to walk back, but returned after ten minutes or so. "She is nowhere in sight. I think I had better drive back."
She reversed and drove to the top of the pass, and was just about to start down when Hilda's car roared round the first of the hairpin bends. It was empty apart from the driver. Then Doris and May came puffing round the corner. Hilda said that her engine had stalled on the hill, and the other two had got out, and when she eventually managed to get the engine to fire she dare not stop for them to get in again. This little contretemps had wasted an hour, though it had given Prim, Cop, and myself a good opportunity to absorb the atmosphere of the Pennines.
Down into Wensleydale and through Sedbergh and Kendal, leaving the east wind behind, we came to Ambleside, Keswick, Borrowdale, and were home, with Mrs Coates waiting to welcome

us, and everyone talking at once and nobody listening.

Many plans were made that night, for we had resolved to break new ground that year, to climb fells we had not done before. In the event, this resolution was mainly fulfilled, but there was also the lure of familiar, well-loved places, the walks we had already done and longed to do again. These, too, had to be fitted in.

* * *

On the first morning, the dale dreamed in the sun and spirits soared. A more auspicious beginning would have been impossible, for this was Lakeland at its spellbinding best.

"What about Grisedale Pike?" asked Cop, during breakfast.

The ensuing silence was broken by various comments.

"Sounds like a grind."

"Too warm to go sweating up there."

"Don't you think we ought to break ourselves in gently?"

Prim looked anxiously from one to another. The idea was to keep the party together as far as possible, especially at the beginning of a holiday, but this was growing increasingly difficult, as the tendency to split into A and B groups was becoming more manifest each year.

"We will leave Grisedale Pike for later. I propose we have an easy day on Honister Crag and Fleetwith Pike, then go down to Buttermere. Agreed?"

"Agreed!" we said.

After lingering over coffee at Seatoller Farm, we took Honister so slowly that it was lunch-time when we reached the old 'Gallows'. We were certainly breaking ourselves in gently!

We walked to the top of Honister Crag, again experiencing the fascination and the shock of precipitous height as we looked down on the pass far below. From the Crag, a short track led to the cairn on Fleetwith Pike and the grandeur of the surrounding fells — Gable, Pillar, the Scafells, the mountains we loved. We spent most of the afternoon lying contentedly by the cairn, just looking at them.

Fleetwith Pike descended to Buttermere in a series of rock outcrops and grassy terraces. It was delightful going — until we reached the final outcrop. This was too sheer to climb, and we were forced to leave the narrow spine of the fell and veer to the left down a steep, slippery slope of dead bracken. The angle looked nasty, and turned out to be even worse than it looked. We did most of it sitting, rolling, or on our backs, unable to brake and completely out of control. It was a ridiculous situation, and the sight of the others in the same predicament made it worse, until the fell echoed with shrieks and yells. It was an impossible slope, and we were more than glad to arrive safely, though battered, at the bottom.

"What a beginning to a holiday!" someone wailed, as we picked ourselves up and staggered to Gatesgarth for a cup of tea.

"Thank goodness it is Sunday tomorrow!"

Immediately after tea, Prim rang up for John to take us back over Honister. We were anxious to get home and take stock of our bruises, cuts, and other damage. We were all bloodied by the vicious sharpness of the hard bracken stalks. Hilda's shoulder straps were in ribbons, May vowed that her bruised knees and back were permanently injured, I had four deep, gory scratches down the backs of my legs, and Prim had torn out the seat of her pants.

"Just look at that!" she exclaimed, bending to show us. "I kept these specially for hiking. I've had them for years, and now they are finished!"

"And so am I!" groaned May. "Why don't you stop planning easy walks!"

Round the fire after dinner, with half the party yawning and grumbling about stiffness, Cop said, "Let's go up Grisedale Pike tomorrow. It looks a gentler sort of fell."

Nobody replied.

Cath asked May if her legs were recovering, and May retorted, "It's not my legs!"

"No," chimed in Cop, "it's the sitting down that hurts!"

Hilda, full length on the hearth rug, wailed "I'm finished! Whiteless Pike began to finish me last year, and now I'm really done!"

Cop eyed her with scorn, then leapt to her feet and started to dance a highland fling, gleefully chanting, "Am I stiff? Am I stiff? I am not!"

She was told to stop making a fool of herself.

* * *

Another glorious morning, hills all a-shimmer with heat haze.

"Grisedale Pike?" Cop made a tentative suggestion, anxiously watching our reaction. She seemed obsessed with Grisedale Pike, so we all agreed to do it, until Doris changed her mind.

"Count me out. It is too nice a day for slogging up a mountain. I shall walk in the woods, and go on the lake, and then climb Latrigg."

"It's a free world!" We told her.

Taking the cars to Braithwaite, we parked at the foot of Grisedale Pike, and started up, and within ten minutes began to wonder why we had bothered. The going was decidedly unpleasant on a loose, earthy track which cut up the grassy slope so sharply that we might have progressed better on all fours. There was much sweat and toil until we gained a long shoulder running from the top of the fell. This promised half a mile of comparatively flat going. Here we sat to regain our breath, and to say what we thought of the part we had already climbed. Then Hilda and May refused to go any further, so we left them sitting there.

The final stretch of slate and boulders was the best part. At the summit cairn we ate our lunch, but the views were almost obscured by haze, which was disappointing. Except for the view from the top I can see no reason why Grisedale Pike should ever be climbed.

We discussed dropping to the Coledale Pass and doing the Causey Pike ridge next — a tempting prospect, except that we should have come down at Stair and the car was parked at Braithwaite. Prim suggested going down Gasgale Gill to Lanthwaite Green, near Crummockwater, which would have taken us much further from the car, though no doubt she would have found some means of getting us back. The only other alternative was to go down the Coledale Pass back to Braithwaite, and because this seemed sensible we did it, but it made a very tame ending.

We headed down thick, bumpy grass towards Coledale Hause. I tried a short cut down a gully, but it turned into a slimy moss-chute, and I had to climb back again. Meanwhile, the others had reached the Hause and were waiting for me.

Next, a track of unpleasantly large boulders led to Coledale Beck, after which a long lane curved down to Braithwaite. This hot, dreary, monotonous walk made us thoroughly fed up with Grisedale Pike. Like Skiddaw, it is very beautiful to behold and very boring to climb.

But on discussing the walk after dinner, we came to the conclusion that it was not the walk but the heat which had got us down. Someone suggested that we should hire seven mules and do our future hill-climbing in comfort.

Prim began to chuckle.

"I was thinking about us rolling round on Fleetwith Pike. We should have come down sitting on seven sheep. They are sure-footed enough."

"How would you steer a sheep?" demanded Cop.

"Easily. One of the car drivers — Hilda, Cath, or May — could steer the first one by its horns, and all the rest would follow. Sheep always do."

Cop sniffed. "I'd sooner go down on my feet than on a sheep!"

"But you didn't go down on your feet!" Prim retorted.

We laughed, and Cop glared.

"I didn't split my pants! Most of the time I was just crouching down and holding onto the bracken. I was not sitting!"

"Like hell you weren't!" I jeered.

May said, "Who suggested we hired seven mules? We already have them — daft ones!"

Then Prim changed the subject.

"What about doing Bowfell tomorrow!"

Cath, Cop and I whooped with delight, but the other three were not so enthusiastic. Doris and May thought it might be too strenuous, and Hilda, after consideration, said "It's a long way from here, isn't it?"

"Quite a long way."

"I don't really feel I want to do it."

"We four do!" I said.

So it was settled that the four of us went to Bowfell, though Hilda said, "You will never do it in the time. You always linger so much on the fells. It will be midnight before you get back, and we shall be wondering what has happened to you."

Prim said, "We shall not rush it, neither shall we linger. We shall go steadily. We can do that, you know, if we want to! And we shall have plenty of time!"

"I doubt it!" and Hilda shook her head.

"What do we three do while you are cavorting on Bowfell?" May asked.

"Find us a nice fell," from Doris.

"We could all start together, and go up Grain Gill onto Esk Hause, then you could go on Great End. That is a fine walk, not too far, and Great End top is a wonderful place for views."

Having sold them that idea, we began to make plans. We would have breakfast early, and get going at once. I went to bed with my fingers crossed for good weather.

* * *

In all the years of the S.L. Club, this was the only occasion on which we kept a time record.

7.15 a.m.
Down to breakfast, with rucksacks packed the night before. Breakfast was scrambled egg and sausage, and there are few things I dislike more, except baked beans. Scarthwaite breakfasts were excellent, and I wondered why Mrs Coates had done this to us at the start of a fairly long day, then realised that she had not had time to cook the usual mound of bacon, etc.

9.10 a.m.
The two cars were parked at Seathwaite. In the freshness of the spring morning the deserted dale was heavenly.

9.35 a.m.
Short pause on Stockley Bridge before beginning the climb. Grain Gill easy going, apart from a little collar work at the top.

11.05 a.m.
Esk Hause. A quick look at Great End, magnificent at close quarters with Central Gully half-filled with snow, and at Great Gable, about which there is always something special.
At the top of the Hause, where a track forks right for Great End, we left Doris, May, and Hilda.

12.15 p.m.
Summit of Esk Pike. Found there were two summits separated by a tangle of rocks. Climbed both, and all the subsidiary rocks with gusto.

12.50 p.m.
Dropped to the reddish track across Ure Gap. Cone of Bowfell on the skyline. Our track followed the contours, to end in a climb up rock slabs.

1.40 p.m.
Bowfell summit.
A sharp peak scarcely large enough for the four of us to stand together. A superb view embracing Great End and the black cliffs of Scafell, Crinkle Crags, the Langdale Pikes, Windermere, Esthwaite Water, Devoke Water, Langdale, Eskdale, the Duddon Valley, and miles of sunlit sea. It was indescribable — a mountaineer's dream, which lasted for twenty short minutes.

2.10 p.m.
Dropping down by Hanging Knott, the shoulder of Bowfell.

3.15 p.m.
The main Esk Hause track.

4.00 p.m.
Top of Grain Gill.

5.00 p.m.
Sitting on Stockley Bridge.

5.25 p.m.
   Dallying over a pot of tea at Seathwaite.

After a day on the tops, in high wild places, the dale had an enhanced beauty, which welcomed you back.
   It had been a day of steady, unhurried walking, without lingering. A specific objective had been achieved with ease, and that in itself had given satisfaction. And yet — over the years our loitering had yielded a richer reward, a closer communion with the fells. We knew them all — rocky tracks, lichened boulders, viewpoints, almost every wind-blown tree. We were awake and aware, absorbing every detail, however small. Taking time to do so often meant a mad rush for home at the end of the day, but it was worth it. I could not help wishing that we had done this with Bowfell. The walk had been excellent, but there had not been time to get to know the fell, to discover its intimate, inner detail. And we never gained this knowledge, for we never climbed Bowfell again, which was a pity.

* * *

The weather changed, and although it remained fine and warm, mist shrouded the fells, obscuring even the lowly Castle Crag.
   "I propose we go hiking in the cars," Hilda said.
   "What about Ennerdale?" Cath suggested. "We could always walk round the Lake!"
   "Barbed wire and the Forestry Commission permitting!" I reminded her.
   "Well, how about Langdale, then?"
   Cop, who had been lolling half-asleep, opened her eyes, to remark, "The only thing about Langdale is that they always have a lot of things about it on calendars and things, and you think 'Oh, bother it' but I don't mind going, I suppose."
   "What is she talking about?" Doris asked in astonishment.
   "Oh, don't mind her!" I said. "She's always talking rubbish!"
   "Any more suggestions?" Prim wanted to know.
   When none were forthcoming, she said, "Right, we'll go there."
   When May asked, "Is it fit to go anywhere to see anything?"
   Prim blandly replied, "Oh, yes."
   May turned to me. "Do you know where we are supposed to be going?"
   "Yes. Cath suggested Langdale, so we go there and explore."
   "What do we explore?"
   "Anything we can find!" and I turned to Hilda. "Are you ready

to play follow-my-leader?"

"I am," she said, and heaved a sigh of resignation.

Dense cloud on Dunmail Raise brought a protesting hoot or two from the following car, which we ignored. We went on to Little Langdale, and the narrow, hilly road skirting the foot of Pike o' Blisco, the foot being all that was visible. At Blea Tarn, where the Langdale Pikes should have been revealed in their true magnificence, we were obliged to use our imagination.

"Oh, why doesn't the curtain rise!" wailed May.

But her plea remained unanswered.

Prim's plan was to climb up Dungeon Ghyll, ignoring the tourist track in favour of the best scrambling route we could find, but as we drove down into Great Langdale it began to rain heavily, and though we waited for a long time, it went on and on as though it would never stop. So we drove back to Borrowdale — it was raining there, too — and up to Seatoller Farm, where we had tea in the kitchen, and listened to the farmer grumbling about the National Trust, who had limited the number of campers he was allowed to have in his fields. The rain had stopped when we came out, and a rampart of cloud lay along Glaramara's crest.

That night we planned walks for good, bad, and indifferent weather, or rather, Prim and I did. We were the last to go to bed, and had just switched off the lights when Cath appeared on the landing, hissing, "There's been a tragedy!"

Her hot-water bottle had leaked, soaking sheets and mattress. The three of us set to work, first draping the sheets round the bathroom, then hauling the mattress downstairs and propping it in front of the fire. Then we decided to bring the sheets down, too. All this was done silently to avoid rousing the household, and by the time we had finished we were aching with suppressed laughter. Cath had to share my double bed, and lay muttering balefully about its hardness instead of going to sleep.

* * *

We walked in deteriorating weather conditions until the last day of the holiday, which was too wet to contemplate any outdoor activity. For something to do, Cath, Prim, Cop and I went into Keswick in the morning, thus, as May put it, enabling the others to sprawl peacefully round the fire. As we returned up the dale, the rain had stopped, the lake was pure silver, and a gleam of watery sunlight flirted among the clouds. Our spirits soared.

"We shall be able to do a walk this afternoon!"

It was a vain hope, quickly dispelled, for after lunch renewed rain savagely obliterated every fell and even the valley itself. We stayed by the fire, gradually getting more and more argumentative. Then Prim and I donned oilskins and went to post the accumulated batch of letters and cards.

"We'll just ignore the rain!" Prim said. It fell with unabated fury, bouncing in streams off our oilskins, but it felt good to be out, away from the fug of the sitting-room. We brought back seven bars of chocolate, which were promptly devoured, although Mrs Coates had just brought in the tea.

Having disposed of that, we ranged restlessly about the room, getting in each other's way and not knowing what to do next. Then in a cabinet we found a stack of song music, ballads and real old-fashioned stuff, on which we pounced with glee. Prim played the piano, Hilda and Doris sang, Cop clowned about like a demented prima donna, and the rest of us accompanied on combs and the fire-irons. The noise swelled to an uproar, until May wielded the poker so lustily that the shovel was badly dented, and Prim closed the piano lid to stop us from going completely wild.

As the noise subsided, May exclaimed, "Look! It's stopped raining!"

There was a wild yell, and we immediately rushed off to Manesty Woods to gather firewood. When we returned, dragging our branches behind us, Mrs Coates tut-tutted when she saw our wet feet. "You are like children! You go through all the mud you can find!"

At the end of dinner, Cop made a speech about Sally's Ladies and their unique President. This, as she had intended, reduced us to laughter, and the more we laughed the more outrageous she became. Prim, when told that she was expected to reply to the speech, could do no more than gasp, "Oh, Cop! Why don't you stop? It hurts!"

The next morning the sun shone and the breeze was fresh. Conditions for walking were ideal — but they came too late.

OCTOBER CAMEO

The four originals had reached the stage when to be exiled from Scarthwaite and Borrowdale from one Easter to the next was unendurable. The call of the hills was too strong, and could be suppressed no longer, so in the autumn we took five days' holiday, and headed north.

"Let's plan five walks!"

Cop was bubbling over with enthusiasm, even when reminded that we should only be in Borrowdale for three days.

"Let's plan them, I say. It will be good to have a few in reserve."

"Why?" I asked.

"In varying degrees of severity," she went on, ignoring me.

"You plan them, then," invited Cath, at which Cop lapsed into silence.

"She's thinking," Prim said, "and it hurts."

Dusk was falling as we drove up Borrowdale, and we were strangely quiet, scarcely able to believe that we were back. It seemed too good to be true!

After dinner, we re-arranged the furniture round the fire to suit ourselves. Mrs Coates brought in the late tea, and stayed to bring us up to date with the news of the valley, and we were so comfortable and contented that we forgot to plan any walks at all.

This was perhaps as well, for we began with a grey day of low cloud, useless for serious walking, though ideal for wandering. By Peace How, through the woods, and up onto the ridge of Catbells, we walked in a silent, shadowy world, so eerily fascinating that we found ourselves speaking in whispers.

As it was Sunday, we attended evensong in Grange Church, and became involved in a series of ridiculous minor incidents. It began with the pew. When the four of us sat down simultaneously there was a dreadful creak, as though the thing was about to collapse. After that, we tried to be cautious, sitting down one after the other, but this caused four successive loud creaks, instead of the one. The lady at the harmonium not only played merry hell with the music but also sang at the top of her voice, with every note so flat that Prim's eyebrows, raised in amazement, almost disappeared into her hair. When we were about to start 'For All The Saints', the vicar gave up the struggle, saying helplessly, "I don't know what we can do about this hymn, it's so long. You had better miss out any verses you don't fancy."

As the collection was being taken, Prim began groping about on the floor, and whispered to the sidesman hovering with the bag, "I've dropped it!" He began searching, and we joined in, all grovelling together, with the pew creaking like mad. Proceedings were held up for several minutes, until the money was found on the seat of the pew in front.

We laughed all the way back to Scarthwaite, Cop admonishing us with mock severity.

"You are not supposed to go to Church to be entertained!"

* * *

The mist persisted, completely blotting out the fells at the head of the valley. Over breakfast, Cop suggested, "Let's go up the slate gully to Lobstone Band."

"Whatever for?" we asked, in unison.

"Oh, I don't know," vaguely. "It would be somewhere to go."

"Where should we go when we get up there?"

"I don't know. Has anyone any other ideas?" No one said anything, so she went on, "Right! Then we will go up there!"

We told her to shut up about Lobstone Band.

Prim said, "We'll take our packed lunch and eat it on Friar's Crag," and was promptly accused by Cop of being nothing better than a tripper.

Friar's Crag was deserted, and we climbed down the rocks onto the shingle to eat our lunch. The lake was a shimmer of silver backed by the red-gold of Catbells, but the high fells were hidden, denying us Ruskin's vaunted view.

Next, we drove to Seathwaite, and walked to Stockley Bridge, but the clouds were half-way down Styhead, so we amused ourselves on the huge boulders near the bridge, practising traverses and balancing on minute holds. It was good fun.

Over a large tea at the Scafell Hotel, we discussed the pros and cons of joining the Fell and Rock Club. We possessed the necessary qualifications for entry, but reached the conclusion that though we should enjoy the annual dinners, the other communal activities would probably leave us cold. Then we drove back down the darkening dale to the mellow firelight of our sitting-room, and a dinner to which we could not do the justice it deserved. Those Scafell teas were quite something!

Mrs Coates, coming in with the late tea, sat down to chat, and the room was filled with the essence of Cumbria, with all its dry humour and remarkable turn of phrase.

We asked her if she had ever climbed the fells, and she said, "Only the once, and that was more than enough. It was up Catbells, and I took my tea in a basket, and when I got down again I said 'Never again!' "

"Next Easter," I said, "I am going to bring a climbing rope."

"You've threatened to do that before, but maybe you've forgotten what I said to you. If you bring a climbing rope here, you'll go straight out of that door again. You would have me fair worried about what trick you would be up to every time you went out, and I'll not have it!"

And she meant it.

* * *

The last day, and though much of the low cloud had dispersed, the high fells remained hidden.

With Glaramara in mind, we drove up to Seatoller to see how good visibility was, and found the fell completely misted, though the Scawdel Fell side of the valley was bathed in sunlight. Glaramara was off. We strolled up Honister, and got into half a gale at the top of the pass. After arguing for five minutes about whether or not to go any higher, we started up Dale Head. I have never been warm on Dale Head. Two-thirds of the way up, we huddled under some boulders to eat our sandwiches. It was uncomfortably cold, but very rewarding, for suddenly the clouds thinned and the Scafells emerged.

From Dale Head we did the ridge to Hindscarth, up Robinson, and down to Buttermere Moss and the slippery track to Buttermere, with the great bulk of Grasmoor burning like fire in the sunset. Prim rang up John, who took us back over Honister, for tea at Seatoller Farm. It was then after five o'clock, and when dinner time came we could scarcely face another meal. Cath suggested taking the soup outside and pouring it on the garden, but we didn't, in case Mrs Coates caught us. Cop eyed the roast pork and stuffing with despair, and groaned, "I wish I were starving!"

Prim pointed out that no one had forced her to eat a lot of iced cake with thick cream at tea-time, whereupon Cop made a solemn vow.

"I shall never do that again. I shall never eat much at tea-time, not even scones. Never!"

"Amen!" I said.

The next morning, we returned to the city, our hearts full of the rich pageantry of Borrowdale in autumn when the birches were torches of flame and the hollies were jewelled with scarlet, when robins sang in the blackthorns, and white gulls hovered and settled in the field beyond Mrs Coates' garden. We had come to love this place so deeply.

Mrs Coates, standing at the kitchen door to wave us off, said, "Remember what I've often told you — the fells will be there waiting for you to come back. The fells will always be there!"

She waved until we were out of sight.

FAREWELL TO SCARTHWAITE

The 'October Cameo' helped to shorten the dark months of winter in the city, and we were eagerly anticipating the coming of Easter. Then, two months before we were due to go to the Lakes, there came grievous news for the S.L. Club.

One morning, Prim rang me at my office, and said in an unsteady voice, "Mrs Coates is dead."

I was shocked into disbelief. Mrs Coates dead? Our Mrs Coates? I did not want it to be true — but it was. She had died suddenly in her sleep, and her daughter, who lived with her at Scarthwaite, had got in touch with Prim. We arranged to let the other S.L. Club members know, and Prim said she had that morning sent a wreath of anemones, Mrs Coates' favourite flower, with the following message:-

To our beloved Mrs Coates
With love from Sally's Ladies.

It was the beginning of the end. Not only had we lost Mrs Coates, but we were about to lose Scarthwaite, too, for although we should be going there at Easter, as arranged, it would be for the last time. With the termination of Mrs Coates' tenancy, the owner of the property would be returning from America in the summer to take up residence in the house, and would not be taking 'visitors'. This bitter knowledge made us all the more determined to extract the last ounce of enjoyment from that final Easter!

* * *

There were six of us, Hilda having gone abroad for a holiday, and there was never a year when we fooled about more and talked greater nonsense. This may have been partly caused by frustrated energy due to inclement weather, but I am sure it was mainly a kind of desperation at the thought of leaving Scarthwaite, and no longer having our Mrs Coates. The kindliness and warmth had gone from the house, and we tried to make up for the loss in the best way we could. Sally was gone, but Sally's Ladies would carry on!

This year's detour on the way north was to Ribblehead, and the two cars, Cath's and May's, went by the Ilkley-Skypton road to Settle, and there took to minor roads. We liked the wild situation of Ribblehead, but deplored its disfigurement by extensive quarrying. We drove down a narrow, winding road to Dent, and enjoyed its cobbled streets and crazy corners. Then it was Sedbergh, Kendal, Keswick, Borrowdale, and Scarthwaite — and no Mrs Coates. Walking into the sitting-room on that first evening was when we felt the deepest sense of loss.

* * *

The weather was in a vile mood, and on the first morning heavy bursts of rain-cum-hail kept us lounging round the fire, assuring each other that we were quite content to be doing nothing. Such assurances were transient, for if we were compelled to remain indoors for long periods we grew as restive as caged animals. By the afternoon we had reached this stage, and took ourselves off to do some mild scrambling above Ladder Brow. Some of us got dirtier than others, but we all got wet.

That evening, the wind howled round the house and rain battered the windows, but by morning the storm had abated. It was fine but exceedingly cold.

"We'll do Walla Crag," Prim said, and waited for comments.

"It's going to rain again."

"We've done Walla Crag once."

"No, we haven't. We couldn't find it."

"We went on a wild goose chase last time!"

"We shall not be going on one this time," Prim said, "because we shall go another way — straight up the front. We are not going to be beaten by a thing like Walla Crag!"

So, in the afternoon, we walked down to the woods fringing Derwentwater, and climbed up near Cat Gill, very steep and messy going, and soon stood on Walla Crag. It was a glorious viewpoint, with the lake at our feet and the high fells brooding under gathering storm clouds. The mood of the mountains was that of savage power, holding us spellbound for some time.

Then we cut over in the direction of the Ambleside road, thus reversing that first abortive attempt. It was ridiculously easy. Once on the main road, we did the mile and a half to Keswick almost at a jog-trot, because no one enjoys walking on a busy road and we wanted to get it over quickly.

Having bungled the first attempt, there was a certain satisfaction in getting little Walla Crag ticked off. I knew we should, ultimately.

* * *

On a wild, wet morning, we drove up to Borrowdale Church, taking some anemones to put on Mrs Coates' grave. Her skyline is the high sweep of Greenup Edge and the great hills are all about her — a lovely place in which to sleep.

The afternoon was spent round the fire, with Cath, Prim and Doris dozing; May knitting with one eye closed because she said she was too sleepy to keep both open at the same time; and Cop and I arguing. After repeated complaints about being disturbed, the others gave up trying to go to sleep and began writing letters. Cop and I went on talking, and a demand for silence was ignored. Then Cop volunteered to post the letters when they were finished, and it was suggested that I went with her.

"Go and paddle in the river, both of you!" from Doris.

"No!" said May. "Go to the top of Castle Crag — and stay there!"

"I like that!" exclaimed Cop. "We were only speaking in whispers most of the time!"

Doris pointed at the window. "Look! The rain has almost stopped!"

Letters were abandoned as everyone rushed for oilskins. We went up the Castle Crag track, which was practically under water, and along by the madly rushing river. A dozen new becks leapt frothing down the fell-sides. It felt so good to be out that we walked until we had insufficient time to get back for the evening meal, and were late.

There followed the wildest, most riotous evening I ever remember at Scarthwaite. We did senseless things, indulging in sheer idiocy. Cop's black skirt was hanging from one of the pictures, Doris was running round the room on all fours, and someone was balancing on the window-ledge. The idea was to do a traverse of the room without touching the floor. The noise was deafening, until Prim started to play the piano, which had a calming effect for a while. Then she was persuaded to play one of her own compositions, and we provided an enthusiastic accompaniment on combs and tissue paper, the fire-irons, and the clashing together of logs of firewood. After giving a loudly demanded encore, she closed the piano lid, saying, "I think that will do, don't you?"

Then we went to bed.

* * *

The sun shone rather half-heartedly, and we set off in high spirits to do the Glaramara ridge from end to end. Starting from 'Mountain View', we took Thornythwaite Fell direct, slogging straight up the steep, grassy contours. We were amazed by the bumper crop of useless cairns which had sprung up like mushrooms everywhere. Knowing that Thornythwaite Fell would be the most toilsome part of the walk, we did it quickly, and were soon scrambling up the rocks to the summit cairn on Glaramara.

A minute later, we suffered maddening frustration, for with the speed of an express train dense cloud raced across the fells, obliterating everything — wiping the slate clean. It became bitterly cold, and we put on all our spare clothes, and ate our sandwiches while we waited, shivering, for the cloud to clear. We waited in vain, for it remained as thick as ever, and visibility was less than a dozen yards. That mist was not going to clear. With chattering teeth, we held a council of war. Did we, or did we not, abandon the walk?

Prim, after considering, said, "I am pretty sure I could find the way along the top."

"I'd go with you," I said, as the chorus started.

"We can't go along there in this!"

"We should lose each other in the mist. Let's go down!"

"We can please ourselves. We don't have to do what the leader says," cut in Cop, for the sake of argument.

"Shut up, Cop!" said Cath. "For heaven's sake, let's decide one way or the other before we freeze."

We all looked at Prim, who gave a little shrug.

"We will go down. If we went on, we should not see a thing, anyway."

"Flaming hell!" I exploded.

We started down, soon dropping below the cold opaque world of cloud into colour and warmth, and I felt savage, for that was the second time I had been up Glaramara and gone back the same way. Was I never to do the ridge walk?

Descending Thornythwaite Fell, with time and energy to spare, we built two necessary marker cairns, and took great pleasure in demolishing the rash of superfluous ones. Then we went to Seatoller Farm for tea.

Round the fire that evening, we wrangled amicably over what to do the next day.

"Why don't we go up Blencathra? We ought to!" from Cath.

"The Dress Circle? That's very good!" I said, hopefully.

Cop immediately objected, "There's nothing to do there except watch people climbing the Needle."

"We could sit on the Needle and knit!" grinned Doris.

May, who looked asleep, suddenly opened her eyes.

"If it is a lovely day, Cis and her friends will go on the Dress Circle, and I shall take Doris to Ullswater. If it is not very good but fine, we will all go up Grasmoor. If it is a really bad day, we will go to Scale Hill for tea. That's settled!"

"Shut up, and go back to sleep!" someone said.

Cop turned to me. "I'd climb Scafell with you — not the Pike but Scafell itself."

"I'm not sure if I could hit off the best way down to Mickledore."

"I like that!" she exploded. "You would get me up a mountain and then have no idea how to get me off! Still," she added, "we could always sit up there until the mountain rescue team came."

"Everybody stop talking rubbish!" cut in May.

Then Prim, who had been absorbed in a map and oblivious to our pointless chatter, looked up and asked, "Has anyone decided anything for tomorrow?" and we laughed.

"We are waiting for you!" we said.

"I haven't decided, either. Let's wait and see, shall we?"

She then said she was going to bed, and bade us a cheerful "Good night", and went, and we looked at each other, and someone said, "Well, aren't we a set of prize idiots!"

* * *

Clouds lay low on the fells, and a drift of fine rain filled the valley.

"Let's go to Eskdale," Prim suggested. "It isn't a good day for going there, but it isn't good for anything else, either."

In worsening weather we went over Whinlatter, called for coffee at Scale Hill Hotel, then on to Ennerdale Bridge. On Cold Fell we were in thick cloud, rather trying for the two drivers, and made more so by suicidal sheep wandering on the road.

We drove up Eskdale to the foot of Hard Knott, stopping there to eat our sandwiches. The rain sluiced down and visibility was nil, so there was no inducement to linger. We went over Birker Moor to Coniston, and then to Hawkshead for tea. On such a wretched day, Hawkshead looked extremely dull and dismal.

No ideas were forthcoming for future walks, because to plan anything seemed a waste of time. But by the afternoon following the Eskdale soaking, the sombre cloud which had menaced Borrowdale gradually lifted, and the sky turned incredibly blue. It acted like a magnet, and we rushed to find lost socks and mislaid boots, and went to do the Catbells-Scawdel Fell ridge.

On Catbells the bracken was gold, and the lake a blue mirror. It was a treasure of an afternoon, highlighting every fell with sharp clarity, and silvering the distant Solway Firth. We went on over Maiden Moor to the top of Scawdel Fell, the easy track enabling us to keep our eyes on the distant hills all the way, instead of on our feet.

The others had started to descend Scawdel Fell while Prim, camera in hand, was still ranging about the top, and I was sitting by the summit cairn. I was in no hurry to go down, as long as I could feast my eyes on the great fells I loved. When Prim had finished taking pictures, she came and sat by the cairn, and we went on looking for almost another half an hour. Then she sighed. "I don't want to leave all this, but I suppose we had better go. The others will be nearly home by now."

She went down the fell at a jog-trot, and I followed at her heels. The pace was a little too quick for me, but from Scawdel Fell down to Lobstone Band was easy ground, and I was sure she would slow up when we reached the slate gully dropping to the Castle Crag track. I was quickly disillusioned, because she went even faster, leaping down like a goat. Teeth clenched, I followed, determined to keep up, and we plunged down the gully at such a speed that if I had stopped I should have lost my balance. By the time we reached the bottom I was trembling at the knees, but the killing pace went on along the track until we caught up with the others near Castle Crag. Thankfully, I fell in with them, and although they were walking briskly it seemed like a gentle amble to me. Prim hared on along the track.

"Where's the fire?" May shouted after her.

She waved a hand, and disappeared round the next corner.

When we reached Scarthwaite, she had washed and changed, and was sitting by the fire.

"You training for the Olympics, or something?" demanded May.

"Me?" innocently. "Certainly not."

"Rushing back hell for leather like that!"

"I thought it would be a good idea to get first turn in the bathroom. Anyway, I like coming down at that speed." She looked at me and laughed. "If I wished, I could go much faster than that."

"Thank heaven you did not wish!" I said.

* * *

The cloud ceiling had returned to an annoying low, and at breakfast time, May said she would take Doris to Ullswater. The reast of us had no desire to go, which drew from May the comment, "It will be a change to get away from you lot!"

Prim suggested two walks — either Esk Hause via Styhead and back by Rossett Crag and Stake Pass, or Langdale and Rossett Gill returning via Stake Pass. Both were shelved because the weather was too thick to do anything interesting. We took the car to Seathwaite to see if the hills were at all possible, and found them completely hidden. We were stymied.

"We could always go to the Innominate Tarn."

"There is no point in going up high if you can't see anything when you get there."

We sat, brooding, until Cath said, "Let's walk round Derwentwater!"

"Remember Ennerdale!" we reminded her.

"Yes, but with Derwentwater we could always catch a bus up the dale for the last part!"

She had a point there, and as we could think of nothing better, we returned to Grange to park the car, and started to walk round the lake, beginning at Manesty.

It was enjoyable through the woods, especially as the clouds were thinning slightly, though this provoked Cop into incessant grumbling because we were not climbing anything. After a while, we were tired of hearing the same thing, and, in no uncertain terms, told her to stop. We ate our sandwiches in a sheltered spot near the water, glad to get out of the wind for a while. We had more dirt on our feet than we ever had on the fells, for in places the mud on the lakeside track was six inches deep. Cop tried to wash her boots in the lake, using her sandwich paper as a towel, but she only succeeded in turning the black mud into thick grey paste.

At Portinscale it was too early for tea, and we walked on to Keswick, caught a bus to Rosthwaite, and had it at the Scafell Hotel, afterwards walking home by the river. Not an exciting day, but it gave us a little exercise. There was no Mrs Coates to grumble about the filthy state of our feet. How we wished there had been!

* * *

Prim had to return to Nottingham two days before we did, and she left most reluctantly on a glorious spring-like morning. As soon as she had gone, there came the question of deciding on a walk, and they looked at me. "You are the Sec. It is up to you to decide," Cop said.

That was no problem. "We'll do Prim's Esk Hause-Angle Tarn-Stake walk."

"Nobody is going to drag me up over Esk Hause!" cut in May. "What about you Doris?"

"Well, I'm not particularly keen."

"Right!" May said briskly, "Then we two will go over Whinlatter and potter about round Grasmoor."

"You poor things!" I said, and she called me a rude name, and the A and B parties then separated, each going their chosen way.

We went by Styhead to Esk Hause, and were soon lolling by Sprinkling Tarn, listening to the rustle of the reeds at the water's edge, and the croak of ravens among the crags of Great End. We were in a situation *par excellence* for lingering, and some time had elapsed before we carried on to where Angle Tarn lay blackly under the buttress of Hanging Knott.

Scouting about, we found an indistinct track running parallel to, but high above, the Langstrath. We followed it until it disappeared in swampy ground, after which there was no further sign of it. Shin-deep, we splashed on, skirting deep holes full of black, peaty water, and getting wet up to the knees because we were looking at the glorious panorama of hills instead of where we were treading.

It was soggy all the way to the Skate Pass cairn, from which we zig-zagged down to the Langstrath, and walked to Stonethwaite. Then came the annoying fact that the car was parked at Seathwaite, in the next valley, and having dallied by the way, we had no time to walk there. We caught a bus at Stonethwaite lane-end, and were late for dinner.

Later in the evening, May drove us to Seathwaite to collect the car.

* * *

Our final walk was the old favourite along Catbells to Swinside and back through the woods, but this time it had an unusual quality, in that there was very little talk along the way. It was a quiet walk, for we were remembering how frequently we had gone that way, how we had quoted and counter-quoted poetry by the lake's edge, how we had gathered cones and branches and taken them home to burn on the sitting-room fire.

All that was over.

* * *

Mrs Coates and Scarthwaite were gone. All that remained were vivid memories — pictures of the russet-brown of Maiden Moor in the morning sun, the sharp upthrust of Gate Crag, the lone pine tree on the skyline of the Castle Crag track, Rosthwaite Fell and distant Glaramara and the sweep of Esk Hause . . . . All these I had seen and loved from the windows of Scarthwaite. The realisation that I should never see them from there again was almost unbearable. It was Cop who, in one of her serious moments, aptly expressed in words what we were all feeling.

"When Mrs Coates died, it was the end of an era."

INTERIM

What would happen now that we had lost our home?

Borrowdale was our special valley, the place where our joyous loitering had originated, and we hated the thought of not returning the next Easter. Other parts of the Lake District were considered, but every member of the S.L. Club voted against leaving Borrowdale, and after endless discussion, it was decided that we would go as usual, providing that we could find suitable headquarters, a place which would hold the seven of us but no other people. Finding such a place was far more difficult than we had anticipated when, at the end of October, Prim, Cath, Cop and I went to Borrowdale for four days to see what we could arrange. We stayed at the Scafell Hotel, in Rosthwaite. Our sole objective was to find somewhere suitable for Sally's Ladies, not to do any walking. This was just as well, for the weather was foul, a mixture of rain, hail, and vilely cold wind. The rain was the heaviest I have ever experienced in the Lake District, which is saying something.

The quest went on without ceasing, and encompassed the entire valley. Prim, who seemed to be acquainted with every second person in Borrowdale, interviewed dozens of people, and we marvelled that she could go doing so without losing patience, but it was all to no avail. Each place we visited was either too small or too large. Half the fun of our Lakes Easters was having a place to ourselves, where we could indulge in our own particular antics — and we could not find one. Every night, after dinner, we sat in a corner of the hotel bar, and planned where we should try the following day. By the end of the third day, we were getting so desperate that we began to consider going to another valley.

Then, on the final day, thanks to a suggestion from the manageress of the hotel, we found a suitable place. It was a house called Peat Howe, tucked out of sight down a narrow lane at

Longthwaite, and it was exactly the right size for us. Prim went into action at once, and all the booking details were quickly settled. Borrowdale for the next Easter was assured, and we returned south satisfied — and, also, feeling that we had done four days' hard labour!

* * *

To begin with, there were five of us. Cop, involved in a theatrical production, was unable to come, and Prim was not free until after the Easter weekend. Until the last day of the holiday the weather was excellent, day following day of blue skies. The fresh green clothed the larches, daffodils shone gold, and the valley basked in the radiance of spring. We were out walking every day, either exploring new ground or yielding to the lure of old favourites. One day, from the crest of the Castle Crag track, we looked down the valley to a distant view of Scarthwaite, but we never went any nearer. We could not bear that.

The following four walks were worthy of mention:—
1. Hilda, May, and Doris climbed Blencathra by the grassy, uninteresting Scales Fell, while Cath and I went up by Sharp Edge. This was before Prim arrived, but there was no doubt about which route she would have chosen. Sharp Edge was interesting, though some of the slabs of slate had a disconcerting tendency to move when you pulled up on them. On the whole, I preferred Striding Edge, on Helvellyn, but Sharp Edge had some airy perches which provided dramatic views of Scales Tarn directly below.
2. The best day of all was the traverse of Glaramara and Allen Crags, particularly rewarding to me after so many frustrated attempts in the past. I loved it, especially when we came upon a perfect tarn, deep blue in a rocky basin. We lingered there, enjoying the rocks, which gave some good balance practice. It was a heavenly spot where I could have stayed all day, just gazing at the great fells and listening to the silence.
3. Up on Brandreth, we went across to spend an hour or so by the Innominate Tarn, another delectable place. Then we climbed every rock outcrop we could find on the bristling top of Haystacks, before descending a series of ledges to Scarth Gap — an unorthodox but enjoyable way down.
4. Prim and I did this short walk on a Sunday afternoon when the spell of perfect weather was ending. Obviously rain was coming, so the others chose to wander by the river where shelter would be available if needed. Prim and I climbed Grange Fell. As we went up through the fiery bracken, the sun was fighting

In Eskdale
Cath, May, Hilda, Doris, Cis

*Setting off from Scarthwaite
Cop, Hilda, Cis, Cath, Prim*

Mrs Coates

May, Cath, Prim, Cis, Cop, Hilda

Prim leading on Haystacks

On Glaramara
Cop, Cath, Prim

Doctor Bridge — Eskdale

Great Gable from Brandreth

Bowfell
Cis, Cath, Cop
Prim

*On Crinkle Crags
Cop, Prim, Cath*

Lord's Rake — Scafell

*In Lord's Rake
Cath, Cis
Cop*

*Red Tarn — Helvellyn
Cath, Cis*

Castle Crag track

High Stile
Prim, Cis

Drinking in Black Sail Pass
Cop, Cath, Prim

Top of Black Sail Pass

Top cairn Scafell Pike
Cis, Cop

Straits of Riggindale
Daisy, Cath, Cis

Beda Fell
Cath, Cis, Daisy

*The distant Scafells
Prim, Cath*

Cath, Cis, Hilda, Doris, Daisy, Prim

a losing battle among the leaden clouds. Above the tree-line, our horizon was a ring of wild, black, mist-wreathed mountains. The approaching storm wiped away Skiddaw and Blencathra, and as we reached our summit cairn the rain began. We stayed for quarter of an hour, getting damp, but entranced by a rainbow spanning the long ridge of Helvellyn. Then, ignoring tracks, we cut straight down the fell-side, a steep but very speedy descent, and within a few minutes we were climbing the wall onto the dale-road. By then it was raining heavily, and we went hotfoot to Longthwaite.

Somehow, this holiday had a 'rootless' air, hard to define. It had lacked the fun and joy of other years. Peat Howe, tucked down its rough lane by the river had supplied all our needs. The food had been outstandingly good. Moreover, we had been free to decide the times of meals, so we were never late. When we first arrived, we were told, "You do just what you like here!" — which we did. Both weather and walking had been fine. It should have been perfect, yet was not.

Borrowdale retained its supreme beauty, and the great fells were as they had always been. The difference, the feeling of restlessness lay in ourselves.

Reluctantly, we faced the facts, and came to a definite conclusion. We had lost our beloved Mrs Coates, and we had lost our Scarthwaite home. The time had come to leave Borrowdale itself.

* * *

The break was complete, for the following year we went to Snowdonia, to a fairly large hotel at Beddgelert. We did not have it to ourselves.

We found the Welsh mountains challenging, and the Welsh weather abominable. In a fortnight, we had one fine day, which we spent on the Snowdon Horseshoe, having great sport on the pinnacles of Crib Goch. For the rest of the holiday, it was rain, rain, and more rain.

We thought these mountains were sombre and austere, unfriendly after our Lakeland fells. Given time and better weather, no doubt we should have come to know and like them more, but we should never have grown to love them.

We yearned desperately to get back to the Lakes.

But where?

The search in other Lakeland valleys would have to be renewed. The alternative was to disband the S.L. Club, which was unthinkable.

Then, out of the blue, the problem was solved, when, purely by chance, Hilda heard of a house which sounded exactly what we wanted. It was at Strands, in Wasdale, and was kept by a Miss Wilkinson and her brother, John Robert. It was large enough to accommodate Sally's Ladies, and no others. It sounded too good to be true. Hilda passed on the information to Prim, who at once contacted Miss Wilkinson, and everything was smoothly and speedily settled. Our return to the Lakes was ensured.

That was how we came to know and love Wasdale and the tiny, beautiful hamlet of Strands. Recently, this name has been changed to Nether Wasdale, which, in my opinion, is to be deplored. Nether Wasdale sounds as though it might be some pretty village in the Cotswolds, whereas there is no nonsense about Strands. It is no-nonsense Cumbrian, and fits the place like a glove.

Borrowdale, where we had our beginnings, would always remain the most beautiful valley, but for surpassing grandeur and ultimate magic of mountains Wasdale stands in a class apart, as the most wonderful of all Lakeland valleys. We came to love it with a deep, abiding love.

Part 2

WESTERN WANDERINGS

STRANDS

As a preliminary to the Easter meeting at Strands, Prim, Cath and I had two days in the far east of the Lake District. We planned to climb High Street on the first day, and Harter Fell (Mardale) on the second. We stayed at Bampton Grange, in the old farmhouse belonging to Mrs Coates' niece.

Our plans never became fact, for the weather was hostile, cold as winter, with a low ceiling of sullen cloud which prevented any serious walking. On the first day, we drove round by Ullswater, up the Kirkstone Pass and back, and to Hartsop, where Cath and Prim walked up to Hayeswater while I sat in the car. On a day so bleak and grey, I could not work up any enthusiasm for mere leg stretching.

The second day was no better, but it was a case of either doing High Street then, or not at all. The idea of Harter Fell had been abandoned. In any case, our first choice had been High Street. We drove to Mardale, walked round the head of Haweswater, and were starting up Rough Crag, the first stage of the route to High Street, when the first drops of rain fell. The sky darkened ominously, but we took no notice and went on. We were enjoying the steep scrambling, and were a third of the way up the crag when the rain became a downpour, and forced us to retreat. After getting to the bottom of the crag, there was a lengthy walk round the head of the lake, and we were very wet indeed when we got back to the car. So ended the abortive attempt on High Street, and many years were to pass before our next (and successful) try. Apart from some map work, the two days in the far east had brought little reward.

The next morning, we went west to Wasdale and the S.L. Club Easter gathering.

* * *

With all the time in the world, we thoroughly enjoyed the short journey from one side of the Lake District to the other. After lingering by Ullswater we had an urge to go up Borrowdale, to picnic by the river not far from Grange. Scarthwaite was less than a mile away, but we had no wish to go to it. We stayed in Borrowdale all afternoon, talking, recalling memorable days in the valley, and wondering a little if Wasdale would yield the same enchantment.

We had tea at the Pheasant Hotel, at Bassenthwaite, then cut up the narrow road by Wythop Mill, and over Cold Fell to Gosforth, and so to Wasdale.

At seven in the evening we came down the hill to Strands, and loved it at first sight. It was so small, so unspoilt, and so serenely peaceful. On the left was our future headquarters. Over the door was a board on which was painted 'WILKINSON, STRANDS, WASDALE'. Opposite was the long, low, pink-washed Strands Hotel, and between the two was a stretch of turf like a miniature village green and the narrow road.

Hilda, who was bringing Doris and May, should have arrived before us, but hadn't, and we thought they must have got lost. However, it gave us the opportunity to choose our bedrooms. Cath and I picked the one we liked best, and Prim annexed the only single. After unloading, we went to Seascale to pick up Cop at the railway station, and on the way we met Hilda's car, and heard about the puncture which had caused their delay.

Our first impression of the house at Strands was very favourable. From the front door we could see the Screes, and by walking a few yards across the grass we looked at Scafell. Miss Wilkinson was most pleasant, and co-operative about small details such as late night and early morning tea. It would be the first time we had had the latter, or even asked for it, but we had decided to start out as we meant to go on. At neither end of the day did we intend to go thirsty in Wasdale. On that first evening we made an effort to behave with decorum to give a good impression, but as the holiday progressed we degenerated into our normal selves.

* * *

Although April was well advanced, it was unseasonably cold, but there was Wasdale waiting to be explored, and to get the first 'feel' of it we strolled towards the lake. We never arrived there, because we passed Woodhow Farm, where morning coffee could be obtained, and our feet automatically turned in at the gate. After that, it was time to go back to Strands for lunch.

By afternoon, it was raining. We drove to Wasdale Head, where the downpour was so heavy that we could not even get out of the cars, and we hastily retreated, abandoning the hills for the coast. At Ravenglass, where the rain had diminished to a fitful drizzle, we had an excellent tea at the Pennington Arms, followed by a long walk on the sands at Drigg. We spent the evening planning walks, and wondering if it would ever be fit to do them.

The next morning was fine but even colder. After coffee at Woodhow, we went down the fields to the foot of the lake. Beyond the gloom of Wastwater, Great Gable rose misty grey, almost invisible against the pale, cold sky.

Rain came with the afternoon. We began to wonder if the weather was always like that in Wasdale, in which case we would ignore it, so to Hilda's, "We don't go out this afternoon, do we?" came an answering chorus, "We do!" and we drove to Ravenglass to inspect 'Ratty', otherwise the Ravenglass and Eskdale Railway. The miniature train was attractive, though not sufficiently so to make us want to ride in it in the rain. 'Ratty' was then in its infancy, and had open carriages with wooden seats. "We'll come tomorrow, if it is fine," we said, and went up Eskdale to have tea at the Woolpack. At the foot of Hard Knott torrential rain blotted out every fell, so we called it a day, and drove back to Strands.

There was much snarling about the weather that evening, but still we went on planning walks. I was particularly interested in doing Lord's Rake, on Scafell, though some pessimist pointed out that we should be lucky if we even saw Scafell, much less went on it.

* * *

The miracle happened, and the holiday really began.

The fells were shrouded in November-like fog, and our teeth almost chattered with cold during morning service in the village church. That, however, was winter's final fling. By lunch-time the mist was beginning to lift, and with the afternoon came blue skies and heavenly warmth.

Spring had finally come to Wasdale!

Heading for Ravenglass and the anticipated ride on 'Ratty', and talking too much to notice where we were going, a wrong turning near Irton took us into Eskdale by mistake. Doubling back to Ravenglass, we caught the train by the skin of our teeth. 'Ratty' was not swamped by hordes of tourists in those days, and we enjoyed the trundling excursion through the fields, the halts at miniature stations, and the shrill whistle toots as we steamed under bridges. At the Dalegarth terminus we watched the uncoupling and turning of the engine by hand, then we rode back to Ravenglass where the cars were parked, and Hilda discovered that one of her tyres was flat. Cursing, she changed the wheel, and we went to St. Bees.

Scouting around, Prim located a narrow lane which ran up the side of the headland to the lighthouse on the top of the cliff. Prim loved lighthouses, and never lost an opportunity to visit one, but on this occasion Hilda demurred.

"I am not going to risk going up that awful road. I have no spare wheel." May and Doris, who were in the car with her, had no choice.

"I'm going up," Cath said.

"I shouldn't, if I were you."

"Why ever not! I'm going up!" Cath repeated.

"Oh, well, in that case we'll wait for you."

We left them parked at the roadside, May calling after us, "Don't take all night about it!"

The surface of the lane, a mixture of pot-holes, ruts and boulders, deteriorated as we climbed, until we reached a part where we appeared to be negotiating a ploughed field. The car leapt and jerked, and the four of us got a good jolting, but we made it to the top with ease.

The lighthouse stood on the edge of the cliff, high above the sea. It was unmanned, and we poked about, climbing steps and exploring everything we could find. We stayed there for half an hour or so, then bumped and lurched back down the appalling road to where the other car was waiting. Hilda asked if the rest of the lane had been as bad as the beginning, and we said, "No" truthfully, because it had been much worse.

We were back in Strands two minutes before dinner time, inclined to be smug because so far during the holiday we had not once been late for meals.

"Perhaps we are reforming!" grinned Cop.

"And perhaps pigs will fly!" May said.

* * *

The bathroom at Wilkinson's was half-way down the stairs, and going, half asleep, for my morning wash, I almost fell over May, who was reclining on the stairs, towel over shoulder, singing a dirge which sounded like a string of curses.

"Are you serenading somebody?"

She waved her towel towards the bathroom. "I'm waiting to get in there. I've been sitting here for twenty minutes waiting for Doris to finish washing."

"Fetch her out!" I said.

"I can't. She's locked the door."

"Yell at her!"

"I have, but she takes no notice. I'm sick of this lark. I'm going outside to wash in the horse trough!" and she got up and went, and as far as I know she actually did wash in the horse trough.

Then I bellowed at Doris, and hammered with my fist on the bathroom door until it opened.

"You have forgotten the S.L. rule!" I said.

"Have I? Which one is that?" Doris looked the picture of innocence.

"No one spends more than five minutes in the bathroom."

"I didn't know anyone was waiting until you started banging and shouting and I wondered what was happening."

"I'll tell May to bang and shout like that next time!" I said.

John Robert, Miss Wilkinson's brother, assuming that we were new to the lakes, endeavoured to be helpful in suggesting small excursions for us. To begin with, we might fancy a nice little walk part of the way up Styhead. We looked at him as though he had gone crazy, while Prim, always tactful, politely told him that we always planned our own walks, and would he be free to drive us to Eskdale that morning.

"Which part of Eskdale do you want?"

"We would like you to take us to Boot."

"And will you be wanting me to fetch you back later?"

"No, we shall go across Burnmoor, and along the top of the Screes, and back to Strands. That should make a nice, ordinary walk."

John Robert never offered suggestions after that.

As he could not get seven people in his car, it was arranged that he should take four, deposit them in Boot, and return for the other three while the first contingent sat and waited on the bridge over the Whillan Beck.

We had a glorious walk over Burnmoor. Larks sang, curlews bubbled, and when we heard the cuckoo we knew that spring had really come. Walking slowly and with deep appreciation, we came to where Burnmoor Tarn shone blue amid the russet-brown of the moor, and there we lingered, eating our sandwiches and quietly lazing, our eyes on the heat-hazed fells beyond the deep rift of Wasdale. Then we went up Illgill Head the hard way. Prim had pointed out the obvious route, but instead of taking it we went straight up, which involved hard slogging up a long shoulder of steep grass.

The walk along the top of the Screes from Illgill Head to Whin Rigg was excellent. It was tremendously exciting to stand on the brink of the shattered, riven precipices, with the awesome depths of Wastwater directly below — and comforting to know that the path beneath one's feet was perfectly safe. All the ferocity of the Screes lies in the face sweeping down to Wastwater. The top, broad and grassy, is easier to traverse than Catbells.

After Whin Rigg came the descent alongside Hawl Gill, which none of us liked. It was abominably steep, which meant that you had to put the brake on hard all the way. Even Prim took it slowly. We all gave groans of relief when at last we were down on level ground.

Prim said, "We should have done better climbing down the gill itself. At least, there would have been stones in the gill instead of all that awful grass."

"Pity we didn't!" exclaimed Cop.

"How much further have we to go?" May asked.

"About a mile along the lane, and on the way we will call at Easethwaite Farm. We can get tea there."

Hilda stopped moaning about her knees to say, "Only a cup of tea! Nothing to eat!"

"Just a drink!" said Doris.

"That is all I want!" agreed May.

The four originals said nothing.

At Easethwaite Farm, we were given an outsize pot of tea and a large dish piled with home-made cakes. The cakes were for the four of us, but in spite of their former protestations, Hilda, Doris and May fell on them like ravening wolves.

Cop exclaimed indignantly, "Well, I like that! They were the ones who did not want anything to eat! Those cakes were for us!"

Prim said, "We can always order more."

Hilda, between bites, moaned continuously about her knees. "Whiteless Pike began the trouble and Hawl Gill has really finished them. I feel as though they will never bend again. What they need is a course of massage with a good liniment."

"I've got some dubbin," offered May, with a grin.

Hilda looked outraged, while the rest of us laughed.

"You will get over it!" I said. "Don't ever expect to get much sympathy from Sally's Ladies!"

It felt good to be alive as we strolled along the lane back to Strands.

* * *

It was a perfect spring day. We were wearing skirts and walking shoes, the idea being to do some exploration of the dale head, studying the different fells and planning. Everyone was prepared for a leisurely, unenergetic day, until I said, "Let's go and have a look at Lord's Rake." Cath and Prim immediately agreed, but Cop seemed a little hesitant.
"Do you mean go up the Rake?"
"Well, we could go and look at it, anyway."
Doris said, "I don't want to be dragged up Scafell today. I shall stay with May and Hilda."
Hilda said she could not go far because her knees ached. Also, she had to get the flat tyre on her spare wheel mended. After that, they would, in her words, have a gentle ride round.
The four of us drove up the dale, and parked among the gorse bushes near the camping ground. We made short work of the track up Brown Tongue, and sat for some time by the big cairn at the top, feasting our eyes on the sunlit valley below.
Cop suddenly broke the silence. "I don't know why I have come up here. I wanted to do seven miles on the flat today."
We paid no heed, assuming it was one of the pointless remarks she so frequently made.
After a while, we headed for the tongue of scree leading up to the start of the Rake. It was biggish, awkward stuff, a nuisance at any time, but especially when you are wearing shoes. We took it slowly, and were glad to get to the top. There we could see into the Rake, and were surprised to find it filled with deep snow. It was the last thing we expected. A narrow trail of footprints ran up it, and the trodden snow had hardened into ice. We considered what to do next, knowing that the scree up which we had toiled would be an even greater nuisance to get down again. Moreover, we did not want to go down.
Prim hitched up her rucksack, and pointed to the footprints. "Other people have been up it. You can see the holes made by the point of an ice-axe. Let's go!"
We started up, stopping after a few yards to look into the opening which is the climbers' way to the Pinnacle. We were awed by the magnificence of the great, soaring cliffs — 'like a great cathedral', Prim described it.
The Rake was steep, slippery, and hard going, and an ice-axe would have been useful. We had bought one several years ago, but had forgotten to bring it to the Lakes. Presently, we came to where a large chock-stone almost blocked the Rake. It could only be

passed by a narrow gap on the right hand side, and this gap was filled with solid ice. Prim tried it gingerly, and retreated.

"It won't go. We shall have to get over the chock-stone."

Every small nick and crack on the chock-stone was iced. Prim climbed it delicately, Cop following close on her heels.

"I'm not climbing that!" exclaimed Cath. "I shall have a go at the side."

She got half-way up the ice before she slipped and came hurtling down. As she shot past, I grabbed the back of her anorak, and held on until she had regained her feet. Then she climbed the chock-stone, assisted by a shove or two from me.

Then it was my turn, and I could not get a toe-hold on the iced rock. I had half a dozen attempts, and each time slipped down again. I was getting cross, for there we were, three above the chock-stone and one below, and it looked as though we were going to stay that way. The others stamped about impatiently, offering all kinds of advice, and asking if I intended to spend the night in the Rake, which made me really annoyed. Something had to be done quickly, so I did it. Yelling "Stand clear!" I charged like a bull at the chock-stone, going up so fast that I had no time to slip, and landing on my stomach at the top to a chorus of applause. As good climbing, it was deplorable.

On reaching the first col, we viewed with some misgiving what lay ahead, for between us and the second col a sixty degree snow slope swept down the mountain. Across this slope was a trail of footprints a boot-sole wide. It looked hazardous. Prim led with caution, balancing with fingertips against the slope, and one by one we followed, greatly relieved when the crossing was over. Prim said quietly, "That was nasty."

Beyond the second col was a large, snow-choked basin, on the far side of which a scree shoot between crags led up to the exit from the Rake onto the open fell-side. We plunged from the col, slithering through the deep snow, unpleasant for anyone not wearing trousers because the quality of the snow had changed from firm and icy to wet and mushy. We got soaked to the waist, and weak with laughing at each other.

The snow in the hollow bristled with half-concealed boulders. As an alternative to the exit-shoot of dirty, wet gravel, we considered climbing some steep rocks over to the left, and had made some progress towards them before we deemed it wiser to stop. To reach the rocks meant finding a way among the boulders in the hollow, and the pockets of deep, soft snow made the crossing dangerous. So it had to be the scree. But on reaching the shoot, we found a wide tongue of ice between us and the scree, and we could not get across it. This, the last hazard of the Rake, was the worst.

Somehow, Prim got over the ice onto the scree. As it moved, she dropped on fingers and toes to spread the balance, slid down a yard and stopped. As soon as she attempted to move, she slid again, and after the third try she was much lower on her side of the ice than we were on ours, and we began to get alarmed. The scree shoot swept out of sight round a buttress, and we were afraid she would be carried all the way down, possibly over a steep drop. She told us afterwards that she had thought quite calmly, "If I am not careful, I shall end up in Whitehaven hospital this time!"

She looked untroubled, remaining motionless for several minutes before beginning to inch in slow motion towards the rocks on the right. We watched, hardly daring to breathe. Then a fully-equipped climber, walking past the top of the scree shoot, saw what was happening. He climbed down the rocks and extended his hand, which Prim grasped, and quickly reached safety. She scrambled up the rocks while the climber was hacking nicks in the ice for us, and we were able to get to the exit. Prim thanked him, and he went on his way.

We looked at each other, and back at the Rake, and said, "Well!" and Prim said, "That was quite an adventure!" and as we laughed, Cop exclaimed, "It's nearly tea-time, and we haven't had our packed lunch yet!"

We sat on the rocks and ate, after which the others decided to go to the top of Scafell.

I said, "I'll sit here and wait for you."

There are times when one needs to be alone on a mountain, and this was one. I looked at the Rake, the tortuous route through the black cliffs. Snow and ice had made it difficult, spicing it with a little danger, but it had been a deeply satisfying experience on a great mountain.

When the others returned, we began the long, monotonous trek down Green How, Scafell's deadly dull side. As usual, Prim went at a jog-trot, while Cath slanted over to the right. There was no track to speak of. Cop strode along steadily, not doing her customary gallop after Prim, and I kept with her because I prefer to go at that pace. For once, she was not talking, but I did not mind. Cop was an incurable chatterer, and I love silence in the hills.

I was quite startled when she suddenly snapped, "Where's Prim?"

"Nearly down by now, I should think. She was heading for the Burnmoor track."

"She should not get so far ahead! Where's Cath?"

"She went down a gully over on the right."

"She has no business to go out of sight!"

She sounded so irate that I turned to look at her — and put my leg in a bog-hole. From ankle to knee I was covered with black mud. I swore. "Bloody hell!"

She turned on me in a fury. "Your language is getting disgusting!"

"Don't listen to it then!"

I did not know what was wrong with her, but whatever it was I was getting sick of it and of her. Then she burst out, "I'm tired of walking on the sides of my feet. I wanted to do seven miles on the flat today."

"Well, why didn't you go and do them? Nobody stopped you."

"Mind your own business!" she snapped.

"Oh, go to hell — bloody hell!" I added with relish.

We did the rest of the descent in silence.

The other two were waiting by the car, Cath with tea flasks at the ready. Cop appeared to have recovered from her waspish mood, but she had annoyed me, and I thought a little explanation was due.

"Now, perhaps you will enlighten us about this seven miles on the flat nonsense, and why you were in such a rotten temper!"

She looked rather sheepish. "Oh, well, it was my toes."

"What about them?"

"It was coming down all that steep grass by Hawl Gill yesterday. My toes were pressed so hard against the front of my boots, and got so bruised that some of my nails have turned black, and coming down Green How was absolute hell. I've had those damn boots for years, and they are finished. The toes have gone soft. I shall wear shoes in future!"

"Why on earth didn't you tell us about your toes?" I said. "You could always have gone for a walk on the flat— round the lake, or something?"

"And let you three go off and do Lord's Rake without me? Not likely!"

We drove home down a valley full of singing birds, and were late for dinner. It had not taken many days for us to fall from grace.

I do not recall much of the Lord's Rake post-mortem in the sitting-room that evening, but I remember Cop chanting loudly as we went to bed:—

'The Lord put down his Rake,
And we all climbed up!'

She went on and on, until May begged her to put a sock in it.

* * *

Eskdale glowed with the fresh beauty of spring. When we parked at the foot of Hard Knott, Hilda said she intended to remain in her car and read, or go to sleep. She did not wish to walk, as coming down Hawl Gill had given her a blistered foot, which news drew a superior smirk from Cop.

"You should have put on some Elastoplast, like I did!"

On the way to Esk Falls, in the peace and solitude of Upper Eskdale, we discovered a veritable heaven for walkers. We lunched by the ancient pack-horse bridge at Throstlegarth, listening to the music of the Esk as it plunged down the gorge into a deep, green pool, and the even wilder melody of the Lingcove Beck waterfalls.

After eating, Doris and May said they would stroll back to rejoin Hilda, Cath and Cop stretched full length on the turf to sunbathe, while Prim and I went exploring, starting up the Lingcove Beck, and climbing until we gained an upland world of rippling tawny grass bounded by snow-capped peaks. Bowfell, Esk Pike and the Scafells had assumed the grandeur of an Alpine range. We sat on a rock, and looked at the perfect cone of Bowfell, tantalisingly near, or so it seemed.

"Shall we climb it?"

A gleam came into Prim's eye as she studied the mountain. Then she looked at her watch, and shrugged. "Better not. We should not have much time, and the other two would wonder where we had gone — and be annoyed because they had not gone with us!"

So we dawdled back, and amused ourselves on the rocks above the Lingcove Falls before rejoining Cath and Cop. We said we had considered going up Bowfell.

"You would have had a mad rush, especially if you had come back to fetch us," Cath said.

"You could not have gone up Bowfell today," I taunted Cop.

"Why not?" indignantly.

"I was only thinking about your bruised toes."

"They are better!" she said. "At least, they are getting better! They are good enough to take me up anywhere you can go!"

"And make you lose your temper?"

We were about to argue when we noticed that Prim and Cath had started to stroll back to Brotherilkeld, so we went after them. We rooted the others out of Hilda's car, and went into the farm kitchen, where Mrs Harrison gave us a superlative tea. Only a large party could have cleared all that was on the table. Mrs Harrison's teas were famous.

We drove back to Wasdale in the glory of evening, with the

setting sun turning the western fells to gold.

* * *

Morning mist laid a blanket over the dale, so for want of something better, we went to explore Gosforth. At that time, we knew nothing of the treasures to be found in the church, or Shelagh's Cross, or even the cork tree, because we had not consulted any local guidebook. Hence, the exploration fizzled out almost before it had started, as we did not know what we were looking for, and we soon lost interest in the few shops.

By afternoon the mist was lifting and the day becoming blue and gold, and we went to Wasdale Head. After pottering about here and there, talking about the pioneer climbers who made this dale head forever famous in the history of mountaineering, we went into the Wastwater Inn for tea. Then Prim and I went round searching for the old photographs for which the place has long been renowned. Some were stacked against the walls, as though the inn was about to be spring-cleaned, and some were missing altogether. Seeing the landlord propping up the bar counter, Prim demanded, "Where is the picture of Owen Glynne Jones!"

He told her that it had been taken upstairs, and asked, "Did you write the article in 'Cumbria'?"

"Yes," she said, to my surprise.

As we went out to rejoin the others, I asked, "What article was he talking about?"

"I have no idea!"

"But you said you had written it!"

She laughed. "I only said yes because I could not tell what he was talking about, so I answered the first thing which came into my head!"

We strolled up the lower part of Black Sail, and before us, soaring above Mosedale, rose Pillar. We wanted it!

* * *

Our last day was like summer.

"Let's go up Pillar!" Cath suggested, over breakfast.

"I can't," Hilda said. "Another of my tyres has gone bust, and I simply must get it put right before we go home tomorrow."

"You need a new car!" commented Cop, rudely.

Doris and May said they would prefer to do some gentler walking, if we did not mind.

"Of course not," Prim said, "you do just what you prefer."

Doris, May, and Hilda were beginning to grow wary about the bigger expeditions, especially after hearing about Lord's Rake; whereas Prim, Cath, Cop and I were getting tougher and more ambitious. In spite of this growing difference, the S.L. Club was flourishing. If the two parties went separate ways during the day, they became united in the evening 'get togethers', and everyone was content.

The four of us set off for Pillar. Under a broiling sun, Black Sail was hot going and seemed twice as long, and we panted so much and stopped so often that anyone seeing us would have thought that we had never climbed a fell before.

"We shall not even get up to the top of Black Sail at this rate!" exclaimed Cop — but we did, eventually, and went to the top of Lookingstead, to sprawl on the warm grass and feast our eyes on the dark north face of Great Gable, and upon fold upon fold of hills which stretched to the far horizon — a noble, soul-stirring vista. The whole Lake District was ours, a priceless reward for the effort of climbing Black Sail on a hot day!

We could happily have stayed there for the rest of the day, but there was Pillar to be climbed. We left our belvedere and went on, up through a belt of rocks and along a grassy escarpment, till we reached what we thought must be Pillar summit. We were mistaken, for in the distance a higher top was revealed. This was the summit, and after climbing up through another belt of rocks, we reached the mossy, bouldery plateau. Apart from the views, Pillar top is not particularly exciting.

Walking along the edge facing Ennerdale, where there were deep cornices of snow, we looked down on the strangely fore-shortened Pillar Rock. We saw the dark green geometrical shapes with which an unimaginative Forestry Commission has desecrated the natural structure of Ennerdale.

"We should go on, over Scoat Fell to Haycock, and come down by Greendale Tarn," said Prim, whose chief delight was to go from one top to the next.

"The car is at Wasdale Head, remember!" was Cath's comment.

"Pity we didn't ask Hilda to pick us up at Greendale."

The worst thing about a walk was having to return to where the car was parked.

We spent some time on Pillar summit, so long, in fact, that when we finally descended to Wasdale Head we were much too late for tea, and had to make do with cider, a passable stop-gap, though its thirst quenching qualities are short-lived.

And so, back down the valley, sunburnt and content, wholly satisfied with our final walk — and with Wasdale.

Wasdale --- It was not Borrowdale, nor did it have a Mrs Coates or a Scarthwaite, but it had cast a spell on us, a spell from which we were never again to be free.

MINOR MISFORTUNES

A full muster of the S.L. Club travelled north. Prim, Cop and I were Cath's passengers, while Hilda, who had a new car, took May and Doris. Spirits were a hundred per cent high, but physical fitness was not. It had been an unfortunate year for some of us. May had been suffering from high blood pressure, Hilda was still having knee trouble, and I was recovering from a virus infection which had laid me low during the latter months of winter. That made three down! The other four were in good form, until Prim came to grief two days after the holiday began, so Cath, Cop, and Doris were the eventual winners in the health stakes.

It rained steadily from Nottingham to Keswick, but as we turned west for Wasdale we left the grey clouds behind and ran into sunlight. The evening was golden at Strands, the peaceful, unspoilt hamlet already so familiar to us that it seemed impossible to realise that this was only the second time we had stayed there.

To Prim's, 'It's nice to know exactly where we are coming!' Miss Wilkinson countered, 'It's nice to know exactly what we are getting!'

That side of it had never before struck us.

* * *

Our first morning was bright and sunny, though the wind was sharp. No definite plans had been made. First, as we strolled towards the lake, there was only the desire to look at everything, to check that it was all as we remembered, to re-absorb the feeling of Wasdale and its high mountains — especially those.

Near Woodhow Farm, Prim climbed a wall and went up a hill to take photographs, the others went down a field to see where the River Irt leaves the lake, and I walked on to sit on a rock by

Wastwater with my face to the hills — the finest view in all Lakeland, or in all England for that matter. I intended to sit for a few short minutes, but was unable to tear myself away, and when I finally did so I met Prim rushing down the road to find me.

"Are you all right?"

"Of course," I said. "Why all the fuss?"

She said that I had been gone so long that they thought I must have collapsed or something, after my recent illness. Hilda had set off looking for me in the opposite direction, and I felt rather sheepish, as though I ought to apologise.

After lunch, we went over a stile at the back of Wilkinson's, and tried to take a bee-line to the main road up Wasdale. It involved pushing through thickets and across ploughed fields, coping with barbed wire and climbing numerous fences, but we got there. Hilda and May then walked on to Greendale Farm, while the rest of us started up Buckbarrow.

Though the going was so ridiculously easy, I found it very tiring, and realised that, thanks to the virus, I was desperately unfit. Even a little thing like Buckbarrow was beyond me, so at the first rock outcrop we separated, Prim and Cop heading for the top, while Cath and Doris accompanied me down. I expect I was swearing.

Walking on the flat was no trouble, and we joined Hilda and May for tea and scones at Greendale. We returned to Strands across the moor, an enjoyable walk, though very swampy in parts. Cath accidentally stepped into a large hole and water came over the tops of her boots, which caused May to laugh so heartily that she walked into a tree and fell in the mud.

Prim and Cop turned up at Wilkinson's half an hour after us. They had been over Buckbarrow and come straight down by a ravine.

"It was awkward," Cop said, "quite hairy, in fact."

"Wouldn't it have been easier to circle round to Greendale Tarn and come down that way?" I asked.

"I don't know," she said vaguely. "I just followed Prim. She swung down on an old tree and jumped into the ravine, so I did the same."

They had been to Greendale for tea, then gone down to the lake and along the minor road back to Strands.

"You must have hurried!" I said.

"We did. We came hell for leather. You know what Prim is like when she has the bit between her teeth!"

After dinner, I was asked to read aloud the detailed diary I had written about the activities of the S.L. Club during the meeting of the previous Easter. The reading was disjointed, due to incessant interruptions, contradictions, and references to trivialities omitted from the script. I was patient for a while — but not for long!

"You can't expect me recall every single time anyone trips over a rock, or makes a silly, fat-headed remark!"

"Oh, but we do. We want everything in minute detail!" insisted Cop.

"Right! You've asked for it! I promise that this year's diary will contain things which would be better forgotten! You will be thoroughly ashamed of yourselves!"

They looked startled, and May said, "You wouldn't be so mean!"

"I certainly would, and I shall do it, unless you all shut up and let me get on with this reading in peace. We will have all comments at the end."

And for once they did as they were told.

* * *

A wild, wet morning kept us round the sitting-room fire, wrangling over a Lakeland quiz which I had just concocted to amuse them. It was a very simple one, consisting of such questions as:— "Which is the highest tarn?" "Where is the Sphinx Rock?" etc.

They should have done the twenty questions easily, instead of which they argued at the tops of their voices, bellowing at each other to such an extent that had Miss Wilkinson been listening at the door, she would have assumed that we were having a free fight. The quiz was won by Prim.

Just before lunch, we went to the Strands Hotel for a drink. We called it 'Going over the green'. The Strands Hotel was unique. Not only was it old, but the proprietors, the Misses Smith, were straight from the pages of Jane Austen. We loved it. The bar was in a kitchen where there was an old-fashioned, black-leaded range, and the drinks were produced from a cubby-hole under the stairs. There was a sofa and several other seats, including a rocking chair for which we made a concerted rush. The winner paid for the drinks.

Drink was, in a way, the reason for a visit to Whitehaven that afternoon. Two of Sally's Ladies would be having birthdays during the holiday, and to celebrate these we had bought sherry, gin, etc. when we came through Keswick on the way to Strands, but apart from tumblers we had no small glasses. Hence the trip to Whitehaven, where we bought some at Woolworth's — for 5d each.

Then we drove to St. Bees, where the others set off on a walk towards the cliffs, leaving me in the car. Before long they were back, half-carrying Prim, who had fallen on the promenade, of all places, and had a sprained ankle and a wrenched shoulder. The ankle was badly swollen, and we had to do something about it. There must have been a chemist's shop somewhere in St. Bees, but we could not find it, and as the entire village appeared to be deserted there was no one we could ask for directions.

We knew there was a general store with a small chemist's section in Gosforth, so we drove there fast. Cath and I went into the store, to be told that the person in charge of the chemist's section had finished for the day and gone home, but if we liked we could go and rummage in the drawers to see if there was anything we needed. The assistant left us to it, and we turned out every drawer, scrabbling among bottles of cough mixture, boxes of tablets, and tablets of soap, until we found a bottle of embrocation and some adhesive bandages. The assistant, with no idea of the prices, said, "Pay me what you think," which we did. Cop, who had also gone foraging, returned with a small bottle of whiskey and a broad grin.

"I don't suppose it will help the sprains, but no doubt it will do you good!"

Back at Strands, we bandaged Prim, and at dinner time besieged her with offers of help, from cutting up her meat to even eating it for her. When it was bedtime, Cop and I helped her to undress. We did our best, but it is not easy to get an injured person out of an Aran sweater, especially when two people are pulling simultaneously in opposite directions, but we finally got her tucked up without causing too much chaos, and Cop thoughtfully left the whiskey bottle on the bedside table.

* * *

Prim was black and blue next morning, but cheerfully limping around. It was a teeming wet day with thick mist, and we could see neither the Screes, nor any other fell. We might have been in the Fens.

We had an unusually quiet and peaceful morning, reading, writing, knitting, and being strangely polite to each other, and even kept this up for a while after lunch, but not for long. There was too much static energy penned up in the sitting-room, and prolonged wet weather always led to a degeneration in behaviour. We became restive, and began milling round and tormenting each other, and in the mêlée Hilda tripped over my foot, and measured her length on the floor.

Cop exclaimed, "We have already had one accident. The next thing we know we shall have another — in the sitting-room!"

To calm us down, I was asked to read aloud. I agreed, but the subsequent harmony was short-lived. After quarter of an hour I was battling against so many interruptions and private conversations that I threw down the book.

"I am not doing this to amuse myself. It is for the benefit of all you silly ---"

"Let's open a bottle of sherry!" cut in Prim.

There was a roar of approval. The drinking of the sherry provided a peaceful interim, which Prim ingeniously tried to prolong.

"Let's measure each other's legs from knee to ankle. Cath and Hilda look all leg!"

May found a tape-measure in her knitting bag, and we set to work. Cath and Hilda had the longest legs, but only fractionally, as we were all tall except Prim.

"We could do all our vital statistics!" said Cop enthusiastically, but just then Miss Wilkinson announced dinner, and we rushed into the dining-room like a pack of wolves.

Afterwards, Cop gave an impromptu lecture on calypso music, demonstrating so absurdly that we laughed until we had to beg her to stop. They were then content to sit quietly and listen to me reading from *Inside The Real Lakeland*.

If Miss Wilkinson had ever had a high opinion of us, she must have lost it that day.

* * *

Sun shining from a sky dappled with fleecy clouds brought a breath of spring to the valley, and we set off for morning coffee at Greendale, walking up the hill from Strands and along the cut-through lane which led to the main Wasdale road. Prim, though limping badly, assured us that she could manage the walk, and declared that before the holiday was over she intended to climb a fell, but it would have to be one of the smaller ones. She knew that the damaged ankle had put the big ones out of bounds for this holiday.

She and Cop started out first for Greendale, and we set off some twenty minutes later, thinking that we should soon overtake them. It was a morning made for lingering. Full sunlight illuminated the bastion of Pikes Crag and the Napes Ridges on Gable, highlighting them so that it was possible to trace each separate climbing route. The valley rejoiced in the music of rippling becks and singing birds.

We reached Greendale to find Prim and Cop already there, sitting by the beck.
"The tortoises won!" Prim greeted us.
After coffee, we walked round by the lake and back to Strands for lunch.
"Bet it will be ham and mashed potatoes again!" I said.
"Same old lunch every day!" May agreed.
"I find ham and mashed potatoes rather boring," Hilda said, "I should prefer something green — something like tomatoes."
"Perhaps she's colour blind!" hissed Cop in a loud stage whisper, which drew an exclamation of annoyance from Hilda and laughter from the rest of us.

In the afternoon, we went to Ravenglass, where we separated, Hilda, May and Doris to visit the gardens at Muncaster Castle, Cath and Cop to laze by the sea, and Prim and I to go on 'Ratty'.

We converged on the Pennington Arms at tea-time. Cop and I went in first, leaving the others standing in a group in the village street, deep in argument over something or other. We ordered tea, and it arrived before they came in. Cop knocked over the sugar bowl, then swept up the sugar from the table and put it back, muttering, "I don't think it is very dirty do you?"
"It is not what you could call white, either."
"Don't tell Prim! She would probably take a dim view of it!"
Cop did not mind the dirt as she never took sugar, and those who did failed to notice its slightly speckled appearance.

Afterwards on Drigg sands, Cath and May began collecting dead starfish, razor shells, and other marine flotsam, which they carried back to the cars while we watched and commented.
"What on earth are they getting all that junk for?"
"I haven't the slightest idea."
"I don't suppose they have, either!"
So I asked May why they were doing it, and she retorted, "Why don't you mind your own business!"

Inside The Real Lakeland was abandoned that night, because we had stoked up the fire too well and pieces of blazing wood kept falling onto the hearthrug. Each time this happened it caused such an uproar that only an idiot would have attempted to continue reading aloud.

* * *

On a dull morning with black clouds at the head of the dale, we abandoned the hills for St. Bees. This suited me, for I felt incapable of tackling anything energetic. Hoping to reach the lighthouse, we climbed the headland, but it had been raining there recently and the clay path was unpleasantly sticky. I soon grew tired of slithering in the mud, and turned back. May followed me down, and when I said, "What about going over to the hotel for a drink?" she replied, "Suits me!" and the next half hour passed very pleasantly. As we returned to the cars, the others were coming down the headland. Baulked by a steep, muddy ravine, they had abandoned the lighthouse.

"A pity!" said Prim, regarding her ankle with annoyance. "Normally, I could have got over the ravine easily."

We picnicked in the cars, and ate ice-cream which Cop had been sent to buy at a beach cafe. Then we looked at the sea and gradually grew bored. Half-way through the afternoon, Prim said, "What about going to Eskdale for tea?"

"To the Woolpack?"

"Need we go as far as that?" Cath asked.

"We'll forage!"

Hilda said very firmly, "May and Doris and I don't want any tea."

The other four replied, equally firmly, "We do!"

Hilda went on, "We will go with you and wait. That is in case you suddenly decide to take off and go somewhere else!"

We went hunting in Eskdale. After drawing a blank at the tea-less Bower House, we tried the King William the Fourth, where Prim, having gone round to the back of the house, reported that they did not serve tea, but would make some for us.

"There was a notice on the front door which said, 'No meals except dinner', so I pretended I hadn't seen it, and went to the back and talked to a man!"

We were ushered into the bar and given large cups of tea, accompanied by a strange assortment of buttered biscuits and potato crisps. Meanwhile, the other three waited outside, patiently or otherwise.

As we were getting into our car, Cath asked, "Where next?"

"We'll go and have a look at Devoke Water," Prim replied.

"What about the other car? They won't know where we are going."

"Oh, they will follow us!"

We drove up the narrow, winding road onto Birker Moor. At that time, the rough track to Devoke Water was unsigned, and we drove past the end of it and parked near a lane leading to a farm. Walking up the lane past the farm, we reached an indistinct track over moorland. It was so marshy that after a while Hilda refused to go any further.

"I'm wearing my best shoes. I did not anticipate paddling!"

"Hilda," admonished Cop, "I once warned you about wearing your best shoes when you are out with Sally's Ladies. Anything might happen!"

We went on, and Hilda turned back, grumbling.

Devoke Water was a silver mirror in a russet setting. Apart from the far-off calling of curlews there was profound silence, an atmosphere of deep, aloof melancholy, and I loved it, even though my feet were soaked.

We did nothing after dinner that night, apart from arguing, and contradicting each other from force of habit.

Cop eyed us disdainfully.

"Look at you! Eating chocolates and drinking gin! It was not like this in the old days! The S.L. Club is degenerating!"

This raised a storm of protest.

"Would you rather go back to the days of no late tea at night?"

"And no early morning tea?"

"And candles?"

"And hard beds?"

"Yes!" retorted Cop.

"Liar!" May exclaimed, and everyone said, "Hear! Hear!"

"In any case," I said, "when we were at Scarthwaite, we should have had to walk about a mile down the road to get a drink if we wanted one."

Cop went on, "We are lowering our standards. The president had better start planning a few walks — hard ones."

"We don't want to do any hard walks!" from Hilda, Doris, and May.

"Yes, we do!" from Cath and Cop.

Prim eyed her bandaged ankle. "Count me out, but there is nothing to stop you others going anywhere."

"Then the Sec. had better plan something," and all eyes swivelled expectantly to me, but I had no bright suggestions to offer.

"I can't do a hard walk either, not this year. Damn it to hell!" I added bitterly.

* * *

Harter Fell, neither long nor tiring, appealed to everyone, and on a grey morning of sullen cloud we set off to climb it. It was raining before we reached Santon Bridge, and pouring in Eskdale. Harter Fell was abandoned, and we drove up the lane leading to Dalegarth Hall, parked, and sat listening to the rain hammering on the cars, and wondering what to do next. Then Prim persuaded Cop to go with her to see the Stanley Gill falls, and they went off under an old umbrella which Cath kept in the car. An hour later they came back dripping, and told us that they had followed a stony track up a gorge, and had crossed three rickety bridges, and the falls were gorgeous, and we really should have gone with them, and we said, "Oh, yes?"

After picnicking in the cars, we went up to the Woolpack for a drink, and stayed talking for a while. Then Hilda said, "I don't know what you are thinking of doing next, but we are ready to call it a day. It's so miserably cold and wet, we have decided to go home to the fire."

They drove off. In spite of the weather, we had no intention of going home. As Cop put it, "It's a waste of time. Let's go wandering!"

First, we went to the foot of Hard Knott, where the nearer fells were grey ghosts cowering under the onslaught of the rain and Bowfell had disappeared.

"Where do we go from here?" Cath wanted to know.

"Nothing to see here!" Cop looked disgruntled.

"There is plenty to see," I corrected her, "only you can't see it."

"I know!" said Prim brightly. "Let's go and find a new place for tea!"

We had heard of several places in the Calderbridge area where one could get a good afternoon tea, which we quickly convinced ourselves we needed, so we drove back down Eskdale, and for the next hour or so the hunt was on.

At the first place, which was along the main road towards Egremont, we found a notice saying that tea was served on Saturdays and Sundays only. The second place we had heard about was a farm near Calder Abbey. We found a farm there, only to be told that it was the wrong one and we needed the next one further up the lane. We went further up the lane to the next one, where a man working in the yard told us that all the women were out, and suggested that we tried the farm up the lonnin by Ponsonby Church.

We drove back to Calderbridge, and up the muddy lonnin by Ponsonby Church to a deserted-looking farm. Prim, who had spent most of the afternoon getting in and out of the car, went to investigate, and found a man in one of the barns. He was no help, for when asked about tea he shook his head, saying, "The women are all awa'!"

"It must be the afternoon for the women's institute," deduced Cop, no doubt correctly.

The frustration of the search made us determined to get tea somehow, even if it meant driving round half the district. In the end, we got it at the Globe, in Gosforth. It was an excellent tea, and in our triumph we overate, forgetting that dinner time was drawing near. We were very muddy about the feet and legs, especially Prim, who had tramped through several farmyards.

Before dinner Cath and I searched the interior of our wardrobe, from which a peculiar smell had emanated for the last two days. We found the dead starfish and other marine oddments which Cath had collected on Drigg sands.

"I'd forgotten all about them!" she exclaimed.

"Go and put them in Cop's bed, or May's," I suggested.

But she told me not to be mean, and threw them through the window.

Cop had a nightly ritual before she went to bed. From a shelf near the piano she fetched a large paper bag in which she kept pieces of chocolate and an odd assortment of sweets. She sat poring over this, ate a little of the contents, then returned the bag to the shelf until the following night. Prim used to refer to it as 'Cop's nosebag'.

* * *

At last came a perfect spring day for Harter Fell.

Starting from the foot of Hard Knott, and strolling up the delightful grassy track, there were so many pauses for gazing down on the sunlit dale that it was lunch-time before we reached the first outcrops of rock, where we stopped for a long, lazy picnic. Then we had to wake Hilda, who lay flat on her back, asleep in the warm bracken.

Harter summit was fine, the top rocks needing the hand and foot work I love. From it one is rewarded by a grand and glorious pageant of mountains striding across the sky. For the lover of heights this rocky top is heaven, and the walk down should never be rushed, for with such easy treading eyes can rest on fells, not feet. A shapely, satisfying fell, Harter, though small in stature.

Five of us went to Brotherilkeld for tea. Hilda and May declined. Though Mrs Harrison had ceased to provide teas for visitors, she assured Prim that she would always do it for us. We were welcome at Brotherilkeld, and free to park our car on their land at any time. I loved that ancient sheep farm, and the perfect cone of Bowfell crowning the valley. For us, the real Eskdale began at Brotherilkeld.

* * *

Our final day was wild but fine, and having wasted much of the morning in illogical argument about whether or not to go for a walk, we went to explore Blengdale. Almost choked with Forestry Commission trees, it was definitely not our sort of country, and we decided it was not worth a second visit.

After lunch, we drove to Brotherilkeld and walked to Throstlegarth. For some reason, we went in Indian file with a good fifty yards between each person. Prim, leading, did not stop at the old pack-horse bridge, but continued up alongside the Esk gorge. Cop, second in line, followed. I came next, and went after Cop. The others stayed at the bridge.

I found the slope exceedingly steep, and began to wonder if I should ever climb a big fell again, a sobering thought. By the time I had topped the first rise I had had enough, and sat on a rock to rest. I saw Prim just disappearing through a gap in the cliffs on the skyline, while Cop had strayed off course to the right and seemed to be paddling through a swamp.

Apart from annoyance at my inability to climb any higher, I enjoyed my session on the rock, listening to the wind and the thunder of the river in its deep gorge. When I came down, Hilda was waiting for me at the bridge, while the others had started back to Brotherilkeld.

It began to rain, first a few spots then a steady downpour, and we went at the double the two miles to the farm, where a great log fire blazed in the sitting-room and the table was being set with a wonderful tea. We had started to eat when Prim and Cop came in, oozing water. They had been on Great Moss heading for Cam Spout when the heavy rain forced them to retreat. Prim said it was wonderful country up there, and well worth getting a soaking, and Cop agreed.

"You should have been there. It is just your sort of place!" Cop enthused to me, and I said, "You needn't rub it in!"

She had shed all her outer garments and was sitting at the table in her underwear.

The sitting-room was in an uproar that night after dinner, as we finished all the bottles of drink, and argued over the bill in an attempt to find out who owed what. Prim, in her customary end-of-holiday speech to Miss Wilkinson, expressed a hope that we had not been too noisy during our stay, and was assured that we had caused no disturbance at all. This was kind, but manifestly untrue. Having reduced the sitting-room to a shambles and tidied it superficially, we went up to pack, and were ready for bed when a loud voice began declaiming Shakespeare on the landing. Doors opened, and we discovered Cop, an impassioned Lady Macbeth in full cry. We told her to shut up and go to bed, or to hell.

The next morning, the two cars left for Nottingham with Prim and I waving them out of sight. We had given ourselves a small bonus. Her sprained ankle and my general indisposition had so curbed our activities during the holiday that we considered we deserved a little extra time in the Lakes. This had quickly been arranged, and we were to spend a few days in Borrowdale, at the house of Mary Pepper, in Grange.

MARY'S HOUSE

Mary Pepper's comfortable house was just beyond Grange Bridge. It would have been ideal as a headquarters for the S.L. Club had it been large enough to accommodate six or seven people, but unfortunately it could not. Prim and I were made very welcome there. Mary was very comfortable financially, and her only reason for having 'visitors' was that she liked talking to people and looking after them. We found the food superlative, and there were electric blankets on the beds — and no other 'visitors'.

Mary had the notion that we needed plenty of food and rest, and was determined that we should have both. Small, wiry, forthright, and with a great sense of humour, she was renowned in the village as a one hundred per cent individualist — a character. Sitting round the fire over cups of tea at night, she held us in thrall with endless tales of her childhood, and with comments on the dale people. She was a Cumbrian herself, but of Cumbrians in general, she said, "Ee, they're just like the sheep, they're that stupid!"

Mrs Taylor, a large, cheerful woman who owned a small café in Grange, was well known to us. We had often popped into her house for cups of coffee, but we had never spoken to her thin, unsmiling husband, who had the appropriate name of Jonah. Mary said, "Ma Taylor is for ever sitting in my kitchen, grumbling, 'I can't think what came over me to marry that man! He's been nothing but a nuisance to me all his life!' and then when she was going she poked her head back round the door, and said, 'When I die, Mary, I'm leaving yer two things — Jonah and me old arm chair!'"

"Do you think she will?" I asked, when I had stopped laughing.

"Indeed she will not. I wouldn't have either of them!"

"Did you ever think of getting married, Mary?"

"I did not. I liked to go my own way too much to get tied down!" and she launched into the tale of John Armstrong, who became owner of the Woolpack Inn, in Eskdale, who had once had his eye on her. "It was a good while ago, when we were young and soft. He always used to come courting with a quarter of Mintoes."

"Not every time?"

"I'm telling you, every blessed time there would be this quarter of Mintoes. Ee, I got so sick of him and his old Mintoes that he stopped coming in the end."

She got up, and gave the fire a vigorous poke.

"Even now, when I go into a sweet shop and see a jar of Mintoes on the counter, I have to laugh!"

Of all Mary's stories, the one I liked best was of when she was a child living at Seathwaite, where her mother kept a guest-house. Many well-known people had stayed there, including 'Woodbine Willie', the celebrated parson of World War I.

Mary said, "I often went walking with him, and once we went all the way to the top of Great Gable. And there he stood, flinging his arms about, and shouting, 'I will lift up mine eyes to the hills'. And I stood there and wondered what the old fool was blathering about. And he would take hold of my hand to help me down the mountain, and it made us so late getting back that my mother wondered where I had got to. And when I told her she grumbled at me, and said I was nothing but a nuisance to him and everyone else!"

Of course, Mary, with the rest of the valley, had long known us as 'Sally's Ladies'. She could tell us very little about the present owners of Scarthwaite, because they were seldom there, and the place was not like it had been in Mrs Coates' time.

"Sally Coates was one of the kindest people in this valley," she said.

We knew, and how well we remembered that kindness!

One evening, we walked up the lane, and paused with mixed feelings at the gate of Scarthwaite. A thicket of tall bushes blocked the superb vista of the head of the valley, and even Castle Crag was hidden.

"They have spoilt our view!" exclaimed Prim, as she opened the gate and walked in.

"They might be at home!"

"Mary didn't think so."

I followed, knowing that she would invent some plausible explanation if we saw anyone. We peered through the windows. Our sitting-room had lost its big table and the sideboard, and Mrs

Coates' ground floor bedroom had become a dining-room. There was a new front door, and the kitchen had so much stainless steel and white paint that it resembled a doctor's surgery. The porch where we had kept our muddy boots and oilskins had been lined with shelves and made into a store-room. Our Scarthwaite had gone for ever. Lost in thought, we walked back to Mary's. How good they had been, those Scarthwaite days!

We enjoyed our stay in Borrowdale, wandering about, doing nothing in particular. There was a silly incident one afternoon when, having dropped from the Castle Crag track to Seatoller Farm, we found the farmer's wife washing her car in the cobbled yard, and stayed chatting with her. Some weeks ago a bishop's son had gone missing on the fells, and some children playing on Catbells had found his body at the bottom of a deep hole. This topic, fresh in everyone's mind, naturally arose in our conversation. The farmer's wife, having regaled us with all the details, finished by declaring, "If those kids hadn't happened to be playing round there, they might not have found him for YARS!" As she spoke, her voice crescendoed up the scale until the last word was a full-throated roar. I saw Prim's eyebrows twitch, and knew that she wanted to laugh, and so did I — badly. It is agony trying to suppress mirth, but we might have succeeded had she not repeated, even more stridently, "They might not have found him for YARS!" Prim gasped, and I gave a strangled sound like a duck quacking, which caused the farmer's wife to eye me suspiciously. Then Prim, a tremor in her voice, quickly said that it was time we were going as we had to walk back to Grange, and how nice it had been to see Seatoller Farm again. We left hurriedly, and went round the corner to laugh.

Prim said, "You could easily make a sound like that if you pitched it high enough," and going down the dale road we practised doing 'YARS' in different keys until we became almost hysterical, and stopped before anyone heard us.

Ever since then, all Sally's Ladies have used that peculiar pronunciation. For example, instead of saying, 'I haven't done that for years!' they say, 'I haven't done that for YARS!' It sounds ridiculous.

Prim and I had no intention of doing any serious hill climbing, and Mary knew that we were quite happy pottering about in the valley. She approved of this, or so we thought, until the night before our last day, when she suddenly announced, as we sat by the fire, "If it is a nice day tomorrow, you will go up Great Gable.'

Startled, we both spoke at once.

"That would not do my ankle much good."

"I can't do it. I haven't enough energy for a big fell."

Mary made no reply, and when she had gone into the kitchen, I said, "I have no intention of going up Gable. I couldn't."

"Neither could I," Prim agreed.

"What can we do? We had better have some plan."

"Well, if it is a decent day, what about wandering up Grange Fell?"

I thought that would fill the bill nicely. "We will climb every rock outcrop we can find, and have an easy time."

The next morning, when Mary brought in the early tea, she said briskly, "It is just the right day for Gable!" and we laughed. We were not going, especially as the high tops were misted.

After breakfast, when we were busy writing postcards in the sitting-room, Mary came in with sandwiches and a lemon meringue pie in a plastic box, and said that John Cockbain was in the kitchen, waiting to take us to the top of Honister. She practically pushed us out of the house and into John's car. Instead of a gentle stroll up Grange Fell, we found ourselves heading reluctantly towards the high hills.

At the top of Honister the cloud ceiling was very low. Being by then in that frame of mind when part of us wanted to go up Gable and the other part didn't, we lingered at the quarry, talking to one of the workmen. He warned us to watch the weather if we were going up Gable. It might clear, but he thought there would be a thunderstorm because he had the rheumatics awful bad.

Half-heartedly, we climbed to the remains of the 'Gallows' and into the mist of the Grey Knotts-Brandreth plateau. We could not see from one cairn to the next, and every small heap of stones looked as big as a haystack. Suddenly, we realised that we were enjoying ourselves, talking as we ambled along, and occasionally sitting down to rest in a ghostly white world of absolute silence. Prim could not stride out, and I had no wish to, but eventually we found ourselves on Green Gable.

Great Gable was a vast, dark shadow looming through the mist. We slid down to Wind Gap, and went up the rough shoulder to the main summit cairn. Visibility was nil, but there was the satisfaction of being on the top of a mountain — always a wonderful feeling, though we both thought it would be equally wonderful if a helicopter could lift us off, and save us the trouble of getting down.

Prim was unhappy on the descent of the shoulder, and took it very slowly. To me it seemed never-ending, though the sky was growing lighter and you could at least see a few yards. I was utterly sick of treadmilling down, especially when I slipped and sat heavily on sharp scree, which made me lose my temper with the mountain and cry aloud, "Damn you, you dirty great pig!" It sounded so silly, but after that I did what I should have been doing all the time, which was looking where I was putting my feet.

On Green Gable we sat on a flat rock, and ate the lemon meringue pie, and witnessed a miracle. The mist rolled away, revealing first the plunging north face of the Gable, than Kirk Fell and Pillar, then the Scafells — all basking in the clear gold of a perfect evening. It kept us rooted to our rock for a long time because it was too good to leave. Also, we did not wish to face the long trudge back over Brandreth. Prim's ankle was very swollen, and I was tired.

When we could put it off no longer, the slow plod began. We did not grumble or say much at all, each being lost in her own private world of misery. We made no attempt to pick a way round the swamp near the 'Gallows', but went straight through the water. Stumbling down to the top of Honister, we reached the tarmac at last, and looked at each other, and Prim said, "I'm finished!" and I echoed, "So am I!"

We were just about to collapse on the side of the road when a large car drew up. The occupants were on their way to Keswick, and offered us a lift to Grange — and getting into that car was the quickest thing we had done for several hours.

As soon as we crawled into the house, Mary made us a pot of tea. She looked at me, and nodded. "That's given you back your faith in yourself!"

She was right. She had given us both the tonic we needed.

RED PIKE (Wasdale)

There were six of us. Cath, Prim, Cop and myself were in one car, and May and Doris in the other. Hilda, involved in business and family affairs, hoped to join us for a few days before the holiday ended.

Near Levens Bridge, Prim suggested a detour to Grange-over-Sands, which we duly made. May's car obediently followed ours, though she complained afterwards, "I never know just where the hell you think you are going next!" Grange was not looking its best at low tide, but we found a good hotel for tea.

Beyond Newby Bridge we reached the final stage of the journey, where hills were sudden and corners abounded. In those days there had been little attempt at road improvement, and there were no straight stretches where Cath could put her foot down. We seemed to twist and turn in all directions.

"This is ridiculous. They should build a road near the sea, to the south of the mountains," commented Cop.

"They have. We are on it," Prim told her.

"I don't see that we are. We are right among the mountains!"

"We are skirting Black Combe, and this is the best road," I said, and told her to shut up. Surprisingly, she did.

We came to Strands as evening lay on the mountains. Scafell had a powdering of snow, and a single white patch gleamed below the summit of the Gable. It was good to be back!

Miss Wilkinson asked if we wished to have our usual bedrooms, which immediately provoked an argument as to whether or not it would be a good idea to change. While the talking was at its height, Prim quietly carried her things to the single bedroom she always had, and Cath and I took ours to our usual room, and the wrangling then fizzled out.

* * *

Although sunlight bathed the nearer hills, the distant fells were lost in haze, and the wind had a sting. We were filled with first-morning laziness, apart from Cath and Cop, who clamoured for us to do a big fell immediately. We told them to get on with it, and after putting their heads together and tossing a map about, they dashed off to climb Kirk Fell.

Packed like sardines into May's small car, we drove to Seascale and spent the morning walking wetly on the beach. In the afternoon, we went to Ravenglass to find Walls Fort, the Roman bath-house. None of us was particularly keen on Roman remains, but as Prim said, "I suppose everyone should see all these places once."

The ruins were almost buried in undergrowth, but we probed around and inspected everything. We knew nothing about the place, and were none the wiser at the end. We explored solo, each going where she fancied, and coming together again when we were ready to leave. Doris was missing. We called and waited, and then heard a loud crashing among the undergrowth and she emerged, rather bloody about the legs, having tripped over some brambles and fallen in a bed of nettles. She was not in a good mood, especially when I said, "What you need is a collar and lead."

After tea at the Pennington Arms, we sat in the car on the green sward by the water — a thing you cannot do now, for Ravenglass has lost its peace. Arriving back at Strands, we found Cath and Cop busy cleaning up, but willing to stop and tell us about their day. They had gone by Black Sail and found the rocks up Kirk Fell good fun, but the long slog back down Gavel Neese had been a bore. Cop was most enthusiastic about the ascent.

"We had to push each other up the rocks! You would have loved it! You and Prim should have come!"

I shrugged, "Maybe. I never thought much of Gavel Neese. You are welcome to that any day."

"You are only jealous because we have been to a top and you haven't!"

She had a point there, but I was not going to admit it, so I told her to get lost.

The wind howled during the night, causing the window to rattle like castanets until I got up and jammed an empty cigarette packet into the frame. After that every strong gust produced a muffled thud almost as annoying as the rattling.

* * *

On a dull, cold day we went to the Duddon Valley, driving over Birker Moor in a mist of fine rain. The moorland grasses blazed like fire, but the high fells, which should have looked perfect from Birker, were reduced to dim ghosts.

In the Duddon Valley it was raining in earnest. We went into Seathwaite Church, and mused on 'Wonderful Walker', the incredible parson of long ago — or some of us did. The others had never heard of him. We found an interesting track by the river, but it was too muddy to explore.

"Still glides the stream and shall not cease to glide," I quoted, and got a blank stare from Cop.

"What are you talking about?"

"You know the quotation, surely?"

"No, I don't. Why should I?"

"Wordsworth," I said, which seemed to annoy her.

"I thought we had made a rule never to blather about Wordsworth and the scenery!"

"You are really an ignorant---" I began, and Prim intervened.

"Let us go on to the end of the valley where Hard Knott and Wrynose meet!"

At Cockley Beck it was raining heavily, and parking was awkward in the deep, slippery mud among the large boulders, and further complicated by the number of cars already stationed there. We sat looking into the gloom of Wrynose Bottom, half-heartedly toying with our sandwiches. Then the car next to us tried to move off and got bogged down, and we all got out and helped to push it clear. We soon grew tired of idly sitting, gazing at the rain and mist, and decided to go back down the valley. Cath led, and opposite Wallowbarrow Crag we pulled up to wait for May, who should have been close behind and was not. We waited for twenty minutes, then Cath said, "I don't know what has happened to her. We had better go back and see."

We had almost reached Cockley Beck before we met May's car. Manoeuvering out of the parking space, she had hit a sharp rock projecting from the bank at the side of the road, and had holed a tyre and buckled a front wheel. A man had helped her to change the wheel. She seemed more depressed than annoyed, because such a thing had never happened to her before. She had been a member of the Veteran Drivers' Association for many years, and she felt that she had let herself down.

It was Cath who said, "Something must be done about that wheel. I wonder if there is a decent garage in Broughton. Could you drive your car there, May?"

"Of course I can drive the damn thing!"

So we went to Broughton, and were fortunate to find a good garage, for not only could they supply a new tyre but they could also beat out the wheel, and they could do it at once. While they were working on it, we found a café and had tea. May would eat nothing. She sat brooding and silent, impervious to commiseration or anything else. I thought she needed a good jolt out of the doldrums, so when we had collected her repaired car, I said, "The others can go back with Cath. I'm coming with you."

"You needn't bother!" she snapped, which was a good sign, because when May started to be rude it meant that she was getting back to normal.

"I'm not bothered. I'm coming."

"Oh, go to hell!"

While we were arguing, Cath took off with her load of passengers, leaving us glaring at each other. May swore at me, and I swore back. Then she called me a few nasty names, which I countered with even nastier ones. It was so stupid that we burst out laughing.

"All right, let's go!" she said cheerfully.

Although it was raining, we opened the car windows and sang at the tops of our voices all the way home. We must have sounded awful.

We had got into the habit of going over the green for pre-dinner drinks at the Strands Hotel, and returning to inflict our high spirits on the unfortunate Miss Wilkinson. Next to the bar at the hotel was the kitchen proper, from which an appetising smell always emanated, and we used to speculate on what the hotel guests would be having for dinner. We were sure it would be better than ours. The grass on the other side of the fence is always greener.

* * *

Sunday brought fleeting spells of sunlight to temper the bitter wind. The tall fells brooded over the dark lake. Prim, Cop and I went prospecting on Irton Pike, but had to dash back for dinner, which was in the middle of the day on Sundays.

After the meal came the usual Sabbath inertia in the sitting-room, until Prim suggested, "Greendale for tea?" which galvanised us into action. At the back of Wilkinson's was the village cricket field, though it was a mystery how cricket could have been played there, as it sloped steeply uphill. Beyond it, we crossed a ploughed field, climbed a high wall topped with barbed wire, and came to the

Sunday traffic infested main road up Wasdale. We always enjoyed an unorthodox approach to an objective, especially if it presented problems, which it almost always did.

After Greendale, as we walked back across the moor to Strands, the Gable was grape-blue, and the fire of sunset lay along the Screes. Although we lingered over the short walk, we were back long before supper-time, and were at a loose end — until Prim remembered Miss Wilkinson's song.

During the winter, Miss Wilkinson had written the words and music of a song, which she had entered (unsuccessfully) in a local competition. She had called it 'Song of Lakeland'. Prim borrowed the manuscript, played it through and sang the words, and her eyebrows almost disappeared into her hair. It sounded remarkably heavy and dull.

"That is dreadful!" exclaimed Doris.

Prim agreed whole-heartedly. "It will not do at all. I wonder if . . . ." and she went to find Miss Wilkinson, to ask if we could play about with the song. She returned beaming.

"Miss Wilkinson says she does not care what we do with it!"

Then she and Doris set to work, altering time and note values, re-scoring the music for first and second sopranos, and introducing an alto part for Doris. When they had finished there was a part for everyone except me, and while I am no singer, I resented being left out.

"What about me? What am I to do?"

"Oh, you had better sing the melody — but very softly!"

"Or not at all!" said Cop rudely.

When they sang the new version of the song, I was astounded, for they had brought it to life.

"That's not bad," was Prim's verdict. "Let's sing it again. And stop acting the fool, Cop. This is not supposed to be a pantomime!"

An incredulous Miss Wilkinson appeared in the doorway, exclaiming, "Well, what a pity it was not in time for the competition."

Prim evidently had the bit between her teeth, for after supper she unearthed a pile of music from the piano stool, and we bellowed lustily, until she said, "Miss Wilkinson ought to throw us out! And I'm not playing this old piano any more. It's hard work!"

Afterwards, Miss Wilkinson said how much she had enjoyed the concert — but she had been listening in the kitchen, at a safe distance.

* * *

On the day Cath, May and Doris drove to Ullswater, the rest of us went to Miterdale. On the map, a clear track was marked over Irton Pike, but as this led though a swamp we ignored it, and took a direct line to the col between Irton Pike and Whin Rigg.

Cop said, "What about going up on the Screes?"

She was told that we had already been on the Screes, but had not yet been to Miterdale, and that was where we intended going.

She gave an amiable shrug. "I don't mind where I go, as long as I am not expected to lead the way!"

Cutting through a forestry plantation, we descended to the River Mite, which we crossed by a foot-bridge six inches deep in mud. At first, the narrow, gated road up Miterdale was asphalted, but the smooth surface ended in a green clearing where another bridge spanned the river. Beyond the bridge, the road continued, unsurfaced and full of pot-holes, for a further half mile to Low Place, the only inhabited farmhouse in the dale.

"I don't suppose we could get a pot of tea here," said Prim, hopefully, "but I'll go and see."

It was such an unlikely place for refreshments that we were amazed when she reappeared and beckoned for us to come. We had a pot of tea and ate our sandwiches by the kitchen fire.

Then, following the rough track by the Mite, we came to the ruins of houses, relics of the days when Miterdale lay on a pack-horse route from Burnmoor to Eskdale. Where once had been life and activity, all was now silent among the heaps of crumbling stone. Having read that this place was supposed to be haunted, we explored everywhere, and the time flew.

Gradually the track climbed, the dale narrowed into a gorge dominated by the bulky mass of Scafell, and the Mite dwindled until it was small enough to leap over. At one point it disappeared altogether under the boulders. We came to the amphitheatre of Miterdale Head, where the turf was short and springy and waterfalls leapt down buttresses of rock. Was it H. H. Symonds who wrote that you could imagine fairies dancing there? That did not work for us. The knife-edged wind prevented such fantasy.

We scaled the rocks, and emerged shin-deep in swamp on Burnmoor. We had left the constriction of Miterdale for a wide world of melancholy beauty, for a sea of wind-rippled grass and shadowy mountains, under a pearl-grey sky. This was the best part of the walk.

Following a track down to Boot, we were outraged when they refused to give us tea at the Burnmoor Inn.

"I'm hungry!" Cop sounded indignant, as though we were to blame.

"You are not the only one!"

"I'm starving!"

We knew perfectly well that it was more frustration than hunger.

"Have we any food left in our rucksacks?" asked Prim.

We foraged, discovered some cake which had been wrapped with the sandwiches, and grumbled about that.

"It's stale!"

"It must have been made a month!"

"I'm not eating that stuff!"

"It is all we've got," Prim said, taking a bite. She pulled a face, and threw the rest of the piece away. "We'll go up to the Woolpack. They will give us something to eat, and a drink, then we will ring for John Robert to come and fetch us."

We walked the long half mile to the Woolpack, and had sausage rolls and a drink, and it was while going to the telephone that Prim fell down a step and almost sprained her ankle.

"You are not safe anywhere except on the mountains," I grumbled.

While Cop in sepulchral tones exclaimed, "Remember St. Bees!"

"Oh, go and look for John Robert!" Prim told her impatiently.

Cop and I went outside and leaned over the garden wall, and waited for John Robert.

"Ah, primroses!" Cop exclaimed, and climbed over into the garden, and picked a bunch. "I'll give them to Prim to make up for falling down the step. You needn't tell her I pinched them from the Armstrongs' garden!"

When we reached home she presented them to Prim. I did not say they were stolen, and Prim asked no questions. John Robert, who had an exceptionally loud, booming voice, talked non-stop all the way back to Strands. Sitting in front, Prim suffered the full volume. Cop and I rode in the back with the rucksacks. It suited us in the back, as we did not have to make conversation.

* * *

A miserable greyness lay over the dale, and we had no urge to do anything except sit round the fire and gradually lose patience with each other. Then Cath, Cop and Doris decided to go for a walk, and poured scorn on the rest of us for not accompanying them.

May said, "I'm going walking by car — to Gosforth."

So Prim and I went, too. We thought May wished to do some shopping, but when we drew up in the car park at Gosforth she made no attempt to get out, and after a few minutes I asked, "Do you want to buy something?"

"No."

"Then why have we come to Gosforth?"

She looked at me vaguely. "I dunno. It was just somewhere to go. You can always walk back to Strands if you like!"

"No fear!" I said.

She looked at Prim.

"Are you ready to go back?"

"Yes," replied Prim, looking surprised.

So we drove back to Strands.

"An idiotic waste of petrol!" was my comment.

To which she retorted, "It's my petrol!"

"Certainly a new way to spend a morning!" said Prim, in an aside.

In the afternoon, we took both cars to Eskdale, and up Miterdale to the end of the tarred road, and walked to Low Place for tea and scones. The wind was so strong when we came out of the farmhouse that we rushed back to the cars, drove to Ravenglass, and sat in silence, watching the sea. We were subdued. We had come to walk the mountains, but so far had been frustrated by the unfriendly weather. I wondered how long it would be before some of us reached the stage when we did what we wanted, whatever the weather was like. The sooner the better, I thought.

While the rest of us went over the green for pre-dinner drinks, May drove to Seascale to collect Hilda from the train. With her arrival the S.L. Club was complete, so after dinner we discussed my Mountain Quiz. I had been asked to write this, and to forward a copy to each member a month before the holiday, thus giving them plenty of time to work on it before returning the papers to me.

Prim, with full marks, had won, with Doris a close second. The post-mortem was lively, with arguments and objections flying about the room. Those with low scores directed their rancour at me.

"You ought to know all about mountains. You have nothing to do except read mountain books!"

This nettled me, though I tried to be patient, and reminded them, "I did not make up this quiz to amuse myself. I did it because you asked me."

"We didn't ask you to bring in things we have never heard of!"

"Just a nice, easy little quiz, that's all we wanted!"

"But you specially asked for one which would necessitate some research."

"You can't do much research when all you have is a one-inch map!" Hilda exclaimed.

"You could always buy yourself a few reference books."

When someone said, "I've no time for bothering with reference books!" I had had enough.

"I'm sick of the lot of you. You go about in the Lakes with your eyes shut, like a lot of dim-witted sheep. Do your own damn quizzes in future!"

Prim, who had taken no part in the altercation, said mildly, "It was a very good quiz. I shall look forward to the next one, if you will be good enough to set it."

Peace having been restored, Cop voiced what was in everyone's mind. "We are getting on one another's nerves. What we need is to work off our energy on the mountains!"

* * *

So we worked it off, in spite of the gale-force winds which were sweeping the tops. But because clouds were massed at the valley head, half the morning had gone before we set out to climb Red Pike. As we drove up the dale the clouds retreated before us, revealing fells newly powdered with snow.

The cars were parked at Overbeck, and we started up the steep track towards Yewbarrow, which towered ahead like a small Matterhorn. It was fairly stiff going, and on reaching a junction of two tracks Hilda and May turned back, while the rest of us climbed a wall, to get to Dore Head by traversing under the rocks of Yewbarrow.

Soon, we were being buffeted by the wind, and when we were hit by a squall of icy rain Doris turned back, leaving the four of us, the old brigade. Then Prim and Cop produced large sheets of thick, transparent plastic with strings attached, and tied them round their waists. The plastic reached almost to their feet. Cop wore hers over her oilskin like an outsize apron, while Prim had hers underneath, which made her look as though she was losing her underwear. Cath and I howled at the sight.

"Whose bright idea was that?"

"Mine!" grinned Prim, "and we shall be a lot drier and warmer than you, whatever we look like!"

"You don't happen to have a couple of spare ones?"

"No, but I'll tell you where you can buy them."

"That's not much use just now!" I said.

"It might be, some time in the future."

At Dore Head the rain had stopped, but the wind was dreadful. Huddled in a niche between the rocks, we gobbled a couple of sandwiches. From that viewpoint the west face of Gable gave the illusion of a wall of sheer, unclimbable rock.

The ascent of Red Pike was roughish, with interesting bands of rock glittering with the stars and ferns of ice crystals. The gale made conditions on the summit almost impossible, but the satisfaction of achieving a top kept us there until our teeth were chattering and we were cold to our bones.

We rushed down, slipping and sliding on the iced rocks, and at Dore Head the wind screaming over the col almost blew us off our feet. Trying to get out of it quickly, we scattered in all directions. Prim seemed to be heading for the top of Yewbarrow, Cop was crabbing sideways across a band of unstable scree, while Cath and I converged on a tongue of rough grass.

"Let's go straight down it!" I said, and we did this, and found it anything but pleasant, though it eventually brought us to the wall. Cop, also, made it to the wall, but Prim had disappeared. Then, as we scanned the top of Yewbarrow, we saw her head pop above the summit rocks.

"There she is!" I exclaimed, pointing. "How on earth is she going to get down from there!"

The head went out of sight, and a few minutes later she came round the foot of a buttress, and trotted down to us. She was grinning broadly.

"Where have you been?" we demanded.

"I thought it would be easier, and quicker, to come along the rocks. It was, until I found that the only way down was by an awful gully. I started, but it was so steep that I got out and climbed down the face of the rocks at the side. They were bad enough!"

"You came down wearing that awful plastic thing! You might have broken your neck!"

"I never thought about it."

Small matters like doing a rock climb with a piece of plastic flapping round your ankles were quite unimportant!

"You know," said Prim, "there is all the difference in the world between Buttermere Red Pike and Wasdale Red Pike. We must explore all these Mosedale fells!"

We were soon at Greendale, clamouring for tea and cakes, then back to Strands and over the green for pre-dinner drinks which we deemed well-earned. We had fought for Red Pike!

* * *

"What about Ennerdale?" Prim suggested one freezingly cold morning when we were idling in the sitting-room. There was an immediate rush for the cars, because any objective was better than doing nothing.

Speeding over Cold Fell, we were soon at Ennerdale Bridge, heading for the lake. I had assured Cath that the road down to the Anglers Inn had been resurfaced. I had no idea where I had picked up that information, but it was not true, and she cursed me as we lurched in and out of the pot-holes. If she had known, she said, she would have parked at the top of the hill and made us walk down, but I pointed out that by taking the cars down we could park on the very edge of the water and have a superb view while we ate our sandwiches in comfort.

The slate-grey lake was fretted with wind ripple, and the mountains at its head were barely visible. The superb view depended on the depth of one's imagination. After eating, we looked round for something to occupy us for a while, and spotted Angling Crag, and decided to walk round it. We began with a drag up steepish grass, on a little path scarcely wide enough for one's feet. We found it boring, until the path ended at a col on the far side of the crag. A skidding descent through bracken led to the water's edge. Then came a delightful scramble over the rocks back to the starting point. This final part was fun. Most of us loved rock, though some appreciated it more than others. We four originals were never happier than when we were using feet and hands.

Storm clouds were gathering as we left Ennerdale Water, and the dale head had withdrawn behind a grey curtain. May and her carload went straight back to Strands, while we, never anxious to call it a day, went to walk on the sands at Seascale. This lingering brought an unexpected reward when the sun came out. The great western fells were bathed in glory, and the snows of Scafell gleamed with a pink radiance. For that alone it was worth being late for dinner.

*   *   *

Although the sun struggled to produce a few watery beams, the unrelenting wind maintained its savage bite. It was no weather for fell walkers, but the end of the holiday was so near that we were getting desperate. So Hilda, Doris and May set out to climb Irton Pike, while the rest of us went to Haycock.

From Greendale, we started up the flank of Middle Fell, a bleak chilly beginning, and before we had gone two hundred yards I realised that this was not going to be one of my days. The arthritis which was slowly developing in my knees did not affect my walking as a rule, but on the occasions when it did it was a confounded nuisance, because it slowed me down. It was as though I had used up all the spring in the joints and needed a fresh supply.

Near Greendale Tarn we crossed the half-frozen beck, to traverse the lower slopes of Seatallan. The walking was over thick, tussocky grass interspersed with bog-holes into one of which Cop stumbled. The resultant mud plaster made her annoyed. Beyond a brown, soggy basin rose Haycock. The passage across the basin was made tedious by a liberality of swamp, but eventually we reached a rock outcrop, and found a sheltered spot where we could eat. I had had enough by then, and having disposed of my sandwiches, said, "This is my turning point."

Cop's mouth dropped open in disbelief. "Aren't you going to the top of Haycock? It's only just up there!"

"You will go twice as fast without me," I said.

"What are you going to do?"

"I shall sit here for a while, then wander back."

"Have you any spare food?" asked Cath.

"Plenty. Bring me back a bit of rock from the top of Haycock."

I collected a small rock specimen from the summit of each new fell we climbed.

"Will you be all right?"

"Don't be daft," I said, and they set off, muffled to the ears, Prim calling over her shoulder, "Order tea for us when you get down to Greendale."

It was very pleasant on the rock, because I was almost out of the wind, and I was in no hurry. But after half an hour the cold began to penetrate. The other three had long since disappeared, and there were no other walkers in sight. I had the fells to myself. I could select my own route.

To avoid the swampy terrain, I climbed high on Seatallan, until I had a wonderful view of the big fells — the dark precipice of Scafell plunging sheer to the Mickledore screes, the dome of the Pike, Broad Crag, Great End, the massive bulk of Gable — all reaching for the sky. For some time I stood, unable to tear myself away.

Then the wind blew, and I cut straight down towards Greendale Tarn, easy going over rough grass until I came to the top of a high wall of rock. The wall looked as though it would 'go'. I climbed down by easy ledges until these petered out about ten feet from the bottom. Hanging from my hands, I let go, landing in a mossy hollow at the base of the cliff. Then I sat on a boulder and felt a little foolish, because if I had sprained my ankle or broken anything the others would not have thought of looking for me up there. My boulder under the rocks was a sun-trap, and I basked there for a while.

Continuing down, I crossed the outlet to the tarn, and climbed to avoid another patch of swamp, and found myself high on the scree of Middle Fell. "Silly fool!" I said to myself, and had to make my way down, first over boulders then by unpleasantly steep grass, until I reached a faint track. I thought Haycock might have been easier than what I had done!

I was soon down at the car, but it was locked, and I had no key. Hunting for shelter from the wind which was howling down the valley, I saw a large flat stone in the angle between two walls. Making for it, I tripped over some barbed wire hidden in the long grass, and cut my leg.

"Double silly fool!" I told myself.

I regretted missing Haycock, but I had enjoyed my solitary wanderings. I estimated that the others would arrive within the next half-hour, which they did, pelting down at a great rate. They said that instead of making for the Scoat Fell-Haycock col, the usual way up Haycock, they had made a bee-line for the summit, clambering on all fours up the scree. A gale was blowing on the top.

"The wind was eighty miles an hour!" declared Cop.

"How do you know it was eighty?"

"Because we were in it. You weren't, so you know nothing about it!"

"Eighty, ninety, or a hundred!" shrugged Prim. "Call it what you like, but don't stand arguing about it. I only took one photograph on the top, because I couldn't hold the camera still."

"What have you done to your leg?" Cath asked, eyeing the blood.

"Cut it on some barbed wire when I got down to the road."

"Clumsy idiot!" she said, and with that we went into Greendale for tea.

The wind had made our eyes so tired that we could scarcely keep them open after dinner that night. We felt that we had been in conflict with the elements, and yet according to the forecast, the Lake District was having the best weather in England. We disagreed, having been there. As far as we were concerned it had not been good at all, in that it had definitely curbed our activities. Nevertheless, it was with deep regret that we left Strands at the end of the holiday. The western fells, the true kingdom of the mountaineer, had grown into our hearts and minds, and were part of our lives, and it was unbearable that another year must pass before we saw them again.

The urge to return was so powerful that Prim suggested, "Why not go up for a week at Whitsun? We could stay at the Woolpack for a change. I know we should not have the place to ourselves, but most of the people staying at the Woolpack are walkers, so we should fit in well."

She then ascertained which of us would be free to go. Four members of the S.L. Club were otherwise committed. Prim, Cop and I were free, so the three of us went to Eskdale.

ESKDALE IN MAY

Having no car at our disposal, we travelled by train, a somewhat lengthy journey, to Ravenglass, where a taxi, ordered in advance, waited for us. To be driving up Eskdale on a perfect spring evening was like being admitted into heaven. The larches shone green, the roadside verges were dappled with primroses and violets, bluebells spread a mist of hyacinth under the trees, and the fells dreamed in brown and gold. For some unknown reason I sat in front with the taxi-driver, and felt obliged to talk, which I did unwillingly. All I wished was to look, and look again, at everything. Prim should have been sitting in front as she usually did, because she seemed able to talk and look simultaneously.

From the start, we felt at home at the Woolpack, with John and Mary Armstrong. Prim and Cop shared a twin-bedded room, while I had a nearby single. Our rooms were at the front of the inn, looking across to Birker Moor and the very shapely Harter Fell.

* * *

The dale was radiant on our first morning. In the lower fields the lush grass was so intensely green that it glowed, and the fells drowsed against a deep blue sky. It was an ideal day for loitering which, as we told each other repeatedly, was the reason why we had come to Eskdale.

We strolled down to Boot, then to Dalegarth, where we climbed by a succession of creaking wooden bridges up the gorge to the waterfalls. We did not care for the oppressive airlessness in the gorge, and soon came down again and cut over to the River Esk, which we followed until we were opposite St. Catherine's Church.

To our disgust, the green sward between church and river had disappeared under a dense mass of parked cars and multi-coloured tents. Radios were blasting, people were shouting, some wore hideous bathing suits, and some were vainly trying to float on lilos. The noise was hideous. Doubtless they were enjoying themselves in their own selfish way, but they were in the wrong place. True, it was a bank holiday, but the simple beauty of St. Catherine's, a haven of peace and sanctity if ever there was one, should never have to suffer mob invasion.

We continued on our side of the river until we were well out of earshot, and the silence was broken only by the sparkling river chattering over its rounded stones. We stopped for a leisurely picnic before wandering on over a carpet of bluebells and primroses. We found this, and the unending chorus of blackbirds and thrushes, so entrancing that somehow we strayed from the track. It had slanted away to the right, and we had kept by the river. Cop was the first to notice this, as she struggled to disentangle herself from a patch of brambles.

"We are not on any sort of track!"

Prim replied placidly, "We seem to have mislaid it, so we will keep by the river."

We followed her through thickets of brambles and nettles, and over fallen trees and mossy boulders.

"Find us some sort of a path, can't you!" wailed Cop, as we inched precariously along the top of a crumbling wall.

"I'm doing my best. At least, we are going in the right direction, up the dale."

After crawling under several lots of barbed wire, we finally hit a path going across a field, and eventually got down to Doctor Bridge. By then we were wilting in the intense heat, and relieved when we got back to the Woolpack. We had tea, as we sprawled in large, comfortable chairs in the cool, deserted lounge.

In the evening, we went by the river track to evensong at St. Catherine's, and shamefully lost this track, also, and found ourselves down by the water when we should have been high on the hillside. We had to climb up through much bracken and gorse.

"We must be crazy!" I said, as we hauled ourselves up.

"We will keep to the proper track on the way back!" vowed Prim, and we did, and found it delightful, as it meandered through thickets of broom in full flower.

After dinner, we went for what we intended to be a short stroll, but found ourselves going up Hard Knott before we remembered to turn back. "It's about time we stopped streaking up and down the dale for one day!" exclaimed Cop; and we agreed.

At bedtime, there began what was to develop into nightly entertainment. For reading aloud, I had brought a book entitled

Below Scafell. It was written by Dudley Hoys, who was actually living at the Woolpack at the time. He was known locally as the 'Captain'. The farm he described in his book was the Woolpack, and all his characters lived there, too, thus making one of the best of all Lakeland books ring true. Each night, when Prim and Cop were in bed, I went into their room and read a chapter or two, and the next day we would discuss what we had read with the 'Captain'. Appropriately, on this first night we had the chapter called, 'Along The River'.

* * *

There were thundery showers during the night, but by morning the rain had gone, never to return that holiday. The air was warm, the sun shone, and puffs of cotton-wool cloud lingered on the summit rocks of Harter Fell.

We crossed Doctor Bridge and walked past Penny Hill Farm, and I expect we were talking too much to notice where we were going, because we lost the track, whereupon Cop admonished Prim "I thought you were supposed to be the leader. We've done nothing but lose the way since we came to Eskdale."

Prim just laughed.

"I know, and isn't it fun? We are not going anywhere in particular, so tracks do not matter. We'll carry on along the fell-side."

This we did, and it involved a fair amount of beck-hopping. During one crossing, Cop lost her footing on a mossy stone, and went knee-deep in the water. I burst into derisive laughter, which displeased her.

"Some people have a poor sense of humour!" she said tartly.

"You didn't see how silly you looked!"

"There is nothing funny about slipping," she began. "It is a matter which should be taken seriously."

"Come on, you two. Don't start a silly argument!" called Prim, who was well ahead.

Cop always loved an argument, sensible or otherwise, but this time it petered out as we went in single file after Prim who was going diagonally uphill. Soon, having climbed an awkward wall, we found ourselves high on Harter Fell.

"Are we going to the top?"

"No," said Prim, "we haven't time. If we hurry, we shall just get back to the Woolpack in time for lunch."

Rushing down to the foot of Hard Knott, we did the mile and

a half along the road at the double, arriving at the Woolpack as lunch was about to be served. As we rushed panting into the dining-room, Cop groaned, "For heaven's sake let's do something really easy this afternoon!"

"All right," Prim said, "we will go exploring."

We went up the rake alongside the spinney at the back of the hotel. The track climbed between grassy hummocks and rock outcrops, and finally led to blue, reed-fringed Eel Tarn, where we sat on a boulder. We had the world to ourselves and the larks. We were half-drowsing when Prim broke the silence.

"Shall we go and find Stony Tarn next?"

Cop said, "We don't know where to look for it."

"Nobody ever seems to locate Stony Tarn."

"I shall find it!" Prim assured us.

"Do you know which way to go?"

"Vaguely. It's over in that direction somewhere. It has to be. Let's start hunting."

After a torturous foray over boulders, around rock tors, across the black aftermath of burnt heather, and through much bog, we found it. In its rocky setting, the dark, quiet water reminded me of Angle Tarn, under Bowfell. We sat on the wall of an ancient sheep-fold, and foraged for biscuits and apples.

Then Prim said, "The quickest and easiest return will be by the way we have come."

As neither Cop nor I had the slightest idea which way that was, having done so much turning and changing direction among the granite outcrops, we followed, sheep-like, and she led us without hesitation back to the Woolpack in time for a drink before dinner.

Surveying our muddy, blackened legs, the result of the encounter with bog and burnt heather, Cop said, "This was supposed to be a very easy afternoon, instead of which we have spent it laboriously chasing elusive tarns hidden among the foothills. I'm going to wallow in the bath," adding, over her shoulder, "You never know what Prim will think up next!"

* * *

At the foot of Hard Knott, the Brotherilkeld intakes were full of tiny lambs, and we were surprised by the predominance of black ones, being unaware that these change to grey as they get older. We knew little about Herdwick sheep, though by the time the holiday ended we had learnt a great deal from John Armstrong and the Harrisons of Brotherilkeld.

After dallying by the bridge at Throstlegarth, we climbed alongside the Esk gorge to the rock gateway on the skyline, where the full grandeur of the great fells is revealed. Cop exclaimed, "We shall be on Scafell Pike before we know what is happening!" to which Prim replied placidly, "I am merely prospecting. I don't have any particular object in mind," and I said, "We've heard that one before!"

After perching on boulders above the gorge to eat our sandwiches, we followed the curve of the river to Great Moss, surely the wettest piece of ground in the Lake District. We avoided getting completely waterlogged by picking an oozy way along the top of the remains of the old turf bank built by the monks who once farmed at Brotherilkeld. Prim ploughed on and we came after, until we were opposite Cam Spout Crag, where the track to Mickledore rises alongside the waterfall, and then I realised what Prim was after — Scafell, by Foxes Tarn.

Unfortunately, the river was in the way. Running high, and with no convenient stones, it was too deep and wide to cross. We prospected up and down stream, but could find no way over to the other side.

"Blow!" said Prim mildly. "That's that!"

"We could always swim across!" said Cop, with a grin.

"You do that, if you wish."

"Where do we go from here?" I asked.

"We go back."

Cop objected loudly, "Why? Can't you find some place — any place to cross?"

Prim said, "No, not unless you want to go waist deep, in which case I shall stand on the bank and watch you. I'm going back to Brotherilkeld for tea. Next time, we will keep the river on our right, not our left."

We retraced our steps down to Throstlegarth, and to the farm for tea and rhubarb tart. Eskdale surely had a cuckoo in every copse that evening, for they called and called all the way back to the Woolpack.

* * *

The red letter day was when we did Crinkle Crags.

Prim asked Alistair, John Armstrong's son, to drive us over Hard Knott and up Wrynose to the Three Shire Stone, from which point we would begin the walk, thus avoiding the laborious motor road up two passes.

The high-powered car very quickly took us to the Three Shire

Stone. A delightful track wound over the moorland along the flank of Pike o' Blisco and past Red Tarn, and we approached the Crinkles with mounting excitement. Their rough rock acted like a magnet, and our pace increased. We could not get to those five tops fast enough!

Then we were there, with rock under our feet — splendid, wild rock!

We went over the first Crinkle, and on the way to the second, came to the Bad Step mentioned by A. Wainwright in one of his guide-books. Prim stood and studied it.

"It looks awkward, but I could get up it quite easily if I had to."

We waited.

"There is no need to go that way at all. I can see good routes on either side. The rocks on the left are the easier, so we will go up that way," and she led what was a delightful scramble.

From the cairn on the second, and highest Crinkle, we sat feasting our eyes on a great panorama of peaks dominated by the magnificent Scafells. The moment of truth had been reached, the quintessence of all that we had lived for so many years was there before us.

As we went on, the track skirted the three remaining Crinkles, but we diverged to scramble to the three tops. As we stood by the fifth cairn, Cop flung out her arms, and declaimed, "Chanel No.5!"

Prim, who habitually used Chanel No.5, looked startled and asked what she was talking about.

"She's crazy," I said. "She always has been."

After the Crinkles came Shelter Crags, followed by a descent to Three Tarns, and the discovery that there were four pools instead of three. There was a close-up view of the deep gullies on Bowfell Links, and also of the rough track to the top, which Prim was studying.

"It looks very tempting, but I suppose we had better not go up there, because of the time. It is quite a walk from here down to Brotherilkeld."

Dinner was always very punctual at the Woolpack, and as yet we had never been more than a few minutes late, so we turned our backs on Bowfell, and wasted some of our remaining time in a flippant argument about why the place where we were standing should be called Three Tarns when there were four. Then we began the long walk down.

After a thousand steep and stony feet, there was bog in abundance as we followed the Lingcove Beck down to Throstlegarth. Resting on the parapet of the old bridge, we wished that we did not have to do the final two miles to Brotherilkeld.

"It is as bad as sitting on Stockley Bridge, and having to get to Seathwaite — only this is further."

"And then rushing from Brotherilkeld to the Woolpack, like we had to dash from Seathwaite to Seatoller."

"Oh, for a mule!" sighed Cop.

"Two mules!" I echoed.

"I'm sorry now that we did not go up Bowfell."

Prim seemed to be talking to herself, not listening to our groans. We sat in silence for another ten minutes, then she got up.

"We are too late for tea, and I'm parched, so I know what I am going to have at Brotherilkeld — an enormous glass of home-made lemonade!"

"The carrot and the donkey — I mean donkeys!" said Cop.

The lure was effective, for we went from Throstlegarth to Brotherilkeld almost at the double, and the glasses which Mrs Harrison produced were pint-sized. It was a most splendid drink. Then Prim after stating that she had no intention of walking down the road, rang up the Woolpack, and John Armstrong came to fetch us.

The radiant evening light lured us out again after dinner, but the walk was of necessity short as far as I was concerned. To save coping with luggage on the train, Prim had arranged with some people who were returning to Nottingham to take our cases in their car. The shoes I had worn to do the Crinkles were being dried in the Woolpack kitchen ready for the next morning, so I was reduced to doing the evening walk in bedroom slippers.

* * *

"Let us spend our last day just savouring the dale."

It was one of those glorious spring mornings which come so seldom, and are heaven when they do. We walked by the river to St. Catherine's, and down to Trough House Bridge, where the Esk deepens into clear, green pools. This is a favourite venue for bathers and picnic parties, but we were fortunate, and had it to ourselves.

The return on the other side of the river was a gentle stroll because we kept mainly to the track, apart from occasional short-cutting to climb a wall or two. I tried to persuade Cop to crawl through a hogg-hole so that I could take a photograph, but she refused.

"I'm not a flipping sheep, and I'm not going to crawl among the sheep dirt for you!"

"You would look beautiful stuck in a hogg-hole!"

"Well. I'm not going to! Go through yourself!" She eyed me, adding, "You couldn't get through, anyway!"

"You're right," I agreed, "But I never act like a sheep, and you often do."

She was about to get indignant when Prim called, "In five minutes time we shall be late for lunch!" and we scurried after her.

In the afternoon, we went up the lane past Bird How, the tiny stone cottage once lived in by H. H. Symonds.

"This is the way we should have gone to get to Cam Spout, keeping the river on the right," Prim said, "but it's too late to do anything about that now."

At Taw House, opposite Brotherilkeld, we hoped to find a bridge across the river. Alistair had told us, "It depends on how the river has been behaving. Sometimes there is a bridge and sometimes there isn't!"

Evidently the river had been behaving badly, for there was no bridge, and we had to retrace our steps and go by road to Brotherilkeld. Mrs Harrison gave us a splendid tea, took us to see some baby ducks, and showed us the ancient brick oven built by the monks of Furness. We stayed at the farm until we were a little late for dinner.

At bedtime, we finished *Below Scafell,* and with the final page came the realisation that not only the book but our loitering in Eskdale was over. There was a short silence before Prim voiced what we were all thinking. "Everything in Eskdale has been good!"

I shall always remember that spring in Eskdale — the bird song, the call of the cuckoo, the bleating of small lambs, the singing river . . . . . These were the things which helped to lighten dark winter days in the city, until with the advent of another spring our blood began to quicken, and we could head north again to our beloved fells.

THE LAST RECRUIT

There was the problem of Hilda. Deeply involved in family affairs, there was little likelihood of her being present for more than a few days at the S. L. Club's Easter meetings, if at all. Consequently, we should be one member short, and if, for any unforetold reason, one or two others were unable to come, we should not fill Miss Wilkinson's house. This would leave room for other guests, and was the last thing we wanted. At Scarthwaite, Mrs Coates would have kept the place half-empty sooner than inflict strangers on us, but we were not so sure about Miss Wilkinson. Prim and I discussed the situation, and concluded that we must acquire a new member.

"I had better think of someone suitable," she said.

This she eventually did, and invited Daisy, from Maidstone, whom she knew well. She said Daisy was a competent walker, and, hopefully, would fit in with the mood and manner of the club. I asked if she would try to organise us, and Prim said, "She is not that sort of person, and she would hardly try to do that when she is only on trial."

That year, the holiday arrangements were like pieces of a jigsaw puzzle. Cath, Prim and I were to go by the Scotch Corner route, May and Doris via Ilkley and Skipton, Cop by train from London, Daisy to join us five days later and the day she arrived Cath was to leave for a conference, and Hilda would not be there at all. It all worked very smoothly.

Our car-load was the first to reach Strands, and we were sorting out our gear when May and Doris arrived. Then Cath and I went to Seascale to meet Cop's train.

The excessive chatter over dinner that night was a sign of things to come, for as day succeeded day so the clamour increased. This became a noisy holiday, probably because the weather was on the whole inauspicious. We needed the calming effect of long days on the tops.

* * *

The wind roared round the house and whined like a lost soul down the dale. The high tops were impossible, and even walking in the valley was unpleasant, so six frustrated people were marooned in the sitting-room. Once again I had been requested to compile a 'Mountain Quiz', but this time I had to give members not one month but two in which to do their research and send their papers back to me. This inclement morning seemed a good time to announce the results. Prim, with full marks, had won, while Doris, Cath and Cop were creditable runners-up. May said she must have mislaid her papers instead of sending them back to me. I accused her of doing this deliberately, and she put on such an air of injured innocence that I knew she was lying.

When I returned the papers to their respective owners pandemonium broke loose. In addition to arguing with me, each turned to her immediate neighbour and gave a loud, impassioned lecture on what she had written and her reasons for doing so. May, with no evidence that she had even done the quiz, gleefully added her opinions. I had to shout to make myself heard.

"You sound like a menagerie! Come to think of it, you look like one, too!"

Then Prim cut in, "Shall we go to Keswick?"

Heads swivelled round and there was silence, until someone said, "Why Keswick? We always seem to be going to Keswick!"

"Yes," Prim agreed, "but this time I propose that we don't go by any of the ways we know. We will go by the shortest route we can find, taking any little road which is at all possible for cars."

"I'm game!" Cath said.

"You lead and I'll follow," from May.

"Anything to get out of being cooped up here!"

"And we don't take maps," added Prim. "It will be more fun that way."

We set off. The first leg to Calderbridge and over Cold Fell was familiar ground, but after that it was unknown territory. By Mockerkin and Mosser we went, and in and out of half a dozen farmyards, with May close behind and no doubt cursing us. We crossed fields by rutted cart-tracks, saw a signpost which was useless because the arms were missing, and came to a narrow lane with outsize pot-holes which made the car bump and sway so wildly that we clung onto the sides. I could guess what May would be saying about that. Prim called out general directions, and Cath drove, and it was a wild, exciting ride until we reached a metalled road near Lorton, and plain sailing over Whinlatter.

When we parked in Keswick, May strode over to our car and glared at us, shaking her head. "That was quite a ride, wasn't it?" said Cath with a grin, to which May replied, "You are a crazy lot of half-baked idiots!"

A malicious wind was driving stinging rain down the narrow streets of Keswick. We scattered, each going to the shop of her choice, but soon came together again. Getting wet on the fells was one thing, but there was no point in getting soaked in a town, so we called at the Pheasant for tea, then went back to Strands by an orthodox route.

After dinner, I produced two more short quizzes, to be done on the spot. They received a mixed reception.

"Oh, good!"

"Not another!"

"Give us a rest, can't you!"

The first quiz, to do with mountain tracks, was supposed to take ten minutes. Prim completed it in five, but the others, copying shamelessly from each other, took half an hour. The second quiz, a mountain walk with cryptic clues, took longer, causing even more cheating. Prim won both.

"What shall we do next?" I asked, having collected the scribbled, untidy papers. May regarded me with extreme distaste.

"Why don't you go and drown yourself!"

* * *

The wind persisted, the high fells were veiled, and we fretted.

"What can we do?"

"Where can we go?"

"It's not fit for a big walk!"

"All right," said Prim, "if we can't do a big walk we will do three little ones. There are plenty of those in Eskdale."

So we went to Eskdale. Parking near Dalegarth, we walked up onto Birker Moor, and came back very muddy about the legs. That was walk No. 1.

For No.2 we climbed the rake at the back of the Woolpack and went to Eel Tarn. We were returning when over the moor came a sudden onslaught of heavy rain. We fled to an old roofless ruin of a hut, where we tried to shelter, until someone sensibly pointed out that we should get no wetter if we went on with the walk. We went on, splashing through becks and soaking bracken, and ten minutes later the clouds rushed away over Harter Fell and the emerging sun filled the valley with diamond points of light.

After tea at the Woolpack, walk No. 3 was by the river to St. Catherine's, one of the best of all low level walks. Almost absurdly elated at having completed the three little walks, we had more than one pre-dinner drink over the green, which probably was the reason for the noise at the dinner-table. For this we were equally to blame, lifting the lids off the vegetable dishes and yelling at the contents, and roaring when Miss Wilkinson brought in the pudding. Prim attempted a half-hearted apology, and Miss Wilkinson admitted that we made more noise than any of her other visitors.

"But you are the ones we like having best," she added, causing renewed roars.

Cop, said, "It's time the president called the club to order!"

Prim replied, "Why should I?"

* * *

The wind howled, the rain fell, the days passed.

We did a succession of low level walks in Wasdale, rushing out whenever the rain stopped, and always getting caught in the next downpour. Scafell, the Screes, and even little Irton Pike were permanently misted.

We had given up hope when the fair day for which we had been longing finally arrived, but it came too late for Cath, for it was the day when she had to leave for her conference, and she was very annoyed.

"I haven't bagged a single damned top!" she exclaimed.

It was also the day when Daisy would be joining us.

"She little knows what she is in for!" Cop remarked.

Cath, still grumbling, drove away. This left May's small car for five people with conflicting ideas on how to spend the day. Three longed to get to grips with the hills, and two did not. This pair, May and Doris, drove up onto Birker Moor, leaving Prim, Cop and myself without a car. However, Prim was an expert in finding the means to go where she wanted, and John Robert was asked to take us to the camping ground at Wasdale Head, and to collect us from there at six o'clock in the evening.

"Where are we going?" asked Cop, as we headed for Brown

Tongue.

Prim answered vaguely, "Oh, anywhere interesting. What does it matter as long as we get up something?"

The Lingmell Beck was in spate, thundering down over the crossing stones, and, reluctant to get wet feet so early in the day, we followed the stream up, looking for an easier crossing. We were high under the Lingmell screes before Prim lost patience, and said, "This will have to do," and we made an uneasy crossing, balancing on sharp points of rock. Then we climbed on a steep diagonal to the cairn at the top of Brown Tongue, where we sat contentedly for a while, surveying the most dramatic piece of England.

Prim was the first to stir. Hitching on her rucksack, she set off for the col between Lingmell and the Pike, and we followed.

Cop asked, "Are we supposed to be going up Lingmell, or what?"

"I doubt if it will be Lingmell!"

I knew Prim's penchant for the highest objective, and with Scafell Pike so near, I was not surprised when we turned in that direction.

In the final hundred feet to the top, we encountered an icy wind, so bitter that it was demoralising. I had never before experienced such an intensity of cold on any mountain top. We huddled by the great cairn and had a bite to eat, but we were too frozen to care whether we ate or not, and Prim got up and set off down the rough track to Mickledore, and Cop and I went after. The cold made my hands feel as though they were being flayed.

Then I saw Prim begin to stagger, and shouted to Cop, "Look at Prim. There's something wrong!"

Cop tried to shout, but her teeth were chattering so much that the words would not come out, and we skidded down in a rush to Prim. Her face was colourless, so we sat her on a rock and began slapping and rubbing her arms and legs.

"Get the brandy flask — top right hand pocket of my rucksack."

Cop fumbled helplessly with numb hands.

"I can't get the strap undone!"

"Tear the flaming thing off then! Here, give it me!"

I managed to loosen the strap, and we gave Prim a hefty dose of brandy, and had one ourselves. Combined with the energetic rubbing, it made the blood begin to circulate again.

"Sorry to have made a nuisance of myself," Prim apologised, but I never could stand cold as intense as that."

"Any excuse for a nip of brandy!" I said.

Cold never affected me much, but the conditions on the top of the Pike that day were abnormal. No wonder we had it to ourselves.

We went on, and after losing a hundred feet of height we were below the level of deadly cold, and it was as though we had walked through a door into another climate, and life was a pleasure once more. We lingered on Mickledore, the supreme grandstand for viewing the details of the magnificent rock-face of Scafell. One cannot gaze upon that and remain unmoved by awe and wonder. The spirit is at the same moment elevated and humbled.

Having launched ourselves on the scree down to Hollowstones, we found the slope extremely steep. Prim swooped joyously down like a skier, and was sitting on a rock at the bottom when we were only half-way. Cop was bent sideways trying to brake with one hand. I dug in my heels and slid until I became unbalanced and finished on the seat of my pants. We must have looked ridiculous, because Prim was doubled up with laughter.

Cop grumbled, "That was not amusing! Look at my gloves! I've taken all the finger ends out on those rotten stones!"

"I'll mend them for you tonight," Prim promised, "but it was fun, wasn't it? I've always wanted to go on Mickledore!"

"Same here!" I said.

We went down Brown Tongue, forgetting about the swollen beck at the bottom until we got to it, and I exclaimed, "Oh, hell, I shall never get over that!"

The roaring water sounded like an express train — and it was deep. There are large rocks at that crossing, but only the sharp tips of two were showing, and they were far apart. I turned to Prim.

"Can you get over?"

"Yes," she said, "but I am wondering whether it would be better . . ."

Before she could finish, Cop made a rush, jumping for the first stone, flinging herself sideways onto the next, and leaping to the far bank — an excellent piece of muscular co-ordination.

"Oh, well!" said Prim, and followed suit.

Then it was my turn. I got to the first stone, could not bend my knee far enough for the awkward jump to the second, and retreated.

"Come on! It's easy!" Cop called, and I told her not to talk rubbish.

"I'll wade across," I decided, but the water was so deep and the pull of the current so strong that I went back after a single step. Then I sat on the bank and cursed all becks to hell and damnation, which was a waste of breath.

Cop watched me with a smug grin. "Swearing will not get you across!"

Then Prim called, "You walk up your side of the beck and I'll walk up mine until we find a place where you can cross."

We walked until I began to think we should finish on Lingmell itself, but finally we came to where there was a largish, sloping stone in the middle of the beck and a small, precarious one on either side. Prim crossed to the large stone, and extended a hand.

"This will do. I'll steady you past this stone, but you will have to move quickly — and don't pull me in!"

I rushed, and landed on the far side, feeling furious with myself.

"I never thought I should be held up by a rotten little beck!"

She pointed out that it was not a little beck. It was in full spate, and if I had not the necessary spring in my knees in order to cross there was nothing I could do about it. We rejoined Cop, who was sitting patiently on a boulder, and went on, reaching the campsite just as John Robert drove up.

Back at Strands, we went over the green for a drink, but Miss Smith could not serve us until 7 p.m. because it was Good Friday or something, and the licensing hours were the same as on Sundays. With half an hour to wait, and nothing better to do, we washed and changed. We should have loved a cup of tea, but nobody offered us one.

Daisy arrived during the evening. She seemed pleasant and rather quiet. Apart from general conversation she said little, though I noticed that her eyes were everywhere, missing nothing. She was to share my room, in Cath's place. Cath and I always bucketed about in the bedroom and made a lot of noise, but on this particular night I did my best to appear more civilised. I lay in bed pondering over Daisy, and concluded that she would fit in when she got used to us. Then I thought about the day's walk — the unexpected layer of deadly cold air above the 3,000 ft. level; the hilarious descent of the Mickledore screes; the obstacle of the raging beck. It had been a good day, because something had been achieved at last.

* * *

The next day, the heavy rain was back. And so it went on, and on.

Getting dressed with almost indecent haste, I cursed the lack of an electric fire, the weather, and everything else I could think of. I had got to, '. . . and this bedroom is like a bloody morgue!' before I remembered that Daisy was a newcomer.

"It is certainly rather cold," she agreed amiably.

At morning service in Strands Church the singing was dominated by one local woman with an astounding, flat voice. As she bellowed and roared the sound echoed round the roof. I was standing next to Prim during one of the hymns, and I was alarmed when her head dropped forward and she began to shiver. I thought it must be the cold, and I had better take her out before she fainted. Then I bent to look at her face, and realised that she was shaking with suppressed laughter.

She said afterwards, "I have never heard anything like those high notes. I thought I should have to go out at one point in case I laughed aloud. She is probably the mainstay of the singing in winter when there are no visitors, so I really ought not to have laughed, but I couldn't help it!"

After more rain, hail, and a thunderstorm, the afternoon cleared. Optimistically, we assumed that it would remain that way, so that we could go and gather primroses for Prim's birthday, which was the next day. John Robert told us that the best ones grew on the banks in the little lane to Santon Bridge, and the Bridge Inn served very good teas.

"I shall walk," Cop said. "It isn't far to Santon bridge, and I need some exercise."

"I'll go with you," Daisy offered.

"I'm a mountaineer, not a road walker," I said, and Prim said, "Me, too."

Cop and Daisy set off, and the rest of us went in May's car. On arriving at the banks where the primroses grew, May let us out to pick some, while she drove on to the Bridge Inn to order tea. We had each gathered a bunch when she returned to tell us that the Bridge Inn did not serve teas. I was saying what I thought of John Robert when Cop and Daisy strode round the bend.

"No tea!" we said, and Daisy replied cheerfully, "Oh, well, we'll just walk back again."

We protested, though half-heartedly, that it was only fair that some of us should walk back while they rode, but this was airily waved aside by Cop.

"We prefer to walk. We are enjoying it."

So we let them.

"What next?" asked May, looking at Prim.

"It seems a shame to come out for tea and not get any. What about going to Gosforth?"

"Shall we get it there?"

Prim shrugged.

"We can try. If not Gosforth we could go somewhere else."
"What about Cop and Daisy?"
"They said they would rather walk!"
May said, "In any case, my car does not have elastic sides."
In Gosforth we had an amazingly good tea at a house called Row Head, and got back to Strands to find Cop and Daisy sitting by the fire. Prim then said, "Anyone coming for a walk? Perhaps you two have had enough for one day, and would rather not," but they said they were quite willing.
"Some people are gluttons for punishment," I commented, causing Cop to eye me disdainfully.
"Some people are bone idle!"
"Oh, I am," I agreed, "but I don't mind staggering a few steps."
We went down the lane by Easethwaite Farm, diving into the barn when a sudden storm swept over, then going towards the lake, squelching through the deep mud. We had no sooner reached the water than black clouds seethed over the Gable and we retreated, again sheltering in the barn until the storm had passed, then racing pell-mell back to Strands, arriving two seconds before the rain lashed down once more.
"Well," said Prim cheerfully, "we are enjoying the worst Easter weather for years!"
It was a pity that Miss Wilkinson had cream-coloured lino in her hall.

* * *

Cop saluted Prim's birthday by serenading her outside the bedroom door. I said later that it had sounded exactly like the noise a cat makes when somebody treads on its tail.
"It did not! I can sing! Prim said she appreciated it very much!"
"You should remember that Prim is naturally polite."
"No one could say the same about you!" she retorted.
For Daisy's first hill walk, we chose Harter Fell. May took Doris in her car and John Robert took the rest of us, and we met at the Woolpack and lingered over coffee.
The beck at the foot of Hard Knott was running wild, but we found a good crossing lower down the valley, and then cut up steeply to the Harter track. It was a good day to be on the hills, a mad day with a strong, wild wind.
We were going well when we had to stop to attend to Doris, who had cut her leg on a bracken stalk and was bleeding copiously.

When she had been plastered she and May decided that they had had enough, and we asked Daisy if she would like to go back, too, but she replied, "Certainly not!" And the four of us went on.

On Harter top the wind screamed round the rocks, but we found a fairly sheltered hollow in the sun at the foot of a buttress. Cop wanted to take Prim's photograph because it was her birthday; so Prim climbed the buttress and obligingly posed with feet balanced on two spikes of rock, and called, "For heaven's sake hurry before the wind blows me off!"

Then the three of us did a little rock scrambling while Daisy watched, no doubt wondering why we felt the urge to climb up and down rocks when there was no need.

Strolling down Harter, we rejoiced over the snowy Scafells, austerely white beneath a band of thunderous black cloud. For that view alone it would have been worth climbing anything.

At Brotherilkeld we rejoined May and Doris for tea, after which they drove back to Strands while we walked down to the Woolpack to telephone for John Robert, and to have a drink while we waited for him. Unfortunately, the gale had put the Woolpack telephone out of order, and the next one was at Boot. Prim promptly button-holed John Armstrong, and we were driven to Boot, where the telephone at Sim's Garage was working, and in due course John Robert collected us.

That night, the Wilkinsons brought in a birthday cake for Prim, and the sherry circulated. There was a sing-song and a lot of larking about, which became more rowdy after the Wilkinsons had retired. It was very late when we went to bed.

* * *

John Robert always cleaned and laid the sitting-room fire before we got up in the morning, and the noise he made was better than any alarm clock. May, who slept directly above the sitting-room, said he sounded like an elephant in clogs.

On our last day, we chose the walk along the top of the Screes, John Robert and May providing transport up the hill from Santon Bridge to the beginning of the Irton Pike track. We followed the grassy ride, skirting the plantations on Irton Pike to the open moorland, where a track comes up from Wasdale and goes over into Miterdale. Where the two tracks crossed, Doris and May called a halt.

"We'll go back to the car and drive somewhere, and you can go on. Break your necks if you like!"

"Where will you go?" I asked.

"Mind your own business!"

May was always refreshingly rude.

They turned back as we began the long upward slant. The sun lit every fell except the one we were on, which was in shadow — a very minor detail when the bleached grass was rippling, larks were singing, and we were on the hills. Nothing else mattered. We picnicked by the cairn on Whin Rigg, with the awesome view down the gully to the lake, nearly two thousand feet below.

A mile or so brought us to Illgill Head. This is the best way to walk the Screes, for you face the great fells. That day, they were placid giants asleep in the sun. Our fell alone remained in shadow. After dropping through gorse and bracken to the Burnmoor track and following it down to Wasdale, there was a mile of road walking to the Wastwater Inn for tea. We showed Daisy the pack-horse bridge over the Mosedale Beck, and the tiny church, and we named all the surrounding fells for her. When John Robert came to take us back to Strands the Screes were bathed in evening sunlight at last.

During our session over the green, Daisy bought a bottle of sherry, which, she said, would be useful later in the evening. The final dinner was riotous, causing Cop to comment, "If Miss Wilkinson did not think we were demented before, she certainly does now!"

"It's all the fresh air!" I said.

"It's all the silly asses!" corrected May.

After dinner came the sorting out of the holiday bill. Prim did this, ignoring a barrage of ribald suggestions from the rest of us. Next, when the sherry had circulated, she called for an S. L. Club meeting to discuss the question of Daisy's membership.

May said bluntly, "She can walk. I think she will do."

"Perhaps she doesn't want to be associated with a gang of lunatics," put in Doris.

Prim turned to Daisy, who was looking self-conscious. "Would you like to become a member of the club?"

"Oh yes, please!" came the answer. "I've never been on holiday with people like you!"

"I'm not surprised!" said Cop.

Daisy was duly elected.

Then Prim gave a review of the holiday, and outlined some ideas for the next one, pausing at intervals to request Cop to be quiet. Cop, meanwhile, was giving an impassioned speech on mountains to anyone who would listen, and talking so fast that she was stuttering. Then May began imitating Cop, and gesticulated so wildly that she kicked a tray of cups and saucers into the hearth. At this point, Prim declared the meeting closed.

One by one, we drifted off to pack. I went last, and found Daisy already in bed trying to go to sleep. After strewing all my gear on my bed there was no space in which to fold anything, so I asked Daisy if I could put some things on her bed. She readily agreed, saying, "I've never been packed on before!"

I assumed that she then went to sleep, for I finished packing and sat reading a guide-book, and was startled when a small voice said, "Can I turn over now?" I had forgotten about Daisy.

In the small hours, Prim and I crept downstairs, with every single stair giving a loud creak, and finished off the sherry.

We never heard the cuckoo that holiday, and there were no warm days of dalliance on the tops, but when we left Strands there was an ache in our hearts.

FULL HOUSE

We had a new recruit, we were prepared for last minute absences, and then, the next Easter, the unexpected happened. For the first time, the eight members of the S. L. Club were together at Strands.

On a misty April morning the two cars headed north, Hilda and Doris travelling with May, and Cath bringing Prim and me. We chose the Scotch Corner route, and found winter lingering in the Pennines, with snow banked high at the roadsides, but when we saw gleams of sunlight in the west we began planning expeditions, a fascinating topic which lasted all the way to Strands.

The sitting-room looked spruce, neat and impersonal until our gear was unpacked. Then it became our club room. After dinner, we collected Daisy, who had come by train to Seascale. She and Cop were to sleep out, at a house a quarter of a mile down the lane. Miss Wilkinson had arranged this because she could not provide beds for eight people. Seven was her limit. Cop had volunteered to go with Daisy to keep her company, but she would be alone for the first night as Cop would not arrive until the next morning.

During the evening, many possible walks were discussed, enthusiastically or otherwise. I wanted to try the West Wall Traverse on Scafell, and Cath thought the High Level Route on Pillar would be good. Daisy listened and said nothing.

"I am not going to break my neck this year," Doris announced flatly.

"We will let Cis and her gang do that!" put in May.

I turned to Hilda. "What about you?"

"Well, I am a bit out of practice, but I suppose I will go where you go — it depends on where, though!"

Prim said quietly, "No doubt we shall think of places where all of you wish to go."

"Well," said Hilda, looking round, "is everything settled then? I think I shall go quietly to bed now. Is anyone else coming?"

Cath pointed out that nothing whatever had been settled, but by then Hilda, May, Doris and Daisy had gone.

"There's enthusiasm for you!" I exploded, and rounded on Prim.

"Why didn't you suggest a definite walk?"

"I shall, in due course, probably two!"

"As and Bs?"

"That's right. It is getting to be that way, but that is inevitable."

The three of us stayed up until the fire burnt out. We were dealing with the pros and cons of the West Wall Traverse.

* * *

The next morning, Cop arrived, having travelled on the night train. The railways had not then been senselessly mutilated, and it was possible to get a sleeper from Euston to Seascale. Cop said she was fit and ready for anything.

"You lead and I'll follow! I don't care where!"

Unfortunately, it was beginning to rain, and the high tops were under heavy cloud. We had a preliminary leg-stretch down to the lake and back, and after lunch drove to Eskdale to walk by the river to St. Catherine's. The rain had lessened to a fine drizzle, and, as always, the walk was a delight, but the high fells, the great ones for which our hearts yearned, remained veiled.

Of course we had tea at the Woolpack, where Prim was accused by Cop of coming to Eskdale solely for the good food.

Prim looked at Cop gobbling fruit cake, and laughed.

"But aren't you glad we came?"

"I shall not be when it is dinner time, and I am not hungry!"

"Then stop making a pig of yourself now!" I said, which nettled her.

"In future I shall not have any cake for tea, and I shall not have any more scones — not ever!"

"Who cares?" I said, and she glared, and helped herself to another cake.

"Starting tomorrow!" she said, with her mouth full.

That evening, we planned what we would do if the weather turned idyllic. We would have a glorious day over the tops in brilliant sunshine.

"Suppose we don't have an idyllic day?" asked a pessimist.

"There is always Buckbarrow!" retorted Prim.

That night the wind howled, the windows rattled, and with the morning came heavy and frequent showers. Prim said, "We'll go down to Seascale and have coffee at the Scawfell Hotel," and there were no objections, as no one could think of anything better to do. When we arrived back at lunch-time Prim banged her head on the sharp corner of the car door and sliced through her eyebrow. We rendered first aid, but the cut was very deep, so after lunch we took her to the Gosforth doctor to have a stitch put in it. The sticking plaster over the eyebrow gave her a dissipated look, "As though she has been in a brawl," Cop said.

We went back to Strands, and joined the others round the fire.

"There's nothing to stop any of you going for a good walk, if you feel you need some exercise," said Prim, looking at Cop.

"Personally. I don't want any."

"Have you a headache?"

"No, I feel very comfortable, and lazy."

Apparently, no one wished for exercise. Some read or knitted, while others lolled around doing nothing, and gradually we began to irritate each other, interrupting the readers and making rude comments. Then I went to my bedroom, and returned with a sheaf of papers.

"I'll give you something to do! You are not using your legs, so you can use your brains. Here are three new 'Lakeland Quizzes'. You should do the lot in half an hour."

They spoke in chorus.

"Good!" (Prim).

"It will be a change to do something!" (Cath).

"It is a pity you haven't something better to do than invent these quizzes!" (Cop).

"I can never think of the answers!" (Hilda).

"My memory is awful these days!" (Doris).

"You are a sickening nuisance!" (May).

"What are 'Lakeland Quizzes'?" (Daisy).

"I'll tell you!" Cop exclaimed. 'The president exercises our legs, and the sec. looks after our minds. She expects us to know every piffling little detail to do with the Lakes. It's worse than the Spanish Inquisition!"

"But I don't know much about the Lake District yet," said Daisy, looking alarmed.

"Don't worry," I told her. "If you don't know the answers, just copy from your neighbour. Everyone else does!"

I gave out the papers, and with a mixture of eagerness, apathy, and groans, they set to work. Prim soon finished, and we began, *sotto voce,* to discuss unusual walks. When I called 'Time!' there was such an uproar of protest that I let them carry on for the next hour.

"It's one way of getting a little peace!" I said to Prim.

Finally, we checked the answers, which apart from Prim's, were a disgrace. They scored most on the quiz about the names of Lakeland inns.

"Anyone would think you had never been near the fells!" Cop retorted, "We come to climb the mountains, not to think."

"I'm delighted that you don't come to attempt the impossible!"

May cut in, "Don't start arguing, you two. I've been thinking so hard that I'm worn out!"

It was a crush for eight people to get round the sitting-room fire. Some of the easy chairs were very comfortable, others were less so, and one person had to make do with a plain wooden chair. Daisy was usually the one, averring that she did not mind in the least. She sat quietly on the uncomfortable wooden chair while the rest of us jockeyed for position like a rugger scrum. We thought that in time, when she was used to us, she would no longer be so polite.

* * *

Though a sharp-toothed wind prowled wolfishly down the valley, it was actually fine.

"Buckbarrow," said Prim, which provoked Cop to scorn.

"What! A tiddly little thing like that!"

"Buckbarrow to start with."

"And then where?"

"And then we shall see."

"What shall we see?" Cop persisted.

"We shall see where we go next!"

"Shut up, Cop," I said. "You talk for the sake of talking."

Doris cut in, "I'm not going on a route march."

"You can all go just as far as you wish," Prim said mildly, "We are doing this for pleasure, you know. It is not an endurance test."

As a group we got on well together. We enjoyed being together, because we liked each other, but I never envied Prim her role as leader. She needed plenty of tact at times.

We cut over the fields and went up Buckbarrow, a fine top achieved by a minimum of effort, and ate our sandwiches on the rocks crowning the precipitous face which juts arrogantly above the dale. Then the party divided. Doris, Hilda and May made their way back to the valley via the far side of Buckbarrow, having been warned to circle round to Greendale Tarn before beginning the descent, in order to avoid becoming entangled in a network of ravines. The rest of us, after visiting the cairn on Cat Bields, went up thick, bumpy grass to Seatallan.

Buffeted by a mighty wind, we sat for a while by the immense cairn. Being a comparatively isolated fell, Seatallan provided a perfect viewpoint, and visibility was excellent. The entire range of the Scafells was ours.

Cutting directly down through boulders, bog and swamp, we dropped swiftly to the valley. Before us, the Screes filled the horizon with a backcloth of dark brown velvet. After tea at Greendale, we walked back over the moor, thus encountering yet more bog.

Not a strenuous day, but an enjoyable one. The wind had reddened our faces, and made us so comatose that instead of the usual backchat, argument, and general larking about after dinner I was asked to read aloud. Some listened quietly, while others went unashamedly to sleep.

* * *

We went to Keswick for a celebration lunch to mark the coming of age of Sally's Ladies. Although this twenty-first anniversary applied only to Prim, Cath, Cop and myself, the four originals, the others were more than willing to participate. They said they did not intend to be left out of any S. L. Club celebration, whatever its nature.

In a bitterly cold Keswick we went round to various hotels, studied their menus and made disparaging comments. Finally we chose the King's Arms, which offered food and drink more to our liking. Some drank very little ("It doesn't really suit me." "Just a very small glass then.") which meant more for those who liked it, so everyone was happy.

Toasts were drunk to the President, Sally's Ladies, and Sally Coates. The President made a much interrupted speech recalling the early days of the club and its subsequent achievements. Then she presented Daisy with a club badge. This made Daisy blush furiously and stammer, "What a surprise! Thank you very much. I do hope I shall live up to it!" after which we drank the health of the new member.

The club badge depicted a Viking ship set in a circle. No one could remember why we had chosen a Viking ship, except that the

Vikings were wanderers, and so were we. We were supposed to wear our badges at all meetings and reunions, but there was always someone who forgot and left hers at home. They were not taken very seriously.

After lunch, we drove slowly up Borrowdale, commenting on every crag and fell, almost on every boulder, in a veritable orgy of nostalgia. At Grange we went over the bridge to Scarthwaite, looked at the house where we had spent so many golden hours, and turned silently away to continue up the valley to Seathwaite, where dark clouds hung low over the so familiar fells.

We told Daisy how often we had hurtled down from the tops and rushed into the farm, clamouring for tea before dashing madly to Seatoller to catch the last bus down the dale.

"Those were the days!" I said.

"And what days!" Doris said. "You never knew what those four would make you do next. They dragged me up Rossett Gill in a howling blizzard!"

"They got me soaked to the skin, and lost; and they ruined my best shoes!" exclaimed Hilda.

May cut in, "I suffered worse than any of you! They made me do the Gable Traverse and broke my toe nails — on my first walk, too!"

By then Daisy was looking rather apprehensive, though she tried to be flippant. "I expect my turn will come, and they will probably make me break my neck."

Cop said solemnly, "Anything could happen! We break all our members in, one way or another. We believe in trial by ordeal."

I gave Daisy a reassuring pat on the back. "Don't take any notice. You will not be expected to do the impossible. Besides, we are much kinder than we used to be!"

"Thank goodness for that!" she said fervently.

We left Borrowdale and turned to the west, to the gold of evening. As the intrinsic beauty of Borrowdale would never change, so would our love remain unaltered, but it was with profound contentment that we returned to the austere, spellbinding grandeur of Wasdale.

* * *

Hilda's short holiday was over, and on a grey, blustery morning we put her on the train at Seascale. I felt sorry for her, having to go while we remained, especially as the weather had prevented her from doing anything exciting, but she was philosophical about it.

"I don't mind not getting in a big walk. Just to be with you all again has been as good as any tonic."

In the afternoon, we drove to Eskdale and climbed the rake at the back of the Woolpack, with the bitter east wind whistling about our ears. I noticed that May was making heavy weather of the uphill going, and looked pale and strained. I thought she had had enough, and I called to the others who were forging ahead, "This is a mug's game in this wind. We are not going anywhere in particular, are we?"

"Only round Eel Tarn," answered Prim.

"Well, I'm going back. Anyone else coming?"

"Yes!" said May promptly.

If I had suggested that she went back, she would have told me to go to hell, but thinking that I was the one willing to abandon the walk gave her an excuse to do likewise.

"Cowards!" yelled Cop.

"Get lost!" I yelled back.

They went on, and May and I began to retrace our steps. When we came to a high wall which gave some shelter we sat behind it. May soon complained.

"It's jolly cold."

"No, it isn't."

I was beginning to wonder how far the others had got, and half-wishing I had gone with them.

"Why are we sitting under this wall?"

"We are bird-watching," I answered flippantly.

May jeered.

"You wouldn't know the difference between a crow and a rook! In any case, there are no birds here, except that solitary stonechat on the boulder over there."

"We'll watch that then!"

We sat in silence, until the cold began to bite, and I suggested that we drove to the foot of Hard Knott. May gave me a blank stare.

"What for?"

"To paddle in the beck!"

"You silly fool!" she said, with a return of her old spirit. "Still," she added, "it would be warmer waiting in the car than sitting under this wall."

We drove to Hard Knott, and while she sat in the car I pottered up the beck until I estimated that the others would have had time to return from Eel Tarn, and we could meet at the Woolpack for tea.

Afterwards, we drove to Ravenglass, where it was even colder

than in Eskdale.
It was late April, but where, oh, where was the spring?

* * *

The pleasure of walking had become a penance, while loitering meant streaming noses and chattering teeth.

After calling at the Gosforth surgery to have Prim's stitch removed, we went via Loweswater to Lanthwaite Green to explore Gaskell Gill, but made very little progress before iced rocks forced us to retreat. Flurries of snow were eddying over the Red Pike-High Stile-High Crag range, and the sky was grey and bitter. We drove on to Buttermere village, where many people were drifting aimlessly around. Our once quiet Buttermere had become the victim of hordes of trippers, and never again would we find there the peaceful solitude we had loved.

Cop began dancing from one foot to the other, impatient to be doing something.

"Who is coming for a walk?"

"Where?"

"Oh, anywhere. We could go round the lake."

"I'm not walking round any damn lake," I said.

"Neither am I," said Prim.

The others were willing to go, and they set off, muttering scornfully about people who never walked anywhere unless they could go to the top of something. Prim and I went to the Fish Inn for a drink, and toasted ourselves by a blazing fire. Knowing how long it took to circle the lake, we allowed ourselves enough time to get to the water's edge to meet the others as they returned full of virtue.

"It was a marvellous walk!"

"It was not windy on the far side!"

"You should have come!"

"Yes, we know," we said, and trooped into the Bridge Hotel for tea.

On the way back to Strands the grass on Cold Fell was white with snow, and I pitied the tiny lambs newly born into a world so bleak. With imagination, one could see the faintest touch of green on the larches, and there were primroses under the shelter of the hedges, but the first wild daffodils were in distress, for the wind had laid them flat.

* * *

On our last day there was fresh snow on Seatallan and the Screes, and the Scafells were lost in murky haze. Climbing up anything was definitely out. Fine snowflakes were drifting across the green at Strands. Because we had to do something, we walked to Santon Bridge and back, though no sane person would have gone out at all.

"That is enough exercise for today," I said, when we got back to our sitting-room. But in the afternoon, with the exception of Prim who hated intense cold, the others put on every warm garment they possessed, and set off to Greendale for tea.

Prim and I dug in by the fire, and were most surprised when the others returned much sooner than we expected. They were grumbling about a fruitless walk, as there had been no one at home at Greendale.

"You should have gone into the kitchen and made yourselves some tea. Mrs Smith would not have minded. She told us we could always do that if she was not there," said Prim.

"She never said that to me!" retorted Cop.

"You never listen to what people say," I reminded her.

"I never like going in other people's kitchens!"

"That's a half-witted excuse!"

Cath said, "Perhaps Miss Wilkinson will make us some tea."

"And perhaps pigs will fly!"

"She's out, anyway."

May cut in, "For heaven's sake stop arguing about tea, and let me get to the fire. I'm frozen!" and she surged forward like a battering ram. We scattered, and she crouched over the fire, which was blazing half-way up the chimney.

Three ambulances went up to Wasdale Head that day to deal with five people who had fallen down Lord's Rake. Four died, and the fifth was taken to hospital with a fractured skull. It was a sobering thought, and made us realise the value of the mountain craft we had acquired over the years. There was a time for the high tops and there was a time to avoid them. They were not for us that year — no lofty heights; no long, strenuous days; no exploration off the beaten track — but did it really matter?

Welcoming or forbidding; friendly or terrifying; they were the mountains we loved; and, whatever their mood, to be in Wasdale, close to them, was in itself the sufficient beauty.

SUMMER PARTING

That Easter the eight members of the S. L. Club had been together at Strands for the first time, but it was never to happen again. Our number was reduced to seven, because we lost May.

At the Easter gathering she had been below form. She seemed abnormally tired, more subdued, and very much quieter than usual. On returning home after the holiday, her condition deteriorated rapidly. She was hospitalised and underwent operations, but without success. She died at the end of the summer.

We were profoundly shocked and saddened. She had never missed an Easter meeting of the club, and her going would leave a great gap.

But a second shock was in store for me, sudden and totally unexpected.

A couple of days before the funeral I spent the day in London, and arrived home at 10.30 p.m. to find the telephone ringing. It was May's sister, and she said that she had been trying to contact me all day, and I wondered why.

She said, "May used to tell us all about your Easter gatherings. She would not have missed one for the world. She loved the walking, and all the carrying on there used to be in the evening. Most of all, she loved the way you read aloud at night."

"I'm glad she did," I said, feeling the first prickle of apprehension.

She went on, "So we would like you to read the lesson at the funeral. I am sure she would have wanted you to do that."

I was utterly dismayed, and wanted to say that I could not possibly do it. At the same time, I could see no way out, and I knew that I could not refuse. It was the final thing I could do for May.

"Very well," I said, "if you would like me to do it, I will," and I spent the next two days worrying about it.

The funeral service was in the village church at Thrumpton, where May had lived, and all the villagers were present. The church was full.

The S. L. Club sat in the front pew. Their trained voices led the singing of the hymn, until something happened which filled me with alarm. One by one, their voices faltered and faded, and died away. They could not go on singing. It was understandable, but after the hymn there would be the lesson, a solo effort on my part, and I had to do well. If I allowed myself to falter, I could almost imagine May saying, "What are you playing at, you silly idiot!"

The hymn ended. I read the long lesson. I sailed through it without any difficulty, but when it was over I felt weak-kneed with relief.

So went May, after all our happy days together. We should miss her dry humour and uninhibited manner of speech. We should miss slanging and cursing each other, which we often did, though entirely without malice. She was a stoic, and on the fells we must at times have driven her almost beyond the limit of physical endurance, but she never complained. She loved the mountains, and was part of the warm fellowship of Sally's Ladies.

She had guts!

ARCTIC EASTER

For several years our activities had been severely curtailed by poor weather conditions at Easter, and this, fortunately the last in that succession of Nature's spring freaks, was no exception. In fact, it was the worst of the lot. It was just as well that we had no advance knowledge of how bad it was going to be, though had we known it would have made no difference. We should still have gone to Wasdale.

Hilda and Doris being unavailable, there were five of us. Cop and Daisy were coming from London by train. Prim and I, in Cath's car, were not exactly in top form, though we were a good average. She had had her appendix out six weeks before, while I was recovering from what the doctor diagnosed as a frozen shoulder syndrome. I never knew exactly what that meant, but it was extremely painful during the fortnight it lasted.

We arrived at Strands on a calm, clear evening when our beloved fells looked glorious under a cloud-dappled sky, and anyone would have said that we could expect a spell of good weather. Cop and Daisy had got there before us, and came out to lend a hand with the luggage.

"Well, I've got them here in one piece," Cath said, pointing to us. "I feel as though I have been driving an ambulance!"

"To an emergency, judging by the speed!" I retorted.

We had purposely made a late start from Nottingham, because Cath had a powerful car and was a fast driver, and we had done the journey in record time.

No plans for walks were put forward that evening. Prim had nothing to suggest, saying, "I don't know what I am going to do yet. I haven't had time to think about it."

This brought an unsympathetic comment from Cop.

"As you and Cis don't seem up to the mark, we had better think of some nice, easy little walks!"

"Not likely!" put in Cath. "I intend to do some decent walking!"

When asked where she proposed to go, she said she didn't know, and didn't care, either, as long as it was high and good.

Cop enthusiastically agreed.

"That goes for me, too. So long as we are out and really doing something it does not matter whether we have an objective or not."

"But it helps!" I said, and turned to Daisy.

"Is there anything in particular you would like to do?"

Daisy gave an amiable shrug and shook her head.

"No, I am quite happy to go along with the herd. I think you are all mad, anyway."

"She is learning fast!" came an aside from Cop.

No dedicated walker would have felt at home with Sally's Ladies, because we never took things seriously enough. It was strange that, with our widely differing temperaments, we should blend so completely into a strong group. The core of our unity lay in our deep love for the fells.

Later, in an aside to Prim, I asked, "How much walking — real walking — do you think you will feel like doing?"

"That all depends."

"Depends on how you feel, I suppose."

"No," she replied, smiling, "on the weather!"

*   *   *

It began with a windy day when the rain never stopped.

Having passed the morning in the sitting-room, stoking the fire until flames roared up the chimney, and making John Robert stump in with a fresh supply of logs because we had emptied the wood box, we faced the distasteful prospect of being house-bound for the rest of the day. This was the kind of situation when things were apt to get out of control, so Cath, in desperation, suggested, "Let's go to Gosforth!"

"What is there to do there?"

"Why Gosforth?"

"Well, anywhere you like, then," Cath said. "You say where you would like to go."

As no suggestions were forthcoming, Cath jumped to her feet.

"I am not going to sit here doing nothing all afternoon. I am going to Gosforth!"

So we all went to Gosforth, where we sat in the car park and watched the raindrops making miniature fountains as they bounced on the asphalt. It was not fit to get out of the car. Soon Cath had had enough.

"We can't walk, and it is too miserable to drive anywhere. Shall we go back?"

We returned to Strands, and I was asked to read aloud, which I did until they became first restive, then argumentative, then rowdy — and I stopped.

That was the first day wasted.

By morning the rain had ceased, but the wind remained to make eyes stream and noses run. In the afternoon, Prim suggested that we went to Greendale.

"Suppose Mrs Smith isn't in when we get there?" someone asked.

"That will not matter. We know where the kitchen is and we can make some tea. We will not go across the moor this time. I'd like to do some exploring, and find a different way. There is sure to be one."

She led us along the lane by Mill Place, after which the going was rough. Occasionally, we saw vague signs of a track, which we crossed because it was not going the way we wanted to go. We picked an oozy way through expanses of deep mud impossible to circumvent, and climbed several walls. This obstacle course brought us exactly to Greendale, where Mrs Smith was delighted to see us, and promptly put on the kettle and gave us a sumptuous tea.

"Are we going to find another new way back?" Daisy sounded rather anxious, and Prim laughed.

"No, we'll go the usual way over the moor, but after that I'd like to try something different — when we get near the end."

In spite of the buffeting wind, we enjoyed the walk back and were able to maintain a reasonable pace until, beyond the moor, Prim began prospecting for any kind of track which would avoid the half mile of road walking and lead back to Strands. She found one, and once more we went ankle deep in mud. This we did not mind, as our feet and legs could not have got more filthy than they already were.

In our Scarthwaite days, Mrs Coates used to take us to task over the state of our foot-gear.

"You are like children, you always go through all the mud you can find!"

But Mrs Coates had a son-in-law who always saw to the cleaning of our boots and shoes. At Strands we had to do it ourselves, or leave it. We generally did the latter, as most of the mud fell off when it dried.

* * *

Hail hammered against the windows during the night, and in the morning fresh snow lay along the Screes. The devilish wind roared unabated. We braved it as far as the lake, but had to fight our way back against gusts which almost swept us from our feet. Once indoors, we spent the rest of the morning discussing the Mosedale fells. Talking was all we could do about them, talking and cursing the weather.

During the afternoon, after everyone had been gorging small chocolate Easter eggs because there was nothing better to do, Cath, Cop and Daisy decided to go for a walk. They set out, and five minutes later a vicious storm of sleet brought them rushing back, with Cop in a thoroughly bad mood.

"This is absolutely sickening! If I can't get up the mountains, I might as well go home!"

I said, "I have heard you say some silly things over the years, but that is the silliest!"

She pondered this for a while, then admitted, "I didn't really mean that. It is good to be near the mountains, even if we can't get up them."

"Now you are talking sense," I said.

"I might as well go on stuffing myself with Easter eggs."

After tea, Prim pointed out that the sleet had stopped and it was fine again.

"You could still go for a walk."

"Are you coming?"

She shook her head. "I've done my fighting for the day."

"Where are you going?" I asked, and they looked at each other.

"Oh, probably along by the Screes," Cath said. "Are you coming?"

"I've been there once today. Now if you were going somewhere like the Pike I might be tempted."

They told me not to talk like an idiot, and started out, somewhat hampered by all the clothes they were wearing. They walked what we called the triangle — down to the lake, along the main Wasdale road, and back by the cut-through lane to Strands. It was all road walking. When they returned we went over the green for a drink.

We loved the Strands Hotel bar-kitchen, with its old, polished range and its rocking chair, and we loved the appetising aroma of cooking which came from the real kitchen. It seemed more mouth-watering each night, and we sipped and sniffed with appreciation, speculating on what was being roasted.

"Roast chicken with all the trimmings," I guessed.

"A pity we can't change over and stay here," Cop said, and looked at Prim.

"Can't we?"

Prim shook her head. "You know we can't just walk out on the Wilkinsons."

* * *

Throughout the holiday to the last day the sleet and snow continued until the fells were white from head to foot. We should have enjoyed walking in the snow, had it not been for the gale-force wind. To be out in it was devitalising.

"I'm staying put!" I said, and firmly resisted all attempts to make me change my mind. Prim had already dug in by the fire, but the other three, muffled to the ears, ventured out, with Cop grumbling, "I'm not going to walk that flipping triangle again!" and Cath retorting, "You needn't come. You can always go for a walk by yourself."

"Go and pioneer a new route!" I shouted after them, and was told to mind my business.

They did the triangle again.

After lunch, we went to Eskdale, and attempted to go by the river to St. Catherine's, but I gave up at Doctor Bridge. My eyes were streaming and we were facing the wind. I went back to sit in the car and watch the Woolpack daffodils being blown out of the ground.

Ten minutes later a violent hailstorm brought the others rushing back. The walk was abandoned, and we went into the Woolpack for tea. Then we drove up to Wasdale Head. The white mountains rose coldly aloof. They had a terrible, beautiful magnetism, but for us they were forbidden territory. Deep snow lay on Beck Head and Black Sail, and a swirl of dark cloud was caught on the Mickledore ridge. We gazed our fill, then turned back down the valley.

It had been a holiday full of frustration, with too many hours wasted in the sitting-room, where we had burnt at least a whole load of logs. Everyone had tried to sit nearest to the fire, and any movement had brought howls of protest.

"Don't tread on the Easter eggs!"

"Don't tread on the ashtray!"

"Mind my feet!"

"Sit down, you clumsy idiot!"

Cop exclaimed, "The only climbing I am doing this holiday is over the backs of the chairs!"

This started a game of trying to cross the room without your feet touching the floor. As the room was full of furniture, it necessitated some complicated gymnastics. It was amazing that no damage was done either to ourselves or the furniture. Often Miss Wilkinson must have wondered what we were doing.

On the whole we remained cheerful and had fun, but it was not sufficient, and we went home consumed by an overwhelming need. We could not wait for another year. It was an eternity away, and the call of the hills was too strong. We had to get to the Lakes again — soon!

HEAT WAVE

As soon as we reached home after that grim, unfriendly Easter, we began considering the possibilities of another short holiday in the late spring. After we had discussed it thoroughly, Prim telephoned to Cop, in London, to ask, "Are you willing to come to the Lakes for a week to do as much climbing and walking as possible?" Cop asked if she meant all the members of the S. L. Club, and Prim said, "No, just the four of us." The answer was a joyful, "You bet I'll be there!"

We did not mind where we stayed, as long as it was among the fells, and Prim was requested to go ahead and make the arrangements. As Strands would have other, no doubt better-behaved, visitors, she chose the Loweswater area, which would be new ground for us. We knew it could not be compared to Wasdale, and anticipated that it would be more pastoral and therefore tamer. We should have known better.

One Saturday in late May, the four of us and our luggage set off in Cath's car, and it rained without stopping all the way from Scotch Corner to Scale Hill Hotel, at Loweswater. We, being in high spirits, laughed about it, saying, "We may as well get all the rain over at one go!" Any regular visitor to the Lakes is bound to be an optimist.

We were put in the hotel annexe because the main building was full, and over the weekend we shared a very large bedroom for four. There was still plenty of space after all our gear had been spread around, and the four beds were literally yards apart.

Sleeping four in a room was hilarious. Cop said, "I feel as though I am back at school in the dorm, and someone will come in any minute to see that we are not up to mischief."

Prim asked, "Does anyone snore?"

"Cis does," said Cath rudely.

"That is a lie."

Cop said, "Anyone who snores will be sloshed with a wet towel!"

"I'd like to see you do it!"

She got out of bed, and was reaching for a towel when Prim intervened. "If you want to fight go into the yard, and let other people go to sleep."

Cop subsided, muttering, "I'll keep the towel handy!"

"Oh, shut up!" Cath said.

* * *

The hedgerows were adrift with wild flowers. The verdance of full spring lay on the land, charging the air with the perfume of new growth. Doing a little preliminary wandering on the first morning, we followed a footpath through Lanthwaite Woods to Crummockwater. We disliked the heavy airlessness under the trees, but delighted in the view from the lakeside, where beyond the calm water majestic Grasmoor dwarfed the neighbouring fells.

After lunch, Prim proposed a walk to Buttermere which would avoid all regular footpaths. By going diagonally through the woods, we should be cutting out two sides of a triangle. This foray, which involved crashing through thick undergrowth and wall climbing, was enjoyable, but brought us all too soon to the lakeside road, which was thronged with cars. To avoid these, we climbed Grasmoor's lower slopes and went along the fell-side, high above the road.

It was a sultry afternoon, and as we neared Buttermere ominous black clouds started to seethe over the summit of Red Pike. They were coming our way, so we dropped to the road and began to hurry, and had reached the belt of trees not far from the village when a thunderstorm broke in a deluge of rain. We were just passing the drive to a house, and a few yards down the drive was an empty garage. We rushed inside to shelter.

The rain hammered on the roof as though it would never stop, and we stood in the garage for what seemed a very long time — until Prim lost patience.

"We look like being here all night!" she exclaimed, and dashed out into the rain.

"Where has she gone?" demanded Cop.

"Towards Buttermere."

"She will get very wet!"

Lightning flashed, thunder rolled, the rain fell, and we went on waiting.

"She will get very wet!"

"You said that before!"

"Why has she gone to Buttermere?"

"How the hell should I know," I said. "Ask her when she comes back!"

Twenty minutes later she returned, not on foot but sitting beside the driver in a van. She had run to the Bridge Hotel and contacted the owner, who had then instructed his son to drive us back to Scale Hill in their van. So we escaped a soaking, and even Prim was no more than damp, having, as she said, gone like the wind to the hotel.

After dinner the storm had passed, leaving the sky washed clear and blue, and we went to look at Mellbreak, which we proposed to climb the following day. We noted that the steepest, most interesting route lay up the north shoulder, so that was the way we intended to go.

* * *

It was heat wave weather.

The north shoulder of Mellbreak gave easy going over short grass up to a band of scree. This was of the slippery variety on which it is difficult to get a firm foothold. However, by reverting to all fours, we were on the summit with surprisingly little effort.

Being an isolated fell, Mellbreak summit was an excellent viewpoint, with deep blue Crummockwater backed by a panorama of sunlit fells, our old friends from former years. Whiteside alone was unknown territory to us, and Prim studied its dark slopes with a speculative eye. It did not look particularly inviting, being dwarfed by its enormous neighbour Grasmoor.

We picnicked by the summit cairn before following the long saddle to the south top. Only the views saved that hot walk over trackless grass from complete boredom. From the south cairn we dropped, still on featureless grass, to the shore of Crummockwater.

Cath and Cop elected to return to Scale Hill by the lakeside path, but Prim and I decided to go in the opposite direction towards Buttermere.

"Aren't you going to finish the walk?" Cop demanded, but Prim merely smiled.

"I have finished it. I have done what I set out to do, which was to traverse Mellbreak."

"And I am not walking any lakeside path. It is much too hot?" I said.

It was further to Buttermere than we thought, though we made a bee-line for it, climbing walls and fences and crossing several streams. It made us very hot and thirsty, and it was a relief to sink into easy chairs in the lounge of the Bridge Hotel, and order a pot of tea — the largest pot they had, we said. They brought one which would have served six people, and we drained it.

"What next?" I asked.

"Next," said Prim, "we get ourselves back the easy way. I'll go and see about it."

The result was the owner's son driving us back to Scale Hill.

Cath and Cop, scarlet-faced, turned up soon after, grumbling about the lakeside path which, they said, consisted mainly of bog, and was more delusion than path. They clamoured for drinks and rushed into the bar, and we followed.

Cath exclaimed, "Surely you two are not thirsty after all that tea!" but we told her that had nothing to do with it.

* * *

It was difficult to feel enthusiastic about fell-climbing on a day so oppresively close, but there was Whiteside, and any fell new to us presented a challenge we could not resist.

Parking near Lanthwaite Green, we skirted a maze of intake walls and began to climb. To our annoyance we soon reached an impasse, because we had gone up the right side of Gasgale Gill when we should have been on the left. It was impossible to cross over, as the rocks dropped sheer to the water which entered a miniature ravine. Obviously, our route was not going to take us anywhere near Whiteside. We stood grumbling gently, because it was too hot to get thoroughly annoyed, and we argued.

"We must have started in the wrong place."

"It was the only way to come without going over all those walls."

"This side of the gill seems hopeless."

"What do we do next?"

"Do we go back and start again over those endless walls?"

"It would take us all morning."

There was silence. Suddenly, Prim said, "Blow Whiteside! let's go to Borrowdale!"

"I thought this was supposed to be a mountaineering holiday."

"So it is. All good mountaineers have a day off occasionally, and this is ours!"

We drove to Borrowdale, to find our once peaceful valley chock-a-block with cars, coaches, and people. If the river still sang over its stones, as no doubt it did, its music was lost. But in spite of the hordes there were still the unknown corners, still the small oases of unspoilt solitude. We knew them all, and sought an old favourite, where we picnicked on some large rocks high above the Stonethwaite beck. As each of us chose a different rock and these were far apart, we were not within speaking range, and anyone climbing up the rough fell-side would have assumed that we were four solitary hikers.

I would willingly have sat there for the rest of the afternoon, had not one of the others called, "Let's go to Seathwaite!" whereupon we came down the bouldery slope and went back to the car. At Seathwaite, Cath and Cop set off for Stockley Bridge, but Prim said she did not see the point of walking to Stockley Bridge and then having to come straight back. I agreed, and we sat on a bank and waited for them, and listened to the voice of Sour Milk Gill as it cascaded from Gillercombe and plunged headlong to the valley. By then the brightness had left the sun, and the mountains brooded under a heavy, brassy sky.

On the way back down Borrowdale, we went into the Lakeland Rural Industries showroom. I am not sure why, because we had no intention of buying anything, but while we were there a thunderstorm started. There was no rain, but the lightning was spectacular, particularly over the lake.

As we went over Whinlatter and turned west, we left the storm behind to rumble and growl among the hills. There had been no storm at Scale Hill.

* * *

We went up Whiteless Pike to lay a ghost. Some years ago, when we had come down Whiteless to Buttermere, several of Sally's Ladies had disliked it intensely. Hilda, in particular, having wrenched her knee on it, always referred to it with loathing. We had never understood why Hilda, May and Doris had made such a fuss, so we went up again to see if there was anything we had missed the first time.

There was nothing. It was exactly as we remembered, steep in parts, but good going on a foolproof path which quickly led to the summit and an excellent view which stretched from Helvellyn to the

Scafells. The only thing I disliked about going up Whiteless Pike was not the fell's fault. It was because the day was so hot that I was half boiled by the time we reached the top.

We lazed on the escarpment overlooking the ridge leading to Causey Pike, and talked of when we had walked that best of all ridges. For some reason, probably because of the heat, Cop was being awkward, and disagreeing with everything we said. We took no notice at first.

"I'd like to do that walk again," I said. "The finish was so good — Grasmoor, Wandope, Whiteless Pike, and down to Buttermere!"

"We did not come over Wandope," Cop said.

"We did, but you might not have noticed. The top is only a few stones on a plateau."

"We did not come over the top. We bypassed it."

I laughed. I felt too lazy to argue about nothing.

"You never know where you are going!"

"I know I have not been to the cairn on Wandope."

"All right, so you haven't."

"Oh, shut up, you two!" from Cath, but Cop would not stop.

"I know where I have been, and I know perfectly well that I have never been to the top of Wandope. I think we should go there this afternoon."

Cath and I said nothing, but Prim, with a gleam in her eye, looked at Cop.

"You want to do Wandope?"

"Yes, I've never done it!"

Prim got to her feet.

"Right!" I'll take you over Wandope, and as we are so near we will do Grasmoor, too."

"Good luck to you!" I said. "We'll see you in Buttermere when you come down!"

They moved off briskly, while Cath and I continued to absorb the view for a while before sauntering down Whiteless Pike. The track was like an uneven staircase, and we had a couple of rests on the way, because it was that sort of an afternoon and we were not in any hurry.

At Buttermere we sat on a grassy bank well away from the horde of tourists. Soon, we noticed two small dots very high under the skyline, and turned the binoculars on them. They were Prim and Cop, coming down like a cyclone, Prim leading and Cop stumbling gamely after. They seemed to flow down the fell-side.

"I'm glad I'm not Cop!" I said.

In an incredibly short time they were at road level, and we went to meet them. Cop, panting and fiery-faced, clamoured for tea. Prim, comparatively cool, had a wicked twinkle in her eye as she said in an aside to me, "Perhaps that will keep her quiet for a bit!"

* * *

"What about doing Crinkle Crags?" Prim suggested. "Cath has never done the Crinkles, and if we make it a there-and-back from the Three Shire Stone we might have time to include Bowfell as well."

It was a very warm day with the high tops misted, but we assumed it was heat haze which would clear as the sun got higher. We drove to Eskdale and up to the Woolpack, where we transferred to Alistair Armstrong's car, and were whizzed up over Hard Knott and up Wrynose to the Three Shire Stone. We fixed a time for Alistair to collect us at the end of the walk.

The mist persisted and intensified on the tops, though we remained convinced that it would clear. It was wishful thinking, for we were in thick, swirling cloud on the first Crinkle. It was a little difficult to see where we were going, but not impossible, and we enjoyed short-cutting the stony track and scrambling up to the cairn.

"Shall we eat our food here?" Cath asked.

"Perhaps the mist will have cleared when we are ready to go on."

"Then we can have a go at the Bad Step!"

But as we sat on the rocks, busy with sandwiches, the cloud thickened and darkened so rapidly that even the second Crinkle disappeared. Day was becoming night, and to make things worse there were several long rolls of thunder. We sat in silence, looking anxiously at Prim, who was peering into the gloom and frowning.

"What do we do?"

She gave a resigned shrug. "If it rains we shall get soaked, which is unimportant, but a storm could be quite nasty up here when we can't see where we are going. I think we had better go back."

There was a chorus of groans. Then, grumbling bitterly, we started back, walking very slowly, partly because we hated leaving the ridge and partly because we should be back at the Three Shire Stone long before Alistair arrived.

Near Red Tarn we climbed among the rocks for a lengthy rest. For the first time, we looked back at the distant Crinkles, and could scarcely believe our eyes. The mist had rolled away and every top was clear.

"Well, flaming hell!" I exclaimed. "They might have had the decency to stay hidden until we had left the district!"

Cop gave a long, wistful sigh. "We haven't time to go back — or have we?"

"You know we haven't. It is just our bad luck."

We sat snarling among the rocks for a long time before wandering on to the Three Shire Stone, where we had a lengthy wait. Cop began jigging and dancing from one foot to the other.

"It's jolly cold up here!"

We told her not to be ridiculous.

"Yes, it is — and windy!"

Prim said, "She's right. It is getting chilly," which gave us another reason for grumbling. We put on all the spare clothes in our rucksacks, and had no sooner done so when Alistair arrived. We hailed him with delight. We were sick of the Three Shire Stone — and the Crinkles.

After tea at the Woolpack we drove back to Scale Hill, and were very late for dinner because we loitered deliberately on the way.

Scale Hill had gradually emptied of visitors during the week, and we were the sole occupants of the annexe. Cath and Cop moved into another bedroom, leaving Prim and me in the big room. It was like sleeping in a large hall with so much unused space that we could never remember where we had put anything. We were like two peas rattling round in a bucket.

* * *

From the hotel terrace we looked at the innocent slopes of Low Fell, and estimated that its ascent would be no more than a morning's easy stroll. This was a mistaken assumption as we were soon to discover, for a more deceptive fell would be difficult to find.

There was no track, but the first part of the walk, across fields and up gentle, grassy slopes, was pleasant — until the same slopes became so steep that we had to go on all fours. It was a roaster of a day, and I could scarcely see where I was going because of the perspiration running down my face and into my eyes. I detest steep grass slopes, in any case, and soon I had had more than enough of this particular one. Climbing up it was not worth the effort involved. I stopped.

"I am not a mule, and I am boiled, and I have had enough?"

"Same here!" said Cath, and we collapsed on the crumbling wall of an old sheep-fold.

"I've got this far, and I'm jolly well going to the top!" panted Prim, and she struggled on, followed by Cop.

I hated Low Fell and the heat. Sitting on the wall was like being roasted in an oven, and the beautiful view of Crummockwater and Buttermere was little compensation. We sat in a daze until Prim and Cop returned, faces like boiled lobsters, having made the top.

"The going was much worse higher up," Prim said, adding, "I don't think you can call it an easy fell."

Cop cut in, emphatically, "I am sure we went the wrong way."

"There was no other way."

"We should have started from the other end."

"We should have walked miles before we started."

"I still think it would have been easier."

"Just shut up, will you! It's too hot to argue!" we told her.

These insignificant heights were often more trouble than the big fells. They could be an absolute nuisance to climb — like Low Fell.

We went to Buttermere for tea, and walked by the lake for a final look at Haystacks and the High Stile range, the heights we had loved for so many years. The next morning we left Scale Hill, the week's dalliance having ended. For the time being we were satisfied. We had known that the fells of the Loweswater area would not achieve the incomparable standard of our unique Wasdale hills, but they had given us many hours of pleasure during the week. They had atoned for the cruel weather we had endured at Easter.

OVER THE GREEN

There were five of us. Cop and Daisy came by train, and Cath brought Prim and me. As Hilda and Doris did not come, Cath's car was the only one available during the holiday. Times had changed since Sally's Ladies had three vehicles at their disposal.

In spite of our speedy run from Nottingham, Cop and Daisy got to Strands first, and were sitting on the seat outside Wilkinson's when we drove down the hill. They leapt up to help with our luggage, and everyone talked at once and got in the way, but eventually chaos gave way to order.

The S. L. Club was facing a critical situation with regard to Wilkinson's. Our Lakeland home was hovering in the balance. Miss Wilkinson was not in the best of health, having developed a nervous complaint which caused sporadic attacks of dizziness. She had been suffering from this for several months, and John Robert had ordered her to write to Prim and cancel our holiday, but she had refused. She liked us, and was anxious to have us as usual, and hoped to manage to cope while we were there, though she would be making changes. Breakfast and dinner would be as usual, but she would only be providing packed lunches in future.

There was plenty to discuss that evening, but Prim, who had been having a long period of intense stress, looked exhausted, and said there would be lots of time later on to think about the situation at Wilkinson's. As far as she was concerned, she needed about twenty-four hours' sleep, after which she promised she would be ready for anything. She then went to bed, leaving us mulling things over in the haphazard way which leads nowhere.

"The future of Sally's Ladies at Wilkinson's looks pretty dim, in my opinion," I said.

"I wonder where we can go next," Cath speculated.

"I like it at Strands and I don't want to leave it! I love Strands!"

exclaimed Cop passionately, glaring at us as though we were responsible for the impasse we had reached.

"Don't we all!" said Cath.

I said, "Why don't we go over the green to the Smiths at the hotel. We have often thought we would like to try it."

"Yes!" Cop leapt up. "Let's change over to Strands Hotel!"

"Tonight?" Daisy gasped, as though she expected us to go there and then.

"Idiot!" I said to Cop. "We can't just leave like that. We shall have to wait and see what happens in the next day or two."

Cop sat down again. "Oh, well, if we can't stay here I expect Prim will find us another place, so we need not bother about it."

I said, "Our immediate concern is where we shall go tomorrow."

"Steeple!" from Cath.

We all wanted to go up Steeple, apart from Daisy who said she had never heard of it.

Cop was dubious. "I don't suppose Prim will feel up to it tomorrow, do you?"

"No," I said, "not unless she is fighting fit in the morning, which is unlikely. We will do Steeple the day after."

As I spoke, the wind howled and rattled the windows, and Cath laughed ironically. "It is not much use making any definite plans until we see what the weather is like. Listen to that wind!"

Cop protested. "I hope we are not going to be stuck indoors all the time, like we were last year. If that is the case it is not much use coming to the Lakes."

"Defeatist talk!" I snapped, and with that we went to bed.

* * *

When we went in to see Prim the following morning, she said she intended to stay in bed and sleep, and would get up when she felt like it, and we could please ourselves what we did as long as we left her in peace.

We hadn't a clue what we wanted to do, and began arguing with each other. The morning was warm, but heavy clouds were massed at the head of the dale, obscuring the high fells. Cath suggested that we went down to the coast, and we agreed. We found sunlight and blue skies at Seascale, and went for a long walk on the sands.

On returning to the car, we had our packed lunch. There were less sandwiches than usual, and they consisted of lettuce, tomato, and a few uninteresting shreds of meat. They were below standard, and Cop began an indignant monologue.

"This would be no use to me if I had done a morning's climbing. I should want a lot more than this."

She went on and on until we told her to shut up and stop making a fuss. At the same time, we agreed with her.

Next, we went to Ravenglass and walked to Walls Castle. We were not particularly interested in Roman ruins, but Cath had made a bet that I could not remember the way to Walls. I did, so she lost her money. Cursing the tangle of nettles and brambles, we explored the ruins, and Daisy, following us, asked, "What is this supposed to be?"

I answered, "The finest Roman bath-house in the country," whereupon Cop asked, "What was it for?"

"It was for baths."

"Who wanted to bath?"

"Forget it!" I said. "Let's go exploring."

We went through woods loud with bird-song and carpeted with primroses and came to a lane. Cath said, "It must be nearly tea-time!" so we followed the lane in the direction of Ravenglass.

On the way, we stopped to investigate what looked like an empty house, and had opened the front door to go inside when we saw a bottle of milk standing at the foot of the stairs. Hastily retreating, we had just reached the garden gate when a woman walked round from the back of the house and peered suspiciously at us. We pretended we were admiring the scenery, which was non-existent because of the trees. Then we walked away.

Daisy stared at us in perplexity.

"Why did we want to go in that house?"

"No particular reason!" I laughed, and she looked rather shocked.

"I think you must be a little mad!"

"Oh, we are, but don't let that bother you!"

"All Sally's Ladies are as mad as hatters!" chanted Cop. "Soon, you will be mad, too!"

Obviously, Daisy was beginning to regard us with some misgiving, for during tea at the Pennington Arms she asked, "Do your egg sandwiches taste all right?"

"Yes," I said. "Don't yours?"

"Mine taste of paraffin!"

We each did some tasting, but failed to detect anything strange, and Cop assured Daisy that she had lost her sense of taste, which Daisy denied.

"No, I have not, but they do taste peculiar, and I was wondering if any of you had put . . ."

We interrupted with one voice. "We never interfere with anyone else's food!"

"That is one of the few things we do not do!"

She believed us, but the sandwiches remained uneaten on her plate.

We returned to Strands to find Prim poring over a map in the sitting-room. She had slept until the middle of the afternoon, and said no one had been up to disturb her or to ask if she wanted anything.

"The rotten lot!" I said. "At least they might have brought you a cup of tea!"

"I didn't want one. I was asleep."

"Well, they might have been up to see!"

"Yes, they might," she admitted, and asked us where we had spent the day. After we had given an account, she went on studying the map.

"Have you been making plans?"

"Yes, lots of plans. I want to do no end of things."

"Weather permitting?" queried Cop.

"Or weather in spite of!"

* * *

After a showery night, morning brought low, uninviting cloud, but the air was warm enough to prevent our teeth from chattering while we dressed.

As it was Prim's birthday, breakfast was followed by a lengthy session of opening of presents in the sitting-room, and for a while behaviour was exemplary. This unnatural politeness was short-lived, and as the morning passed the larking about began until the place was in an uproar. Daisy was trying to sort out a lap full of postcards until Cop sent them all flying when she took a wild leap over the settee and yelled, "Three cheers for the President! I propose a toast!"

"Nothing to drink it in!"

"Let's go over the green!"

"We need something to fortify us before we tackle a packed lunch indoors!"

Accordingly, we rushed over the green, and the toasting was done, and we returned to face indoor sandwiches about which scathing remarks were passed. In the afternoon, we were horrified when Cop suggested walking to Wasdale Head.

"What! Walk along the road!"

"Yes, it would be a nice, easy walk."

"I'm not walking along any flaming road," I said. "You know my views on that sort of lark."

"Well, I shall go!"

"I will walk with you," volunteered Daisy.

Cath shrugged. "No sense in walking when I have a car. Who is coming with me?"

"I am." Prim and I spoke together, and Prim added, "We will all meet at the Head at tea-time."

Cop and Daisy, striding out as though they were on a route march, had covered the first mile up the valley when we passed them. We parked at the campsite near the Head, and walked along the lakeside path, discussing the crags on Yewbarrow, and aiming to get back as Cop and Daisy arrived.

After tea at the Wastwater Inn, we walked up Mosedale. I kept with Daisy. I wanted to find out how much she knew about expeditions into the fells. She admitted that she had never done any really rough scrambling, but was not afraid to have a go at it. She said two things really made her nervous. One was climbing high, awkward walls, and the other was crossing wide, swift streams — known to us as beck-hopping.

"When I find myself on a wobbly stone in the middle of a stream, and don't know where on earth I can put my next foot, I'm terrified!"

Prim, behind us, evidently overheard, for she suddenly stopped and said, "Let us see if we can get to Burnthwaite without using any tracks!"

We agreed with gusto, for it was the kind of thing we loved, and the rougher the better. This time it meant six successive beck-hoppings. Daisy was thoroughly instructed in the art of crossing streams, and her fear disappeared.

We went into the tiny church, and looked at the rough, ancient beams and the etching of Napes Needle on the window-pane, then outside to see the climbers' graves — all the things we had known for so many years, we wished Daisy to know.

The Eskdale and Ennerdale hounds were to hunt on Buckbarrow the next day. The 'loose' was to be at Littleground at 9 a.m., and we decided to be at the farm to see them start.

* * *

Cop and Daisy were too lazy to get dressed in time, but Cath, Prim and I were at Littleground for the 'loose'. The dale head was lost in dark cloud, so low that even the summit of Buckbarrow was invisible. When the doors of a small van were opened, out flowed the hounds, an endless stream of white and tan streaking up Buckbarrow, with Edmund Porter, the huntsman, hard on their heels, while we stood green with envy, wishing we could climb at even half that speed. Within moments the pack had vanished into the mist, and there was nothing more to be seen.

We followed Prim into the farmhouse, and chatted for a while with Mrs Tyson before returning to Strands for breakfast. We were told that Miss Wilkinson had had another dizzy turn, and a neighbour had come in to look after us for the day. Our Strands home was hanging perilously in the balance, and we were growing restive, and began clamouring for something to be done. Prim assured us, "Something certainly will be done."

"What?" we demanded.

"I'm not sure yet, but I will do something when the time comes, so stop worrying."

After grumbling for half the morning, we went to Santon Bridge, where daffodils made a carpet of gold on the banks of the River Irt and every larch was shining green. It was a day for looking, lingering, and doing nothing in particular — at which we were adept. Our philosophy, perfected over the years, was that rushing up fells and trying to break our own records was not the way to achieve the deepest appreciation of mountain scenery.

We picnicked on the green at Ravenglass, critical of the sandwiches and throwing most of them to the gulls. The tide was out, and we started to cross the estuary to Saltcoats, but after becoming bogged down in the muddy ooze we retreated to the Pennington Arms for tea.

Next, we went up a rough lane to have a look at Irton Church. There we found some beautiful stained glass windows, but even more beautiful was the view from the church door — the vast breath-taking sweep of the western fells. If ever there was a place in which to stand and rejoice it was by the door of Irton Church.

"This is a day of doing bits and bobs! Where are we going next?" demanded Cop, and we looked at Prim.

"To Littleground, to see the hounds fed."

The hounds ate from long, wooden troughs filled with a yellowish mash, the smell of which was only endurable if you kept your distance. The hounds loved it, almost choking as they wolfed it down. They had not made a kill that day.

On returning to Strands, and learning that Miss Wilkinson had been ill during the day, Prim said, "Well, this is it!" and went into action. She saw Miss Wilkinson, and intimated in the most charming manner that we must find another place at once. Miss Wilkinson agreed, most regretfully as we were her favourite visitors, she said. She suggested that we might try Burnthwaite Farm, or Row Head in Gosforth, or perhaps we might fancy Strands Hotel if they could have us. We pretended to discuss it with her, knowing perfectly well where we wanted to go, but not wishing to appear too eager. Then Prim asked me to go with her to the telephone-box down the lane.

"Why the telephone?" I asked, as we came to the box.

"I'll do a little ringing round — mainly for form's sake," she replied, somewhat enigmatically.

"Who are you going to ring up?"

"I think I will do Burnthwaite Farm first."

"Burnthwaite Farm?"

"Yes. It is right at the foot of all the climbs, so it could be interesting. We could mend our ways and make early starts and all that," and she laughed and began to dial.

Burnthwaite Farm replied that they could accommodate five people in single rooms, and Prim said that sounded very nice, and if the five decided to come she would ring again later.

"We will keep that in reserve," she said to me. "I'll try Row Head next. What is the name of the people who keep it?"

"I haven't a clue, so we can't ring there."

"We can. I'll ring up the police station and get the name from them."

This was done, but when she rang Row Head there was no reply.

"What next?" I asked.

"That is enough telephoning. Next, we will go to the hotel and interview Miss Smith."

"Good!" I said, "we can have a drink at the same time!"

When the drinks arrived, Prim invited Miss Annie Smith, the barman, to come and sit with us, and proceeded to interview her. We could have five bedrooms, each with hot and cold water. Morning and late evening tea would be provided. We could have either packed lunch or a midday meal at the hotel. They could have us the next day, and we should have the place to ourselves.

Prim made the booking on the spot. "It sounds exactly what we want. We will come tomorrow morning."

As we went back over the green, she said, "Now we'll go and talk it over with the others."

"There's nothing to talk over!"

"You never know. They might decide that they want to go to Burnthwaite!"

But there was no talking over, as the unanimous choice was Strands Hotel.

"That's good," said Prim, "because I've already booked us in for tomorrow morning!"

Daisy, who looked as though she did not know what would happen next, said anxiously, "Had we better go and start packing now?"

"Good heavens, no! There will be plenty of time in the morning!"

"No need to pack properly, anyway!"

"Hot and cold in all the bedrooms!" gloated Cop. "That means that for the first time since the club started we shall have no excuse for not washing!"

"I have always kept myself reasonably clean," observed Prim mildly.

Cath said, "There's another good thing. We shall not have to have a packed lunch whether we want it or not."

"Even better," I said, "we shall not have to go over the green for a drink. We shall be there!"

We went up to bed for the last time at Wilkinson's. It had never been another Scarthwaite — no place could ever be that — but we had had some good times there, and leaving brought a measure of regret, almost submerged beneath a feeling of excitement and anticipation, as though the holiday proper was about to begin — which it was.

* * *

There was something special about Strands Hotel, and the three Misses Smith. The eldest, Miss Hannah, who was the licensee, did the cooking. Miss Margaret was responsible for all the cleaning, and Miss Annie was barman, waitress, and general factotum. Between them, they ran the place like clockwork, a model of smooth, quiet efficiency. We found it fascinating, and loved it from the first day we were there.

The morning was fair, but the high tops were veiled when we moved to the hotel. After the transfer was completed we planned to go up Scoat Fell and Steeple. Breakfast over, things were crammed into suitcases, lids forced down by sitting on them, and with shoulders and arms festooned with clothes which would not go into the cases we staggered over the green, shedding garments on the way and having to go back to retrieve them, and then dropping others. Fortunately there were no spectators.

Miss Annie received the avalanche with aplomb, as though it was quite usual for visitors to arrive in such an unorthodox manner. The luggage was piled in a heap in one bedroom, and we said we would deal with it when we came back in the evening. We could not stop at the moment, as we wished to go walking. If Miss Annie was surprised, she gave no sign of it.

"She'll get used to us!" Cop said, as we went to the car.

After all the luggage-hauling, we considered that we had earned a break, and drove through Gosforth to Boonwood for morning coffee, over which we dallied for so long that when we returned up Wasdale and parked at Nether Beck, our starting point for Scoat Fell, it was too late to do the walk.

Prim said, "We had better make up our minds to do it tomorrow even if the clouds are low on the top. If we are not careful we shall not have enough days left for all we have planned."

Cop said virtuously, "I did not want to waste time over coffee!" but Prim ignored that.

"We will go up to the ravine, and picnic by the waterfalls."

"And then what do we do?"

"And then we do some exploring!"

The type of exploring Prim liked often proved more strenuous than climbing a fell, but we all enjoyed it, some more than others. After a few hundred yards up the right side of Nether Beck, the ground became so swampy that we returned to the bridge and tried the left side. This was as bad, but we carried on, grumbling amiably. We grumble on principle about swamp. The waterfalls in the Nether Beck ravine are only second to those of the Esk, and not too far second, either. Above the gorge we came to a semi-circle of fine cascades, an ideal spot for a picnic.

After eating and voicing our opinion of the sandwiches, the last ones we should be having from Wilkinson's; we climbed about the rocks for a while, practising traverses and delicate balances for the sheer fun of it, while Daisy watched. Presently, Prim started wandering up a track which led on and on as far as we could see, and we followed, in single file as usual.

"Where are we going?" Daisy asked.

"Nowhere in particular!" Prim called back, and we carried on for some time, until she stopped. She was looking at the steep fell-side rising sharply to the right.

"If we crossed the beck and climbed up there we should see all sorts of things."

We scattered to find a good crossing place, which was not easy because the stones were at awkward angles. Cath crossed first, balancing on a wet, sloping stone in the middle of the beck, and I followed. Cop had gone further up-stream, and seemed to be paddling. I watched her stand with both feet in the water and dive for the far bank, where she landed on her stomach. It looked ridiculous. Meanwhile, Prim and Daisy had come to Cath's crossing place, and Cath had jumped back onto the wet, sloping stone to demonstrate how easy it was. Just as she said, "Look how I do it, then you do the same," her foot slipped off the stone, and she sat heavily in the beck, and we laughed until it hurt. Prim, towing Daisy, was bent double as she crossed. We staggered about, howling for the next five minutes.

Running up the fell-side was a high wall, in which was a narrow tumbled-down gate on which the words 'No Road' were crudely painted. I waited with Cath while she emptied the water out of her boots, and by then Prim had climbed over the wall and was going up on the far side. Cop and Daisy jibbed at the wall and went up on the near side, with the wall between them and Prim. They were all out of sight over the bulging contour of the fell before we were ready to follow. I eyed the wall, and said, "It would be less trouble to go through the gate."

There was a sea of mud near the gate, and after ploughing through that we saw that the gate was tied up with a tangle of rope, with which we struggled until Cath lost patience.

"Cut it with your knife, and I'll tie it up again afterwards!"

It was a job to make the cut ends of the rope meet again, but we managed. Slogging up the fell, we joined Prim at the top. At the same time, Cop and Daisy reached the top on their side.

"What are we supposed to do now?" Cop called.

"You get over the wall," Prim called back, "because we are going up those rocks over on the right."

"Wait for us!" came the cry.

Cop climbed over with ease, but not so Daisy judging by the time it took her to reach the top of the wall. She was starting to descend on our side when her nerve failed, and she wailed, "I'm going to fall! I'm going to fall!"

There are two ways in which to get a stuck person down a high wall. One is to coax them down gently, which takes a long time. The other is to use insulting shock tactics, which is much quicker. I used shock tactics, snarling, "Get down, you stupid clot!" which annoyed her so much that she climbed down at once. She did not speak to me again that afternoon, and several times I caught her eyeing me with distaste — but after that she could climb walls with the best of us.

We climbed up to the rocks, and sat there for some time. From Yewbarrow round to Haycock the fells were sharp and clear, and there was much to discuss. There was good walking for us in the Mosedale fells.

From the rocks we went in a bee-line down to the road, climbing over whatever obstacle lay in our path, paddling through a swamp, and finally getting over a wall into a farmyard. Walking sedately past the farmhouse windows, we reached the road about a mile higher up the dale than Nether Beck where we had left the car. We were dirty and happy, and did not mind a little easy road walking for a change.

After tea at Burnthwaite Farm, where we were confronted by so much food that we had to leave half of it, we drove back to Strands to begin a mammoth sorting out and clearing up. Miss Annie carried off our wet footgear, and we settled into our respective bedrooms. The windows of four faced good views. The fifth, which was Cop's, faced a blank wall, but she waved aside our commiserations.

"When I am in my bedroom, the last thing I want to do is to look out of the window. I go there to sleep, and when I am not sleeping I am busy getting up."

"Then how fortunate you are to be the one overlooking a blank wall," I said.

"Naturally, I like to see a lovely view, but it is not all the world if there isn't one!"

Pre-dinner drinks were taken in the sitting-room, which was already strewn with our maps, books, and other paraphanalia, and looking like home. Dinner was excellent, with perfect service. Miss Annie did not hover over us as we ate, but was invariably there when needed.

We knew that Strands Hotel was going to be good.

* * *

Early morning tea came on attractively laid individual trays. The china pot held sufficient for two cups. The solid silver teaspoon was engraved with the letter 'S'. I felt that we had risen in the world.

The morning was fair, and we hoped that the mist on the tops would disappear as the day warmed up, but in any case we were definitely going up Scoat Fell.

Breakfast over, we set off, and had driven a mile before Prim discovered that the film in her camera was almost finished and she had forgotten to bring a new one. Cath turned the car, and we went back. Then we set off again. As it transpired, we need not have gone back, because the new film was not used.

At Nether Beck we began walking, quickly getting above the ravine and the waterfalls. The track was good, very muddy in places, and frequently meandering across drifts of boulders. It climbed gradually up a long, twisting valley, and as we gained height we expected to see Scoat Tarn at any minute. Then, as we circled a large area of bog, there was no more track. It had disappeared, which was a nuisance, but even more annoying was that at two thousand feet we hit the ceiling of cloud, and it was much thicker than we had anticipated. It was dense, reducing visibility to under ten yards. It also reduced our speed considerably. When an outcrop of boulders the size of haystacks loomed before us, we stopped to have lunch, hoping the stones would give some protection from the wind. They didn't, as it seemed to be blowing from all directions, swirling the mist instead of dispersing it.

Strands Hotel sandwiches were good, but we were too cold and damp to appreciate them, and in ten minutes we were ready to move on. It did not occur to anyone that it might be a good idea to get down out of the clouds, or if it did they kept it to themselves.

We started up a slope of trackless, tussocky grass, and in the thick mist soon lost all sense of direction. Prim set a good pace, and in single file we panted after, our one concern being to keep the person in front in sight. This upward treadmill went on until suddenly we reached a wall, and I remembered reading that a wall ran along the crest of Scoat Fell. I called over my shoulder to Daisy, "Don't get excited, but I think we have got to the top!"

"We can't have. We have to get to Scoat Tarn first."

"We lost that in the mist!"

Following the tumbled-down wall and finally crossing it, we arrived at the summit cairn which is actually built on the wall.

Prim flung out her arms.

"Scoat Fell! We made it! And we can't see a thing!"

"Not very hopeful for Steeple," I said. "Only about ten minutes away, and we can't even see where the track starts!"

"I can find it," Prim said confidently, and strode off into the mist, and we followed. We came to the cairn marking the beginning of the Steeple route, the start of a thin, jagged spine disappearing into the white obscurity of territory unknown to us. Although we could not see, we sensed the depths on either side of the narrow ridge. We stood in a group by the cairn, and for several minutes no one spoke. Then Prim looked at us, shrugged her shoulders, and said, calmly, "Well, that's that. We don't go." We all agreed, but it was terribly frustrating.

We left the cairn and wandered along the top of Scoat Fell, praying that the mist would lift a little, just enough for us to get to Steeple, but if anything it became more dense. We found ourselves stumbling among big, awkward boulders, and it was rather exciting, until someone gave a plaintive cry, "Where are we going? How on earth shall we find the way down again?"

We played follow-my-leader after Prim, among the boulders and round outcrops of rock, until she suddenly made a right-angle turn down steep grass, and led us to the identical boulder where we had halted to eat our sandwiches — a remarkable piece of navigation. We were loud in our congratulations, Cop shouting, "Hurrah for the President!"

"How on earth did you know where to find the exact spot?" I asked.

Prim laughed. "I did not know. I must have found it by instinct. I had no idea of the right direction!"

So ended our abortive attempt on Steeple.

Eventually, we dropped below the clouds, becoming mildly excited when the landscape appeared again and we could see where we were, but it seemed a long, long trail down to the road, though probably disappointment made it appear longer than it actually was.

Wasdale dreamed in the sun. Only the tops of the high fells were crowned with white clouds. They looked so innocent — from the valley.

Tea at Greendale had its problems.

"I only want a drink."

"I'm not going to stuff myself with all those scones."

"I wouldn't mind a piece of cake."

"I'm not going to spoil my dinner, but I'd like something."

Finally, we ordered tea for five, cakes for two, and scones for one. The girl who took the order gave us a strange look, but we all got something to eat, and there was no grumbling.

Back at the hotel, where Miss Annie was waiting to carry off our damp gear, drinks were followed by a perfect dinner, the pudding especially being greeted with shrieks of approval, slightly subdued because we were still at the stage where we wished to create a good impression. During the holiday this phase passed with remarkable celerity.

The inquest on the day was held round the sitting-room fire, the general impression being that the thick mist had made it fairly strenuous, but nevertheless enjoyable. No day is ever wasted on the fells. There is always a dominant urge to attain those heights where the sky seems close and the world far away and the spirit takes wings. Once experienced, that compulsion is there for life.

* * *

"It is time we ticked off Lingmell."

We agreed with the exception of Daisy, who looked anxiously from one to another, and asked, "Do we all have to go?"

She was assured that no member of Sally's Ladies was compelled to go anywhere against her wish. She was free to choose what she did.

"Count me out, then. I shall go for a walk by the lake today and take my time. I shall enjoy that."

We knew that she had found Scoat Fell long and arduous, particularly wandering in the mist, so we left her to enjoy her solo.

We climbed Lingmell by the nose on a green track, easy but very steep. The treading was uniformly good, apart from one short band of scree. Reaching the skyline at Goat Crags, we found we were nowhere near the top, and there was a long, upward-tilted plateau to be crossed. This was trackless, and as extensive grass slopes are boring, we took it at speed.

A rock outcrop crowned the summit, where we sat by the tall, beautifully built cairn — a wonderful spot for lingering. Clouds swirled over the high fells, opening now and again to reveal glimpses of the sunlit valleys below. Visibility was good one minute and poor the next. The Pike, Mickledore and the dark Scafell precipice appeared and were wiped out. Styhead Tarn and Borrowdale cleared and vanished. We gazed into the mighty chasm of Piers Gill and then it was gone.

We moved across to the rock escarpment fringing the Styhead face of Lingmell to see the well-known picture-book portrait of Great Gable, and we were thrilled. Clouds moving over the south face of the mountain magnified its proportions to give an impression of vast bulk and sheer, plummeting depth. We could scarcely bear to tear ourselves away from such mountain magic.

To return to Wasdale we had only to reverse our line of ascent, but first we spent some time scrambling about the rocks. This took us well away from the summit cairn, and also proved our undoing, for just as we decided to start down to Wasdale the clouds came down as thickly as they had done on Scoat Fell. Every mountain and valley was blotted out, making it impossible to pin-point any landmark. A fleeting glimpse of the Lingmell cairn would have been useful, but it had disappeared. We were in the fog again.

We trudged on and on over the grass for some distance. We were becoming convinced that we were walking in a circle when, as suddenly as they had descended, the clouds lifted, and we found ourselves above the scree of Lingmell Scars. Wastwater was over to the right. By dropping gradually towards it, we picked up the thin green line of the track down the nose. Having gained that, we dropped rapidly — or three of us did. For me, the angle of descent was too acute, and I had to keep the brake on hard all the way, which played havoc with my knees. I hated that damned grassy nose!

The others were soon trotting well ahead, while I had to come like a cat on hot bricks. I got further and further in the rear, which did not please me, but I could do nothing about it except bend my back to take some of the strain from my protesting knees. I bent it for so long that I could not walk upright when I reached the bottom of the slope, and my legs went mechanically as though they had nothing to do with the rest of me. Once off the treadmill, however, I soon recovered.

We had had Lingmell to ourselves, with no other walkers on the fell. The previous day, there had been no one else on Scoat Fell, though as Cop was quick to point out, only a lunatic would have been on Scoat Fell in those conditions.

At Greendale, where we went for tea, Cop began her usual chant.

"I don't want any scones. I am not going to spoil my dinner. I could easily eat some, but I'm not going to."

"Oh, shut up!" I said, and she gave me a hard shove.

I promptly retaliated, at which Cath said, "We are not waiting while you two have a fight!" and Prim added, "Just let me get on with ordering the tea!" The order was for scones for two and cakes for one, which, surprisingly, easily fed four.

As a vantage point, Lingmell had been excellent. We thought it would be a good fell to be on in almost any weather, but to be there when clouds were swooping and coiling over the tops gave an extra bonus. I was curious why Prim, with her unfailing instinct for route-finding in mist, had gone astray in the cloud on Lingmell top.

"Did you know that you were not leading us straight off?"

She laughed. "Oh, yes, I knew. I was just curious to see which part of the plateau we should be on when the clouds rolled away. I had myself a little game of pretending I was lost in the mist."

"Suppose you had fallen into Piers Gill!"

She gave me a hard look. "I was not pretending to that extent!"

We talked a lot about Lingmell that night.

I said, "Just to sit up there and watch the clouds roll across Gable is my idea of heaven."

Cop, who had just stood up to go to bed, turned and said, "My idea of heaven is a nice house to stay in, good food, and a fresh fell to climb every day."

"And a pair of good, strong legs!" I said.

"Of course, you would have good, strong legs if you were in heaven!" and with that she went to bed.

* * *

We had often talked about the High Level Route to Pillar Rock, but Prim's suggestion of doing it that day, when every top was bathed in sunlight, was not received with enthusiasm. It was such a perfect spring day, why not laze in the dale and enjoy it? We never seemed to have time to do that, and it would be good to be thoroughly idle for a change.

Prim said, "I don't mind. We still have one more day left. We can do the High Level tomorrow."

I was quite relieved, because my knees had taken a hammering on the nose of Lingmell, and I was sure a day's rest would be good for them.

We parked on the green at Wasdale Head, and within five minutes Cop became restive, demanding, "Are we going to sit here and do nothing all day?"

"You said you wanted a lazy day!" I reminded her.

"Not all that lazy!"

"I think I could do with a little exercise, too," Daisy said.

"I'll take you for a walk," offered Cath.

So the three of them set off for the Styhead track, while Prim and I strolled into Mosedale, where we sat on a boulder and studied Stirrup Crag, on Yewbarrow.

"I should like to climb up that," I said, "if I didn't have to get up to Dore Head first."

The scree shoot from Dore Head to the valley looked naked, countless feet having dislodged every last one of its stones.

"Looks nasty," I said. "I shouldn't like to come down there."

"I wouldn't attempt it. I would climb down the rocks at the side."

As we had no intention of going to Dore Head that day, we next turned our attention to the bristle of rocks on the Mosedale side of Red Pike, and speculated on a possible route up, one which had not been mentioned in any guide-book. We traced one which would be an interesting scramble.

On returning to the car, we were surprised to find the others already there opening their lunch packets.

"I thought you would have been sitting by Styhead Tarn!"

"Or half-way up Gable!"

"We had to come back," Cath explained. "We were hungry!"

Having disposed of the sandwiches, we walked along the narrow track under the Screes, but after a mile Prim and I stopped. The others were striding out, but we knew that they would not have time to do the whole length of the lake, because we were going to Greendale for tea. We meandered back, looking at the sunlit fells and arguing about the nubbly rocks on the nose of Yewbarrow. Picking out a line of attack on any mountain was something you did automatically. Climbing a fence, we went down to the water's edge and followed the undulations of the shore line to the bridge over Lingmell Gill. The others soon joined us, Cath commenting that the track under the Screes had been dull, uninteresting, and not worth doing.

At Greendale, we ordered tea, scones, and cakes for five. Cop ate her share without comment, causing such astonishment that she burst out, "I can please myself, can't I? I never said I couldn't eat scones! I only said . . ."

"Whatever you said was crazy!" I exclaimed, and she subsided into mutterings, unintelligible because her mouth was full.

The evening was so perfect that we stayed by the lake, while the westering sun lit the fells with bright gold, highlighting every detail of the crags. A man in an orange anorak was sitting on the top block of Napes Needle, and I envied him. We said, "Why couldn't it have been like this for Scoat Fell and Steeple?" Lingering by the lake, the spell of Wasdale held us in such bondage that we were very late for dinner.

The unenergetic day was followed by a lazy evening in the sitting-room. Some of Wainwright's routes were criticised, and the odd passage from H. H. Symonds's *Walking in the Lake District* was read aloud. Cath knitted spasmodically, Prim's nose was buried in a map, Daisy tried to write letters, and Cop argued with anyone who would listen. Then someone mentioned the High Level Route, and Cath said, "It should make a good, strenuous day!"

Cop pretended to groan. "Do you think we should go to bed at a reasonable hour, so that we are fresh in the morning!"

Daisy looked up in alarm. "Did you say strenuous?"

"Oh, yes, it is bound to be!"

"Then I think I will go to bed — now!"

"Oh, it will not be as bad as all that. Of course, it may be even worse. You never know!"

Daisy gathered her correspondence, and got to her feet. "I don't trust you lot. Good night, all!" and she departed.

Cop tut-tutted, frowning reprovingly at me. "You should be ashamed of yourself, frightening Daisy so much that she has to go to bed!"

"I don't see why I should take the blame. I was no worse than the rest of you!"

"Then we should all be ashamed!"

Prim threw aside her maps, yawned, and announced, "I'm not ashamed — never have been. Besides, she has only gone to bed to get away from the noise, so that she can write her letters in peace."

The four of us sat up very late, for I produced the diary containing the account of the escapade in the snow in Lord's Rake, and we were reading it aloud, with hoots of laughter.

* * *

The mountains were perfect that day.

When eyes are upon the surrounding heights one is apt to forget one's feet, so it was fortunate that the Black Sail track presented no problems. My enjoyment, however, was tempered with misgiving about my knees. They felt tired almost from the start and had no spring, though they were a good excuse for frequent halts, ostensibly to admire the view.

From Black Sail top we turned onto Lookingstead, to eat our lunch facing a great array of fells. We knew them all by name, and had climbed most. As we lay on the dry turf, our gaze ranging to the far horizon, time ceased to matter.

Then Prim sighed, rose and hitched on her rucksack, and we collected our scattered gear. Rejoining the Pillar track, we began looking for the cairn at the beginning of the High Level Route, the climbers' way to Pillar Rock, and we almost missed the small, insignificant heap of stones on the first rocky outcrop. From that tiny marker, a faint track led down through the crags and disappeared round a buttress. Rough and scrambly, it was the kind of route we loved!

Daisy baulked, and refused to go any further, protesting that she had never done that kind of rock scrambling, and did not like the look of it at all. I baulked, too, but with anguish in my heart. I longed to follow that track, but my knees were so tired that even a small thing like Black Sail had been a drag. Common sense told me that the High Level was not for me that day.

I sat on a rock and watched the other three climbing up and down until they were out of sight. Several minutes elapsed, and I heard Prim's voice calling, "Are you all right?" but there was no reply. They had gone. On my rock, I seethed and cursed aloud. I used every swear-word I knew, and invented a few more. I must have sounded awful.

Daisy stood looking at me with an expressionless face, but I was too furious to notice her. When I had calmed down, I realised that I was wasting my breath. It was not Daisy's fault, anyway, so I turned to her, and said, "I suppose we had better start crawling back down Black Sail.

"Yes," she replied, eyeing me a little apprehensively. "I think I will just go over to the top of Lookingstead again for another look round before we go down," and she walked away. I think she was glad to be rid of me for a while. I made a bee-line for the top of Black Sail, striding out, and taking a perverse, painful pleasure in making my knees work harder than they should have done. I was below the big boulders near the top of the pass before I remembered that I was supposed to be with Daisy, so I sat on a rock and waited for her.

We strolled down, with the odd stop or two, first to eat cake, and again when Daisy produced an apple. Black Sail is tedious when taken slowly, so to relieve the boredom I named every fell, crag, and beck in sight, then asked Daisy which of them she could remember when I pointed to them.

We were down by 5.30, and sat by the beck near the old pack-horse bridge to wait for the others. I did not know what conditions they would have encountered, but I had a good idea of the distance involved, plus the time it had taken us to come down Black Sail. At a rough estimate, they should be back in another hour. I was quite content to sit quietly by the rippling water, until Daisy began worrying.

"What time do you think they will get down?"

"In another hour or so."

"Surely they should be down before that."

I made no reply, and she began again. "Do you think they will be all right?"

"I am sure they will."

She got up and began pacing about, looking up the pass. "There is no sign of them. Don't you think they should be here by now?"

"No, I don't!" and I told her there was no need to worry.

"What shall we do if they don't come?"

"They will come!"

"Suppose they have had an accident?"

"They will not have an accident!"

I was getting irritated, so when she started again, "I'm sure they should be here by now!"

I said, "No, they should not. They have not had time to do the walk and get back here yet!"

I got up, and walked fifty yards further along the beck, to sit in peace. Another half-hour, I thought, and was amazed when they turned up at 6.10.

"You must have come down Black Sail at a gallop!"

"We did!" they said, Cop adding a heartfelt, "I have never been so sick of Black Sail in my life! It seemed endless!"

In detail, they described the High Level, and Robinson's Cairn, and the Shamrock Traverse. We had read that on the High Level Route you walked out horizontally into space, which, they said, was not true, because it was anything but horizontal and you needed to watch your feet all the time, but it was great fun, and they had enjoyed it immensely.

"Don't tell me any more!" I begged.

They declared they were dying of thirst, but it was too late for tea at the Wastwater Inn, so we made do with cider and shandy. Although beer and spirits were available at Strands Hotel, the Misses Smith did not stock wine in those days, and half-way through her cider, Cop said, "It's a pity we can't get wine, because I would have treated us to a bottle or so tonight."

"You still can!" she was assured. "We can buy the wine here, and take it back with us!"

This we did, returning laden to Strands.

Great cleaning up and changing of clothes was followed by a gin session in the sitting-room, then a memorable dinner, ending with liqueurs provided by Prim.

As we left the dining-room, Cath cannoned into a chair, and remarked to Miss Annie, who stood in the doorway, "I feel merry tonight!" to which Miss Annie replied with a twinkle, "You should, after all you have had!"

We were making for the sitting-room when Prim said, "We must go over and say goodbye to the Wilkinsons."

"Oh, must we?"

"We want to get to the fire!"

"We needn't go, need we?"

"Of course we had better go."

We went, and when we came out of Wilkinson's, Prim headed for the vicarage. "Now we have to say goodbye to the vicar and his wife."

We followed, Cop muttering an aside to me, "How many more dratted people does she know in this valley!"

"Almost everybody, I should think, so you had better be prepared!"

But after the vicarage we went back to the hotel, and got the bill sorted out. We noticed that the late evening tea and the half-pint of milk consumed by Cop had not been included. We thought we would say nothing about it, but Prim said, "They might think of it later, and wonder why we had said nothing. I had better go and mention it."

She was told by Miss Annie that the omission of a charge for late tea had been deliberate, because we had not had flasks filled to take out with our packed lunches. We were surprised, for we had never even thought of taking flasks on the fells!

Finally, there was the unwelcome job of packing, but with separate rooms we could neither grumble nor get in each other's way. I had almost finished when I found one of Prim's books, which I took to her room, and we spent the next hour sitting on the bed amid a welter of maps, planning for the future, and discussing the two bases we had found in the west — Strands Hotel in Wasdale, and the Woolpack in Eskdale.

Both were good.

* * *

The three Misses Smith, in their black dresses and snowy-white aprons, stood at the front door and waved us off the next morning, and Miss Annie called after us, "It has been a pleasure to have you! We shall look forward to the next time!"

"They do not yet realise what we are really like!" was Cop's cynical comment.

"Maybe she has already found out," I said, "and why shouldn't it be a pleasure to have people like Sally's Ladies? There can't be many like us in the Lake District!"

TERRACE ROUTE

In June, Prim, Cath, Doris and I went to Eskdale to spend a week at the Woolpack. None of the other club members was free to come, which was their loss, for the weather was excellent — warm, sunny, and ideal for walking. We were out on the fells every day, and after dinner at night there was Captain Dudley Hoys to answer all our questions and regale us with a wealth of Lakeland lore and legend. He knew every walk and climb in the district, and we were absorbed by his detailed descriptions and intimate knowledge of Eskdale.

One evening, we told him that we planned to do the Terrace Route to Slight Side and Scafell the next day. He said it should be a very good expedition, and gave us a warning, "Don't get into the Cowcove basin, or you will go shin deep. Circle round to the left on harder ground, and approach Slight Side obliquely." He took a scrap of paper and drew a rough sketch to indicate the best route. We forgot to take the sketch the next day, but could remember its main features.

At the last moment, Doris cried off. "I am never very happy when you go fiddling about on Scafell. I am not at all keen on breaking my neck!"

"Neither are we!" we assured her.

Prim suggested, "Why not come part of the way, and go back if the going gets tough?" but Doris did not think much of that idea.

"No, I shall do my own sort of walking, probably a good, long stretch in the valley. I never know what is going to happen next on your high jaunts."

So the three of us set off, turning up the fell-side opposite Wha' House and quickly reaching the track known as the Terrace Route.

We found it delightful, and said, "Doris would have loved this!"

The track meandered round outcrops of rock and heathery bluffs, following the edge of an escarpment, and giving a grandstand view of the wild solitude of upper Eskdale and the majestic mountains at its head. It was ideal for lingering, which we did, sitting on a rock. Far below, Brotherilkeld looked like a child's toy farm. The sheep had been gathered, and there was much shouting and barking and general activity in the little fields. Watching men working with sheep in mountain country has always fascinated us, and we could have stayed in the warm sun, contentedly watching for hours, had not Scafell called.

We went on, passing a swamp covered with white flowers. The wet ground made it difficult for Prim to get near, but by balancing precariously with toes and fingertips on four tussocks of grass she eventually got her picture of them. Beyond the swamp, we came to the end of the Terrace track, and were on open ground. To the right lay the Cowcove basin, about which we had been warned. Also, to the right was a long spur running down from Slight Side.

Our instinct was to make a bee-line for this spur, but having been told to go left to avoid the soggy basin, we accordingly turned left where the ground was supposed to be drier, though we did not notice any difference. In places it resembled paddling rather than walking, but this was of no consequence. We were used to getting our feet wet, but the fact that we were walking with our backs to our objective seemed ridiculous. After covering some distance we stopped, turned to look at Slight Side, and with one accord decided to go straight for it, Cowcove basin or not.

The going was no wetter, the only difference being that we came to a series of long ditches filled with black, slimy water. The narrower ones were easily jumped, and the wider ones contained a convenient stone or two. We were going well until we reached a very wide ditch which had no stones. By taking a long running jump we all cleared it with several feet to spare, but it was my undoing. Instead of landing squarely on the far side, I came down sideways, giving my left knee a savage twist.

"Flaming hell!" I roared, hopping about on one leg, while Prim and Cath looked on with consternation.

"Are you all right?"

"Had we better go back?"

"Wait a minute," I said, and looked ahead to see if there were any more ditches to jump. There were none, so my luck was in. I remembered the tired knees which had stopped me from doing the High Level Route. I was jolly well not going to let that happen a second time, especially as the knee was not tired. It was only wrenched, and a bit of knee trouble was not going to stop me getting up Scafell.

"It is nothing serious, so let's carry on. I shall be a bit slower, but I am all right — I think!" I added to myself.

So we carried on, and I found I could go uphill without much trouble, which is usually the case with a wrenched knee. The difficulty lies in going downhill, but that problem could be shelved for a few hours. I told myself that no doubt my knee would have recovered by then, and added, "Liar!"

The final steep pull up Slight Side culminated in an enjoyable scramble over rocks to the summit cairn, a lofty perch where we fell under the spell of all high, wild places. We climbed all the rocks at hand before embarking on the barren ridge to Scafell, a long mile which was too enthralling to be taken quickly. We lingered above Cam Spout Crag, marvelled at the vast sea of boulders flooding down the Eskdale Pike, and were lost in wonder over the great fells ringing Eskdale. Great Moss and the narrow, silver ribbon of the Esk lay three thousand feet below.

The rough track ended on the summit of Scafell, and we had a short halt for food by the cairn before crossing to the rock face. This, not the actual summit, had been our real objective, and it exceeded our wildest expectations. In all Lakeland, there is nothing to equal the beautiful, terrible majesty of those black precipices dropping into space. This is the edge of the world, a harmony of depth and space so absolute that it strikes an answering chord in one's inmost being.

We explored along the top of the crags, and from Pisgah watched climbers at work on the Pinnacle. Far down in Deep Gill we noted the thin line of the West Wall Traverse, and half wished we were on it. We scrambled down to the beginning of Broad Stand. We were in our element, having lost all track of time until a casual glance at a wrist-watch brought us to our senses, and we had to tear ourselves away.

But which way? The steeper the descent, the worse it would be for me. If we retraced our route as we had originally intended, the immediate drop from Slight Side was wickedly steep, so that was ruled out.

"The easiest way would be down Green How," said Prim. "Then we could cut over and go back by Burnmoor."

"A longish walk!" Cath pointed out.

"It would be easy, though. Once down Green How there would be no big ups and downs."

"We shall be late for dinner."

"We shall be late whichever way we go!"

"Who cares!"

We started down Green How, and had barely passed the Lord's Rake exit before my troubles began. Sometimes my knee would bend properly and sometimes it wouldn't, so my progress gradually became slower and slower. Cath, like a watchful sheep-dog, kept pace with me, while Prim went ahead. I had to keep stopping to rest — and to grumble, which I did whole-heartedly. I hated that interminable trek down Green How, and I hated my stupid knee. We were resting on a large, flat boulder when Prim came trotting back to ask if we intended to sit on the mountain all night.

"We are coming as fast as I can!" I retorted.

She stood pondering, then said, "We shall never get over Burnmoor at this rate. The best thing will be to go down to Wasdale. I'll go ahead to Brackenthwaite, the Fell and Rock Club place, and ring up the Woolpack from there, and they can send a car to fetch us."

She set off at a jog-trot, and Cath and I followed at our snail's pace.

"You had better lean on my shoulder," Cath said, after I had fallen a couple of times. That was a great help, and we were getting along quite well until my knee bent suddenly, throwing me heavily against her.

"Hold up, you fool!" she shouted, struggling to keep her own balance.

It happened several times, and we must have looked like a couple of lurching, stumbling drunks. When any other walkers came in sight, we stood and pretended to be admiring the view until they had gone. It was so ridiculous that we could scarcely get along for laughing, but it was also slow purgatory. I cursed with every stumble, until Cath said, "You would do better to save your breath for getting down instead of swearing!"

She looked at her watch.

"They will just be going in to dinner at the Woolpack!"

I said, "I don't care! Mrs Armstrong will save ours, though at the moment I don't mind whether she does or not!"

At last, we arrived at Brackenthwaite, the Fell and Rock Club house at the foot of Scafell. Prim stood waiting for us.

"There is no telephone here. The nearest one is at the inn, at Wasdale Head."

We groaned, for the inn was a mile away, and though the flat valley road would have presented no difficulty, we had no wish to walk another mile.

Then Prim went on, "Cheer up! I've been talking to a man and a girl here. They are just going up to the inn for a drink, and they have offered us a lift."

Just then the pair came out of the house, and we literally scrambled, almost fell, into the car. We thought our troubles were over at last.

The Wastwater Inn was packed with climbers, and the entrance hall was so littered with rucksacks, discarded boots, and coils of rope that to reach the bar was an obstacle race. We made it, for we were parched, and a drink was priority number one. Then Prim went into another part of the inn to find the telephone, but was soon back again.

"It's engaged. I'll try again in a minute or two."

I looked at the clock in the bar, and it was just coming up to 8.15.

At the second attempt the line was still engaged, so we went on drinking, and Prim wandered off to buy some picture postcards. Every few minutes, she tried to ring the Woolpack, and it was 8.40 when she finally got through.

"I spoke to Dudley Hoys. I said I had been trying to ring for the last twenty-five minutes. I explained that you had twisted your knee slightly, so we had come down to Wasdale. A car is coming to collect us."

While we waited for the car we had another drink and several bags of potato crisps, for by then we were hungry.

A large, cheerful man arrived with our transport, looked at us, and asked, "Which of you has the injured knee?"

"Me," I said, "but I wouldn't exactly call it injured."

"Can you walk?"

"Well, I walked down Scafell, didn't I, but I had to come slowly, and that is why we are late."

"That, and the fact that I could not get through to the Woolpack," added Prim. "Somebody there must have taken root at the telephone!"

The man hooted with laughter.

"Oh, we've been having fun and games there, I can tell you!"

"What has been happening?"

With obvious enjoyment, he told us, stopping every now and then to chuckle. The gist of it was that when we did not turn up at dinner time, Captain Hoys had started a non-stop session on the telephone, alerting people near and far, including the Eskdale Outward Bound School. He had organised them into parties, and told them to stand by for a rescue.

"What rescue?"

"You three! You were to be rescued!"

"No wonder I could not get through," observed Prim calmly.

"He sent a man to drive up to the top of Hard Knott to see if you were there, but you weren't."

"Why should we be up there?"

"Blest if I know. People were dashing all over the place. The captain had organised three search parties."

"Good heavens, three?"

"Yes. One was to go on the top of the Pike, another to go up to Esk Hause, and a third to look into Piers Gill."

"Good heavens!" said Prim again. "Didn't he arrange for one to go up Scafell? He knew we had gone up there."

"No, Scafell was not mentioned. All the parties were to stand by, and he would telephone them when to start. Then you rang up, and he had to telephone them not to stand by any longer!"

"Good heavens!" said Prim, for the third time. She sounded amused, but I could tell she was hopping mad.

"Your friend, Doris, was so upset when you did not turn up that we took her into the bar for a brandy."

Cath and I burst out laughing, and I said, "She would like that!" but Prim cut in, "Doris was upset? That's nonsense. She knows perfectly well that we have a habit of turning up late — sometimes very late."

We drove in silence for a minute or so, then she turned to the man, and asked, "Tell me honestly, were any of you really upset by all this carry on?"

"Not a bit!" he assured her. "As a matter of fact, we all thoroughly enjoyed it!"

"Good!" said Prim. "We will sort things out when we get back!"

As we drew up at the Woolpack all the guests came out and gave us a round of applause, and I felt that we should bow or something. They insisted on taking us into the bar for drinks, ignoring our protests that we had already had several drinks. Everyone crowded into the bar, until there was scarcely room to move. The captain said they were delighted to see us back, and explained that as we were late, he had thought it prudent to arrange rescue operations. Prim, smiling, waited until he had finished, then proceeded to demolish his argument in a most affable speech, the essence of which was that we were not novices in mountain craft — far from it! — that there were three of us and had we had an accident on

Scafell obviously one would have gone for help while the other stayed with the injured person, that it was a public holiday and the fells were swarming with people who could have come to our assistance if necessary, that Doris was well aware of our habit of turning up late as we had been doing it for years, and that she would have contacted the Woolpack much earlier had the line not been engaged every time she tried to ring. Finally, she regretted the fuss which had been made, all of which had been quite unnecessary.

This speech was made with such charming and convincing aplomb that when she had finished everyone clapped. We had inadvertantly provided good entertainment for the Woolpack that day, and in spite of the Wastwater Inn potato crisps, and the lateness of the hour, did full justice to the dinner which had been kept for us.

"Cop would have enjoyed all this carry on!" I said.

Prim and I were sharing a bedroom. We inspected my knee, which was swollen but not painful.

"A bandage and a couple of easy days, and it will be back to normal."

She said drily, "You had better limp a little tomorrow, whether you need to or not. It will create a good impression!"

We got ready for bed without saying another word. The night was very warm, and neither of us felt sleepy, so we lay in bed reading, at least, I read and Prim flipped over the pages and frowned.

"What's biting you?" I asked.

"They must have thought we had never been on a mountain before!"

"Oh, forget it!" I said. "They know differently now!" and went on reading.

Suddenly, she leapt up, seized a towel, and chased a large moth round the room, swiping in all directions and knocking several articles off the dressing-table. When she narrowly missed my face, I protested.

"Don't you think you had better stop crashing about before you wake everyone in the place?"

"I've settled the moth, anyway!" and she went back to bed.

She had completely recovered her equanimity by then.

"Mrs Coates would have told us we were proper daft, and promptly made us a cup of tea. And she would have grumbled at you for leaping over ditches!"

"Good old Scarthwaite days!" I agreed.

Then she said, "You know I got half a dozen postcards at the inn? Well, with all the rushing to and fro trying to telephone, I forgot to pay for them!"

"Then you have got six free postcards. Lucky you."

"No," she said, "the next time we go to Wasdale Head I shall put some money in the Mountain Rescue box."

We began to laugh, and she said, "We are both laughing at the same thing, aren't we?"

"Yes, the idea of us being rescued willy-nilly!"

"And those three search parties!"

"We were nowhere near the Pike, or Esk Hause, or Piers Gill, so none of them would have found us!"

"It was utterly crazy! It was proper daft!"

"Still," chuckled Prim, "I'm glad none of the parties had started out, or we might have had to go and bring them back!"

"Not I!" I said. "They could have footled round on the mountains all night for me!"

"There is one good thing," Prim said. "They will know in future at the Woolpack that we seldom turn up when we are expected. We never care about the time, because we like to enjoy our mountains."

"Complete independence, no fussing about, no interference, no clock watching — that's the motto for the S. L. Club!" I said. "Here's to Sally's Ladies!"

* * *

TREASURE OF HEIGHTS

The purpose of Sally's Ladies, and the goal towards which they aspired, was to achieve a complete understanding of mountains by climbing them, lingering among them, looking, listening, and feeling. This account of how far they succeeded is by no means complete, but a time always comes for a chapter to be closed....

Love of mountains has an almost tangible quality which can never be lost. It is as abiding as the hills themselves. For that love to be entire means experiencing the heights in all their transient moods, to be blistered by relentless sun, soaked by merciless rain, flailed by knife-like winds, plunged knee-deep in bog and deeper still in snow — and all to reach that far-off summit cairn. By such endurance and endeavour is born the feeling for the hills. To read a map as easily as a book, to use a compass with precision, to interpret winds and clouds and every portent of the sky, to memorise landmarks automatically, to pioneer a route, to go safely in mist, to deal confidently with rocks, and, of paramount importance, to be so fully aware of your own capabilities that you are never tempted to go beyond your limit — if, with ease and joy, you are able to do all these, then you are not a mere fell-walker but a true mountaineer.

Not all hill-lovers are mountaineers, but the S. L. Club was of that category. When Prim died, we never elected another president, and it was left to me, the secretary, to ensure that the thread remained unbroken and nothing was lost — a fitting memorial to one who was a dedicated mountaineer. So I carried on the business of the club, planning, arranging and organising, and gradually widening its horizons. To our bases in Wasdale and Eskdale, we added the Patterdale Hotel by Ullswater, the Haweswater Hotel in Mardale, and the Sun Hotel at Coniston. In Baddeley's *'Top Twenty'* only Fairfield had never been climbed by us, so Cath and

Cop ticked that off, not by the humdrum way from Ambleside, but via Deepdale and Cofa Pike.

Gradually, Doris and Hilda withdrew from the longer, more exciting expeditions, but Cath, Cop and I, the three remaining originals, progressed from strength to strength, and Daisy proved a faithful follower.

We climbed everything, everywhere. I may not have been an inspired leader, but I knew my mountain-craft was adequate. I loved wild places, and always sought them out, for the well-worn trails were not, and never had been, for us. Ours was the freedom of the hills.

I recall our beginnings, those unforgettable years at Scarthwaite — the mornings when we ran, boots unlaced, over the bridge to catch the bus up the dale, the long glorious days on the tops, the sunburn and the blisters and the soakings, the long treks home with Prim trotting ahead to explain why we were so late for dinner, the tremendous meals we ate, the evenings lolling round the fire with wet socks steaming on the fender, the dark quiet nights when a hard bed was bliss to tired bodies — and Mrs Coates, who looked after us so well because she liked us to be there though she was often anxious about what course our next escapade might take, who looked askance at our ice-axe, and refused to allow us to bring a rope (we were often in places where a rope might have been advantageous, but she never found out about that). In Mrs Coates was the heart and soul of Cumbria.

From beautiful Borrowdale to the ultimate, which is Wasdale. The Lake District has nothing greater than this western dale. Upper Eskdale is a close second to it. Both are enchanted places.

But Lakeland has so much to give that to list all its riches would be an endless task. I give the ones I love the most . . . .

The feel of rough rock rasping the hand, sliding scree beneath the boot-soles, all summit cairns, little stone bridges, long views where hills lie fold upon fold to the far horizon, stone walls snaking up steep slopes, high tarns, the first green of the larches in spring, sunlight dappling birch woods carpeted with primroses and bluebells, cloud shadows drifting, drifting across the mountains, stark rocks thrusting against the sky, snow-drifts, becks tumbling and chattering, lark song, the mournful cry of the curlew, and the deep silence of the heights — that essential silence which is greater than sound.

And for scents, the one I recall most vividly is of meadowsweet on the banks of the Derwent, in Borrowdale. I smelt it in the dusk of my very first evening in the Lakes, and I can smell it still.

To sit by the Westmorland Cairn on Great Gable, poised on the edge of space, listening to the thunder of Piers Gill and gazing down upon the triangle of tiny fields in the valley below — that is my heaven.

And there is a seat at the foot of Wastwater from which one looks down the long, dark lake up to the high mountains — beloved territory which we have made our own. These are our hills!

These I have loved,
Still love, and in my heart shall hold
For ever, as my treasury of gold.